SIMON WOLF

Sincerely
Simon Wolf

SIMON WOLF

Private Conscience and Public Image

Esther L. Panitz

Rutherford • Madison • Teaneck
Fairleigh Dickinson University Press
London and Toronto: Associated University Presses

© 1987 by Associated University Presses, Inc.

Associated University Presses
440 Forsgate Drive
Cranbury, NJ 08512

Associated University Presses
25 Sicilian Avenue
London WC1A 2QH, England

Associated University Presses
2133 Royal Windsor Drive
Unit 1
Mississauga, Ontario
Canada L5J 1K5

Library of Congress Cataloging-in-Publication Data

Panitz, Esther L.
   Simon Wolf : private conscience and public image.

   Bibliography: p.
   Includes index.
   1. Wolf, Simon, 1836–1923.   2. Jews—United States—
Biography.   3. Statesmen—United States—Biography.
I. Title.
E184.J5W77   1987   973'.04924024 [B]   86-45378
ISBN 0-8386-3293-9 (alk. paper)

Printed in the United States of America

For David
who has always sought for a world at peace,
that our grandchildren may one day enjoy

Contents

Acknowledgments
Introduction

1	The Urban and Urbane Politico	17
2	Recorder of Deeds	34
3	Building a Constituency	61
4	Egyptian Interlude	70
5	Champion of the Immigrant	79
6	Challenges to Power	92
7	Justice for the Stranger	99
8	In the Shadow of Restrictionism	121
9	Toward Racism: "An Expense of Energy"	132
10	In the Russian Maze	140
11	Wolf: Classical Anti-Zionist	161
12	The Search for Lasting Recognition	176

Notes 182
Bibliography 211
Index 218

Acknowledgments

Many years ago, the late Dr. Solomon Grayzel, former editor of the Jewish Publication Society, asked me to write a biographical study of Simon Wolf, his life and times. Other commitments intervened to prevent its completion. But even then, in the early days, in addition to Dr. Grayzel's encouragement for this project, I was privileged to receive constant assistance and a sense of direction from Dr. Jacob Rader Marcus, director of the American Jewish Archives on the Hebrew Union College-Jewish Institute of Religion campus at Cincinnati. During the same period, Dr. Isidore S. Meyer, editor emeritus of the American Jewish Historical Society, remained steadfast in his help, reading early versions of manuscripts of the work and providing meaningful comments toward its improvements. Dr. Nathan Kaganoff, librarian of the American Jewish Historical Society, made a host of necessary documents available to me in the summer of 1982 when I spent a few days at the Society's library in Waltham, Mass.

I am exceedingly grateful to Congressman Robert A. Roe of New Jersey and his staff who spared no effort on my behalf in obtaining federal records and legislative accounts normally inaccessible to the general public. In addition, I should like to thank my many friends and colleagues whose own writings made this work ever more valuable. In this connection I am indebted to Dr. Naomi Wiener Cohen, Dr. Lloyd P. Gartner, Dr. Marc Lee Raphael, Dr. Melvin Urofsky, and to the late Dr. Oscar Janowsky. Dr. Jack Wertheimer of The Jewish Theological Seminary deserves my thanks for having shown me which pitfalls to avoid in the writing of the manuscript.

I must thank the librarians of the American Jewish Archives, those at the Blaustein Library of the American Jewish Committee, others at the Jewish Theological Seminary Library, and the staffs of the Manuscript Divisions of the Library of Congress and the New York Public Library, who facilitated my research at their respective institutions.

Permission to quote from the writings of Zosa Szakowski, "The Alliance Israelite Universelle in The United States 1860–1949," from my own earlier articles on immigration, entitled "In Defense of the Jewish Immigrant,

1890–1924" and "The Polarity of American Jewish Attitudes Towards Immigration, 1870–1891," and from a study written in collaboration with my husband, Rabbi David H. Panitz, "Simon Wolf as United States Consul to Egypt," has graciously been granted by the American Jewish Historical Society.

I should like to thank the Union of American Hebrew Congregations for the right to quote from the *Annual Reports of The Board of Delegates on Civil and Religious Rights of The Union* (1891–1924).

B'nai B'rith has kindly given me permission to reproduce a twelve-line poem by Justice Wendell Philips Stafford, which was dedicated to Simon Wolf on the occasion of his eighty-fifth birthday.

Thanks are also in order to the librarians at the school where I taught for sixteen years. Mrs. Mary Lee Miller and Mrs. Carole Washnik, at Northern Valley Regional High School in Old Tappan, New Jersey, have been indefatigable in their efforts at locating appropriate historical material for this book. May I also extend my appreciation to my dear friends, Mrs. Ruby Schepps of Little Falls, N.J., for having read portions of this manuscript years ago; to Mrs. Ruth Walter Spingarn of Chevy Chase, Md., Simon Wolf's great grandniece, who helped me reconstruct the Wolf family tree; and to Ms. Beth Gianfagna, managing editor of Associated University Presses, who is responsible for seeing this work through publication.

My largest debt is to the members of my own family: to my parents, Robert and Gittel Allentuck for their help in securing and translating early immigrant accounts; to my sons, Chaplain Jonathan A. Panitz, USN, who procured out-of-print works for me relevant to this study; to Dr. Raphael I. Panitz, without whose yeoman service in tracking down elusive sources this manuscript would never have seen the light of day; and to Rabbi Michael E. Panitz, whose incisive ideas helped shape this book. Most of all I am thankful to my husband, David, for his love, patience, and constant encouragement.

Introduction

At the present time, Simon Wolf has merited only a footnote on the American historical scene.[1] Yet in an era when personal contacts marked the relationships between government officials and representatives of the American Jewish community, he exerted an influence far beyond the limits of his own abilities, knowledge, and financial significance. How he gained access to the corridors of power in America is the theme of this study.

Wolf possessed a unique talent to reach those in command. As an immigrant youth in rural Ohio, as a young attorney in a feverish capital aflame with the passions of war, and as a cantankerous old man fighting to preserve his image, he left an indelible impression upon everyone he met. His influence was such that the government of the United States came to regard him as a steward of the Jewish community in this land.

Such achievements, which flowed in the wake of the power he wielded, were not to be minimized. He reunited disparate elements of the Reform movement in Judaism and shaped a civil and religious rights organization to suit his purpose. In this way he endowed his public statements with a measure of authority. In return, executives and legislators acknowledged his concern for the constitutional rights due all individuals, both native and alien alike. Much of his public career was spent in seeking ways to protect the immigrant on these shores and the stranger abroad.

Wolf's battles to insure the legal freedoms for the downtrodden made his name a household word in his day. In his role as chairman of the Board of Delegates of the Union of American Hebrew Congregations and as representative of the International Order of B'nai B'rith in Washington, he was on close terms with every president from Lincoln to Wilson. He was a loyal Republican who not only stumped for Rutherford B. Hayes, but who also tried to advise him, Theodore Roosevelt, and William Howard Taft on appropriate campaign strategies.[2]

Like other public persons, Wolf wanted most of all to be thought of as an author of note. The bulk of the material about him consists of self-assessments and evaluations of the times in which he lived, contained in reams of essays and speeches for every important occasion. In addition, his published works note the immigrant's constant amazement and gratitude for the freedoms bounded by law, which were the marks of the America he knew. At times, such thankfulness was tempered by his outrage at examples of racism he encountered in the form of anti-Semitism. Unfortunately, neither the moral earnestness that characterizes his writings nor the eloquence of his Germanic prose is sufficient to transform his literary output into a memorable undertaking.[3]. Yet his biographical sketches, compositions, and reminiscenes reveal a charming egotist, albeit basically a good man, impelled by humanitarian motives to act as he did. Justice Wendell Philips Stafford, of the Supreme Court of the District of Columbia, called him "the representative American Jew," and Father Walter, a prominent clergyman of the period, thought of Wolf as the "best Christian in Washington."

In appearance he was both handsome and meticulous. The number of his friends was legion and his personal life exemplary. At his death, the near and the great mourned him in regal terms. In his honor, even the Supreme Court recessed on the day of his funeral.[4]

The obituaries that limned his accomplishments grew long and rich in detail. He had served as president of the Washington Hebrew Congregation, and of the Schutzenverein and the Schillerbund, German-American societies devoted to cultural and philanthropic endeavors. As founder and director of the Hebrew Orphan Asylum in Atlanta and of the Christian and Eleanor Ruppert Home for the Aged and Indigent in Washington, D.C., he proved his steadfast support for the young and old of all faiths, The Cleveland Orphan Asylum, established by B'nai B'rith, received his constant care and attention. As a loyal friend and coworker with Adolphus Solomons, who helped establish the American Red Cross, Wolf labored diligently on its behalf. Other service organizations included the Board of Charities of the District of Columbia and the Kesher Shel Barzel, a Jewish institution whose presidency he held for twelve years. He was a 33d-degree Mason and claimed a life-long association with the Shawmut Club.[5] To further the need of his compatriots from the land of his birth, Wolf represented the German-American Alliance.[6]

This book is a selective biography, for only the more notable of his experiences deserve public attention. These include his attempts at negotiating with the federal government on a score of issues that affected both Jews and Christians, and his activities as a leader in the American Jewish community. Could Wolf, representing the relatively insignificant Jewish group in this land, be able to stem the tide of restrictive immigration legislation? Might he, speaking for the few, accumulate sufficient power to moderate anti-Semitic czarist policy? Could his constant emphasis on the unalloyed patriotism of those he stood for be sufficient to deflect the barbs of the bigots, or mitigate their charges of dual allegiance brought against a minority in the United States?

In his attempts to secure favorable responses to these questions from government officials and other notables, Wolf relied on his lobbying skills. His arts of persuasion consisted of personal contacts, private meetings with the prestigious few, occasional petitions, letters to those in authority, and presentations of oral or written testimony. In all of these communications, Wolf cleverly fashioned an image of the public man, the official spokesman to whom legislators and executives and diplomats would have to turn whenever matters of Jewish concern held center stage. Only on occasion, in his voluminous correspondence with the power brokers in Washington, did he allow himself the privilege of communicating as a private person. He preferred to regard himself as an emissary for others.

Whenever possible, Wolf tied his abilities at parleying to his personal relationships with those at the helm of government. Partying, glad-handing, quietly accepting a favor granted for an obligation undertaken, and graciously acknowledging failure when all opportunities for victory had vanished, were the ways he endeared himself to officialdom. Essentially, Wolf measured the extent of his polite pourparlers with politicians and diplomats by the depth of their friendship for him. He hoped especially that such warm associations would never be broken, even when he had come, hat in hand for some special request, and was rebuffed.

Once, such obsequiousness invoked the ire of Louis Marshall, jurist and civil libertarian, Marshall accused Wolf of "palavering with the high and the mighty"[7] to insure his personal advancement. Marshall himself was one of a group of younger men who, in 1906, rose to challenge Wolf's leadership. Marshall's colleagues, most of whom held significant posts in law, letters, finance, and academia, disdained Wolf's techniques of personal persuasion. From the bastion of their newly organized American Jewish Committee, Oscar Straus, Jacob Schiff, Cyrus Adler, Cyrus Sulzberger, Herbert Friedenwald, Marshall, and others battled to secure political and religious rights for Jews both at home and abroad. Of this coterie only Max Kohler, a former district attorney and Wolf's heir apparent as chairman of the Board of Delegates of the Union, was able to placate the old man. The rest scoffed at Wolf's graciousness in his meetings with well-known politicos. Yet until the very end of Wolf's career, Marshall and his friends could not ignore him. They were forced to channel their need for tidbits of political or diplomatic information through this aging functionary, to whom they sneeringly referred in private correspondence as "Lupus Washingtoniensis."[8] Sometimes they fretted that the rumors he dispensed were deliberately misleading. Yet his influence and political clout forced them to manipulate him as best they could.

They found it difficult to dislodge Wolf from his vaunted position as spokesman for the Jewish community in this country. For more than three decades, prior to the formation of the American Jewish Committee, he had been guaranteeing his entrée to the highest levels of government. He had secured his niche in Washington's political establishment because he believed wholeheartedly that at all times personal friendship was the keystone in the arch of successful negotiation.

To his advantage, he was able to operate within an open society. In such a milieu officials from the lowliest subordinate to the chief executive himself were readily available for consultations of all sorts. To his political encounters Wolf brought an innate sense of bargaining where no one would lose face. Such failures as he did sustain were not discussed publicly, but became matters of private concern. But whether he succeeded or was defeated, he never abandoned the opportunities present in America for continuing his courtly exchanges with those in command. For this the committee never forgave him. Instead, it charged him with resorting to expediency more frequently than principle, embracing irrelevent causes, and clinging to outdated methods of influence peddling.[9] Justifiable though such criticism was at times, it merely exemplified the notion that even a "giant of justice"[10] may have clay feet.

What follows then is an account of how Simon Wolf achieved his objectives and why on occasion he missed the mark. This study includes references to his personal life when these illuminate his public goals. This story of his career is characterized by the paradox that here was a man who was not an intellectual, not a leader by virtue of his wealth, not a professional social worker, not a historian, and not a theologian. Yet he was able to speak freely and authoritatively for thousands who had no authentic voice of their own.

1

The Urban and Urbane Politico

On the occasion of his eightieth birthday, Simon Wolf was the guest of honor at a banquet tendered him by the Hebrew Immigrant Aid Society. The place was the Hotel Savoy, New York City; the date, 28 October 1916.[1] There, the evening stretched forth endlessly, with its paeans of praise[2] to an old man who thought of himself as the doyen of Jewish ambassadors to the federal government.[3] The words spoken that night were heralded in the Anglo-Jewish press.

> During the many centuries of exile . . . during long, long years . . . of oppression, here and there appeared beacons of light calling on the people of Israel to march on. Many of our treasures have been lost on the way. . . . Many of our offspring forsook the tents of Jacob for the camps of Esau. . . . But God ordained that at least a few of our sons. . . . alleviate our pains, soothe our outraged feelings . . . light our weary countenances with rays of hope and happiness. We need not go back to search for these great men in Israel—the last century alone gave us a Simon Wolf.[4]

Wolf, it has been said, "for more than fifty years stood guard at the nation's capital as a faithful Jew and a loyal American patriot."[5] In 1916 he was called "an American Jew, lawyer, statesman, philanthropist, publicist, spurred on by dreams of his people's eventual deliverance."[6] A former commissioner of Immigration wrote a fulsome poem on Wolf's noble qualities of heart and mind.[7] Other observers vied among themselves to extol Wolf's virtues; even the more restrained of commentators felt obliged to place Wolf in the company of Moses Montefiore, Adolphe Crémieux, Baron Maurice de Hirsch, Theodor Herzl, and other Jewish luminaries of the nineteenth century.[8]

Is it possible that some of this high-flown prose meant more than honeyed words to sweeten an octogenarian's life? Wolf's own belief to live disciplined in freedom was genuine enough. Throughout his life he clung to the doctrine that man, given the opportunity, would always seek the obligations and rewards of democracy. He was forever consumed by the twin passions of liberty and responsibility. It was this that endeared him to his admirers, who in their zeal to do him justice may have exceeded their bounds but did not wholly depart from the truth.

Wolf's romance with freedom was the product of two environments. Though he had to contend with Germany's strident anti-Semitism, his attitude to that country was one of nostalgia and reverence, reinforced by a sense of duty to its people and to its cultural values. Willingly, he transferred such bonds of affection to the United States. The occasion was one for rejoicing: to swear undying fealty to this land, noted for freedom and justice, where individuals were to be judged on merit alone, became his enduring hope.[9]

Such devotion to American democracy found its rationale in his view of religion. An ardent follower of Reform Judaism, he was convinced that his faith was a universal creed that ought to forego old rituals and ethnic associations. For him, Reform Judaism contained the dynamic necessary to alter a talmudic regimen, directing a group's way of life, to a universally inspired statement of a faith community. In pursuit of this goal, he regarded himself as an American citizen beyond the walls of his temple, and a Jew within its precincts.[10]

Tied to his religious worship by a shared acceptance of a rational way of life, his Americanism became his secular creed. His perceptions of that belief grew inordinate. Here was the land where the social, religious, political, and economic troubles of the old world were gone. Here was the country where liberty reigned supreme, and where human beings would be recognized for their intrinsic worth. When, however, evidence of bigotry in America challenged such attitudes, he would harp on the theme of his people's spiritual, legal, and cultural achievements. He saw no discrepancies between the Jews' distinguished collective past and his own insistence that each person had always to be judged in terms of his own individuality. His measuring rod for a Jew's true worth was the intensity of his allegiance to his native or adopted country.[11]

He extended this obsession with liberty backward in time, to encompass his most formative years. Then, as a lad growing up in Rhenish Bavaria in the 1840s, he imagined that such traits as a devotion to duty and a concern for truth would flourish best in a democratic society. To prove how quickly he matured, even though he had not yet tasted America's freedoms, he recalled that as a six-year-old he had already added to the family's income. By reading the romances of Eugene Sue to wealthy, illiterate neighbors, the Simon Peter Langs, Wolf earned enough to help run the household. Meanwhile, his mother looked after his learned father, who was an invalid.[12] Many years later, in 1881, when Wolf was a middle-aged man of forty-five, he revisited his hometown of Hinzweiller. There he met an old lady who remembered him as a boy at school. There are no other references to his early education, no documents to indicate how he acquired his knowledge of Judaism. This would imply that Wolf was either self-taught, or tutored privately (his father was a teacher of Hebrew), or perhaps he attended classes intermittently. Yet by 1909, he was to donate 800 volumes of Judaica, half of his private library, to the Freemasons.[13]

If, intellectually speaking, his was to become a rags-to-riches story, there was still no sign of this when he came to this country in July 1848. Twelve years old at the time, Wolf reached America with his grandparents, Benjamin and Rosa Wolf. They settled in Uhrichsville, Ohio, then a rural outpost not far from Cleveland. Here Wolf clerked in his uncles Abram and Elias's general merchandising store.[14]

Growing up in a provincial settlement, he combined the financial rewards of ordinary work with social contacts. Life for him was most meaningful only in the presence of others. To this end, he even made a virtue of his daily schedule. Rising at five in the morning to complete his chores about the store, he looked forward to the "business or barter" of numerous items ranging from "wheat and oats" to "slaughtered meats and live poultry for mercantile wares." Such exchanges, he insisted, formed the basis for his ongoing relationships with neighboring farmers, villagers, and salesmen who would come to the Wolf establishment from near and far.

Though publicly Wolf was later to eschew group identification for Jews lest it lead to a ghettolike isolation, privately he cherished those ties he had been able to form with his coreligionists in Uhrichsville. In reviewing his adolescence, he waxed eloquent over the sense of family and grew misty-eyed at the thought of the religious atmosphere that prevailed in that isolated homestead. He delighted in the personal warmth exuded by those itinerant German Jewish peddlers who made it their business to reach the Wolf home before the Sabbath.

> Around the family groups there ranged itself twenty to thirty Jewish peddlers who with their packs, weighing from one hundred to one hundred and fifty pounds, would start out into the rural districts of the state, returning in two, three and four weeks, with a diminished load on their backs and an adequate return in their pockets. These peddlers became known far and wide in the farming community and looked upon as so many friends who were bringing them things that they most need.

Wolf marveled that despite their daily contacts with their Christian neighbors, these drummers stood "firm and fast in their adherence to all the glorious tenets and traditions of Judaism." They somehow "managed," he said, "always to return on a Friday, so as to be with us on Saturday when in

the house of one of my uncles we had services, and were constantly reminded by the loving care and attention of the hostess that the Jewish heart
had not died out in our women. . . ." In Wolf's eyes, those "travel-stained"
wanderers showed more "real piety" than was to be found in any synagogue
or temple in the world.[15]

When, years later, these incidents faded from Wolf's memory, his recollections centered mostly on the gastronomic delights of "Matze and Apple
Chalet, Zimmet Kuchen, Kertoffel Pfankuchen, und Saure Fish." These
were the foods that the mothers of the Wolf clan, the "Amelias and Marys,"
and other untutored but morally upright German Jewish housewives placed
on their tables in the new world.[16]

Although the Wolf homestead was a rural center for social and religious
activities, as a young man Wolf was not bound by its environs. He found his
friends and formed new associations in neighboring Cleveland and the more
distant Chicago. In Cleveland he was active in the Young Men's Hebrew and
Literary Society. There he met Benjamin Franklin Peixotto, scion of a
distinguished Sephardi family, who was to exert a profound influence on
Wolf, lasting for four decades. Now, however, before the Civil War erupted,
both young men led carefree lives, enjoying their roles as amateur actors in
theatricals sponsored by the local Young Men's Hebrew and Literary Society.
Sometimes they were even joined by a professional, John Wilkes Booth,
whose acting would in time pale before his notoriety.

When Fort Sumter was fired upon, Wolf and Peixotto in a moment of
inspired patriotism, raised the flag of the Eagle Street Synagogue in
Cleveland. Later, during that summer of 1861, when Wolf was about to leave
to enter a law firm in New Philadelphia, Ohio, Peixotto and other friends
wished him godspeed and presented him with an elaborately engraved
resolution to mark the occasion. In it, they urged him to remember his
friends, never to forget his Jewish heritage, and to strive for success in all his
undertakings.[17]

In Chicago, Wolf came to know some of the subsequent leaders of German
Jewry in America: his future wife's cousin, Henry Greenebaum, banker and
Republican politician; Abraham Hart, a well-known furniture merchant;
Henry Brentano, a relative to the famous booksellers; and Edward S. Sal-
omon, who would serve with distinction in the Union Army. Wolf included
Adolph Moses, ex-Confederate Army officer and prominent lawyer among
his Chicago acquaintances. But since Moses first settled in Chicago in 1869,
Wolf could not have met him on earlier visits to the city. Wolf recalled,
however, that when he came to lecture in Chicago, in 1870, Moses offered
him the hospitality of his home.

For Wolf, those early times in Cleveland and Chicago were days of "politics, music, song, wit, humor, good cheer, and comradeship." Wolf remembered that on his first visit to Chicago, in 1853, when cousin Hannah

Greenebaum and Gerhard Foreman were engaged, he, Wolf, Edward Sa-lomon, and Simon Wolfe Rosendale, who was to become attorney general for New York State, were "in a high state of humor at two in the morning." At dawn, they carried David Greenebaum across the fence to his house. At that moment old Uncle Greenebaum appeared and scolded them not only for drinking all night, but for not calling him to join in the fun.[18]

Other anecdotes, which Wolf chose to record for his salad days, show him to have been scarcely green in judgment even then. He made much of the fact that as an adolescent of sixteen he had been called upon to serve as a witness in a $50,000 lawsuit. Though he was subjected to three days of grueling cross-examination, he did not repudiate his testimony. This led the prosecutor, John A. Bingham, a future Congressman and judge, to predict that Wolf would "someday be a great man."[19]

It is no wonder, then, that four years later, in 1856, Wolf managed adroitly to salvage his own political reputation. He had joined the Democratic party, and though the Democrats, with James Buchanan as their presidential candidate, won the national election, locally the Republicans carried Uhrichsville. Thereupon, Wolf, "determined to steal the evening's thunder," turned personal defeat into victory. Organizing a social ball for the occasion, he sent for the finest delicacies in food and drink, brought musicians from a fifty-mile radius, and spent $1,500 of his own money on the affair. Dr. Brisbane, State Democratic Chairman for Tuscarawas County, where Uhrichsville was situated, found the proper expression to mark the occasion. Word went out that while "the Republicans were celebrating their political victory by feasting on dead venison, the Democrats were enjoying the hospitality of a living Wolf."

Wolf admitted that his insulated, provincial life, so characteristic of outly-ing towns and villages in mid-nineteenth-century America, was the nurtur-ing force of American democracy. Township meetings and primaries became the proving grounds for political hopefuls. Specifically, these settings pro-vided opportunities for local party workers to reach significant national levels.

In 1860, Wolf served as an alternate to the Democratic National Con-vention. He there met Stephen A. Douglas, who reckoned that Wolf's support, and that of his friend from Chicago, Henry A. Greenebaum, would provide ample protection against statements made by that "renegade Jew, Judah P. Benjamin [who later became Secretary of the Confederacy.]" Such a rejoinder may well have constituted a politician's attempt to flatter his followers. Aside from its stereotypical allusion, Douglas's response bore witness to the rapidity with which Wolf rose on the political scale. Only in a frontier society could a presidential candidate have spoken so freely with a relatively unimportant party man from an insignificant area.[20]

As a youth of twenty, Wolf once rode bareback to the county seat on an

election night to discover if his candidate "had run ahead of his ticket."[21]
Later, he would translate such activity into fostering relationships with those
at the highest governmental levels. In large measure, his involvement in the
American political system sprang from his innate sense of ease with other
people. It had all begun with a ball back in 1856, and was to continue for the
rest of his life, spelled out in thousands of variations on the basic need for
human contact. This, combined with his keen delight in the workings of the
political marketplace, helped him rise very fast, very far. It almost did not
matter who the political candidate he was backing was, so long as his man
won. Of course, Wolf went to great lengths to explain his transfer of allegiance to the Republican party. In his memoirs he credited a Lincoln speech
with effecting his conversion.[22] Somewhat more realistically, Wolf acknowledged that, like all immigrants, he too was drawn to the egalitarian call of the
Democratic party, but that when that organization faltered on the slavery
issue, he joined the Republicans. For the remainder of his life he was an
ardent party man. By the time he acquired that stature in the Jewish
community which could command the attention of the Anglo-Jewish press,
the official account of his political change of heart took on a different hue.
Now, he was certain that back in 1860 he was determined "to align himself"
with the "new patriotism" of the Republican Party. He would have to
abandon Democratic "partisan passions."[23]

This ability to reconstruct motives to his own purposes served Wolf well.
As he reshaped parts of his earlier life, it would appear that Prosecutor
Bingham's compliment had convinced him early on; he was destined, he felt,
for a far greater future than that warranted by clerking in a country store.
Meanwhile, by 1856, he had become the sole manager of his uncles' ware-
house, and in the following year he had married Caroline Hahn, of Suffield,
Ohio.[24] But the depression of 1857 played havoc with his mercantile pursuits. In the future, he was to expatiate on the political insights to be
garnered at the level of the town meeting. Now, however the very thought of
remaining an obscure village proprietor was stultifying. His first step, then,
was to read law in the office of Judge Joseph C. Hance. He also attended
lectures at the Cleveland Law School, and was admitted to the bar on 16 July
1861, the day of the Battle of Bull Run.[25]

To hear Wolf tell it, his examination consisted of only one question put to
him by Frank Hurd, who later became a congressman from Ohio. Hurd
asked Wolf what the first duty of an attorney was. Wolf promptly responded
"to get a retainer." With these words, the interview was over, and Wolf
speedily was admitted to the bar. Without further ado, he entered into a
partnership with Alexander L. Neely, in a law firm in New Philadelphia,
Ohio.[26]

This lasted for only one year. The effects of the Civil War were such that his
legal business collapsed, and in July 1862, Simon Wolf moved his family to

the nation's capital. This time, unlike the previous occasion, when he had gone to great lengths to explain his political conversion, there was no need to refine his motivation.

> I was determined to win a position that should be an encouragement to others and at the same time prove that the government under which I lived had found in me . . . [an advocate] of that which was best and purest.

Not one to hide his light under a bushel, Wolf had come to Washington armed with a request for a government job. He wanted a clerkship in the War Department and had a letter of introduction fron an Ohio politician, George W. McCook, to Secretary of War Edwin M. Stanton. Wolf did not get the position, but he managed to turn the rejection aside. The secretary responded to Wolf's request by observing that "If [McCook's estimate] is correct, stay out of this department, for you will become a fossil with no chance of development."[27]

It would be idle to speculate how great was the favor Stanton granted Wolf by refusing him a lowly post. In time, the course Wolf chose would take him far away from a lackluster existence as a minor bureaucrat. Instead he entered private law practice, and he soon was alluded to as a "rising member of the Washington bar."[28]

At the outset of the Civil War, Washington was fast becoming the hub of the nation. It may have lacked the physical, social, or cultural amenities of Paris or London. There were "no street cars, no palatial mansions, no sewage, scarcely any sidewalks, dirt, dust, and magnificent distances everywhere." But Wolf overlooked these impediments. "To me," he wrote years later, "it was a novel experience, coming [as I had] from a provincial town in the West into the great and busy political mart of the nation, without experience, without funds, without prospects."[29] Yet when he reached Washington, he knew precisely what he had wanted; he had come "to better [his] life." As it turned out, Washington did not disappoint him.

The city Wolf chose to live in had taken on all the paraphernalia of the War. There were armed sentries at street corners, and the surrounding countryside was dotted with forts and armaments. On entering and leaving the city, "civilians were marched through double files of bristling bayonets."[30] It seemed as if the queues of people waiting their turn would never end. Washington was crowded with newcomers, party hacks, and men on leave from the army. They competed with one another for hotel accommodations and waited in long lines at restaurants for the next available table. They besieged politicans for jobs, and were likely to stop President Lincoln himself whenever he would be driving down the road in his carriage. The favorite meeting ground for these hangers-on was the stairway leading to the president's office, on the seond floor of the White House. There, two steady streams of visitors, one ascending the stairs to Lincoln's study, the other descending, were to be seen round the clock.[31]

By January 1862, Washington had a sizable Jewish community. True to their middle-class heritage, its 2,000 members were engaged mainly in trade and merchandising. Others had entered the professions. As early as 1855, Congress had granted the Washington Hebrew Congregation a charter of incorporation,.[32] By the time Wolf reached the city, members of the congregation worshiped in a spacious room on the second story of a building at 12th and G Streets. It was large enough to accommodate 200 people. In one-half year they would build a more permanent edifice on 8th Street, not far from the Patent Office.[33]

In the years prior to the Civil War, the Jews of Washington had united to secure their civil rights. Then, they had protested to President Buchanan against certain discriminatory resolutions in a treaty between the United States and the Swiss Cantons. After long and involved diplomatic negotiations, lasting for more than a decade, the matter was finally adjusted to the satisfaction of American and Jewish interests.[34] In time, Wolf would be able to benefit from similar instances where governmental intervention on behalf of persecuted Americans abroad had become an accepted procedure.

Rapidly Wolf assumed positions of leadership in the Jewish and general communities. No sooner had he reached the nation's capital than in his capacity as an attorney he began defending Jewish refugees fleeing the South.[35] Soon this brought him to the attention of the authorities. Never one to remain silent in moments of tension, Wolf also found time to protest against the anti-Semitism expressed in some of the journals of the day. So quickly did he emerge as a public figure, that the national convention of B'nai B'rith, held in Philadelphia in 1868, suspended its rules to allow him "unanimous admission." He was deemed an accredited delegate from the newly formed Aaron Lodge in the District of Columbia, which had not yet been qualified to participate in national conventions. At this conference he was quickly appointed to committees dealing with the organization's constitution, its territorial jurisdictions, and the general state of the order. In this new capacity he was able to use his knowledge of parliamentary procedure to insure executive control over district lodges in the organization of B'nai B'rith. This was in indication of times to come, where at every opportunity he would eagerly consolidate his own power in communal affairs. More immediately, the social advantages he gained by being present at the convention were not to be minimized. He now was able to renew his friendship with Peixotto, who then refused the presidency of B'nai B'rith, and to meet with Adolph Moses of Quincy, Ill., who thereupon was nominated to the post. As shall soon be seen, it was Moses who would later question General Grant on the origin of Order No. 11.[37]

Always busy asserting his own importance among friends and associates, Wolf made certain not to neglect his involvement with intellectual matters. He proclaimed his readiness to pursue enlightened ideas, and boasted that he was part of an intended Academy of Science, Literature, and Art. Modeled on a French prototype, the school numbered several illustrious founders, including Ulysses S. Grant and Salmon P. Chase.[38]

Wolf's concern for culture first expressed itself in the formation of a private club, devoted to the arts and humanities and frequented by young men avid for learning. There were no exclusionary policies. Membership was open to people of all faiths. Soon, Simon wolf was named president of the Washington Literary and Dramatic Society. On a Sunday afternoon, 2 August 1862, in a rented hall at 481 Ninth Street and only a month after he reached Washington, Wolf spoke to the society's young audience. He told his listeners that the club could serve as a happy hunting ground for husbands—women were always welcome. But it was high time to avoid frivolous pastimes, such as draughts and cards. Instead, he would urge his hearers to seek knowledge and concentrate on the achievements of the great thinkers of the world.

Were pride and ambition his only motives in seeking the intellectual life? Clearly, Wolf hoped that if he and his friends would devote themselves to the pursuit of learning, they would deflect the prejudicial statements of their Christian neighbors. Wolf was upset that terms such as "money-changers," "cotton traders," and "clothes-dealers" had become words of reproach. What better way was there to improve the reputation of an entire generation than to furbish it with the trappings of a cultural club, whose noble ideals might effectively overcome age-old hatreds.[39]

How well the association succeeded in affairs of the mind or of the heart is not known. But locally, the group's theatrical productions received a good press. Wolf, who often would play the Ghost in *Hamlet* or Shylock in *The Merchant of Venice*, bore an uncanny resemblance to John Wilkes Booth, Lincoln's assassin. Earlier in Cleveland, Booth had joined Wolf and Peixotto in dramatic performances. Years afterward, Wolf remembered that he had met Booth once again at the Willard Hotel, on the morning of the day Lincoln was shot. There, at the bar, Booth explained that Senator John P. Hale's daughter had just rejected his marriage proposal. Wolf attributed Lincoln's murder to this personal tragedy in Booth's own life. Wolf himself was not present at Ford's Theater that fateful evening in April, only because his wife Caroline did not care for Laura Keene's acting talents. Keene, of course, was scheduled to play the lead role in *Our American Cousin*. Wolf also recalled that once he sat for a picture entitled, "The Assassination of President Lincoln."

Far less morbid were Wolf's personal associations with the president himself. Instead, these reveal Lincoln's deep humanity at all times, whether it was a matter of soliciting his attendance at a performance of the Washington Literary and Dramatic Association, or pardoning a deserter about to be executed, or pledging his cabinet members to earnest cooperation with their political enemies.

Once, Wolf and a friend, Newton Gotthold, who had recently returned from London where he had been studying drama, asked the president himself to attend the Association's premiere performance of *Hamlet*, honoring Shakespeare's tercentenary. Lincoln refused politely but wrote a check for $25.00 to help defray expenses. Told that Wolf would play the Ghost, the President asked: "Why could I not be the gravedigger of the evening for am I not a fellow of infinite jest?"[40]

On a more serious note Wolf once intervened with the president to spare the life of a young Jewish soldier from a New England town. He was to be executed the following morning as a deserter. Having been denied a furlough to visit his dying mother, he left, nevertheless, was caught and condemned to death. Thereupon, Wolf contacted Senator Thomas Corwin of Ohio, an intimate friend of Lincoln's, who warned Wolf that Secretary of War Stanton deeply resented Lincoln's readiness to pardon deserters. Corwin still managed, however, to arrange an interview for Wolf with the president.

It was at two o'clock in the morning, prior to the execution scheduled for ten, that Corwin and Wolf were ushered into the Executive Office.

"Impossible to do anything," said Lincoln. "Stanton has put his foot down and insists upon one of two things: either I will quit or he will quit."

Corwin, sensing the hopelessness of the situation, was about to leave. But Wolf pleaded with Lincoln. "Mr. President," said Wolf, "the charge has been made there are few Jewish soldiers in the ranks. You know better, for you have promoted any number of them. This is possibly the first instance of a Jewish deserter and this one not without cause; he has gone home to kiss for the last time the lips of a dying mother and see her decently interred."

President Lincoln looked at Wolf for one moment and said, "Wolf, that will do." He rang for his secretary John Hay, who then sent a telegram stopping the execution.

Later, the young man died at the Battle of Cold Harbor, the flag draped round his body. When the president heard of this, he had tears in his eyes and said, "I thank God for having done what I did."[41]

Still another incident that lent credibility to Lincoln's unparalleled concern for others may be found in a handwritten, unsigned note, dated August 1862, whose outer fold revealed the signatures of the president's cabinet members. Lincoln had requested that Secretaries William H. Seward, Salmon P. Chase, Edwin M. Stanton, Edward Bates, Montgomery Blair, Gideon Welles, and Caleb B. Smith underwrite an unknown pledge, to be opened at a later date. When they finally read its message, it contained the proviso that should Lincoln fail to be reelected, each one of the signatories to the note was to promise his cooperation to the next administration.[42]

Having grown accustomed to interceding for others, Wolf had also to plead for himself. As a young attorney, Wolf defended Jews from the South. Lafayette C. Baker, chief of detectives for the city of Washington, saw the matter in another light when he accused Wolf of being an agent for a disloyal organization that aided rebels and assisted blockade runners. What Baker had in mind was the International Order of B'nai B'rith, the Jewish service institution Wolf represented. Specifically, Wolf was arrested for having secured the release of imprisoned Southern Jewish refugees. He was held at the Carroll Street Prison. Present at Wolf's interview with Baker was Captain Wood, warden of the jail, who realized the justice of Wolf's statement. As a loyal subject of the Union, Wolf was merely fulfilling a lawyer's role under the Constitution. Wood accompanied Wolf to Secretary of War Stanton, who dismissed the charges.[43]

"Defending Southern refugees and speaking up when larger issues of human dignity were involved prepared the way for Wolf to fight three instances of anti-Semitism that arose during the Civil War. One referred to General Grant's Order No. 11; the second consisted of a series of bigoted slurs by a Union general; and the third included slanderous remarks in the press."

Wolf had been declared innocent of any involvement with blockade runners. But in 1862, illegal trade between the Northern and Confederate forces was so pervasive that General Sherman wanted to ban all such contacts across the lines. However, Lincoln's Administration, pressured by speculators, big business, and cotton entrepreneurs, refused to go along. Different agencies of the government, including the War and Treasury Departments and the White House, were accustomed to issuing contradictory rulings. Conflicting permits for commercial dealings were commonplace. Official reports indicate that both the civilian and military branches of the federal establishment were involved in this illicit exchange of goods and services. Treasury agents themselves, sent to investigate the frauds, were not above suspicion. It was rumored that even Jesse Grant, the father of the General, was actively engaged in promoting such illegal dealings. He supposedly derived a profit by enabling certain cotton buyers to obtain trading licenses from his illustrious son. President Lincoln referred to this practice of rampant thievery when he said that the "army itself is diverted from fighting the rebels to speculating in cotton."[44]

"How this matter might have ended none can tell; for on 17 December 1862 an order bearing General Grant's signature was issued from his headquarters in Holly Springs, Miss. [It read as follows:]

> The Jews as a class violating every regulation of trade established by the Treasury Department order, are hereby expelled from the Department within twenty-four hours from receipt of his order. Post commanders will see that all of this class of people be furnished passes and required

to leave, and anyone returning after such notification will be arrested and held in confinement until an opportunity presents itself for sending them out as prisoners, unless furnished with passes from headquarters. No passes will be given these people to visit headquarters for the purpose of making personal applications for trade permits.

"Reaction to this first overt act of governmental discrimination was quick and varied. Delegations of Jewish notables from various cities . . ." came to Washington to meet with congressional representatives, with spokesmen for the War Department, and with Lincoln himself. Jewish periodicals devoted a great deal of space to this military directive, called Order No. 11, and letters and resolutions denouncing its contents were sent to the White House. After having personally heard the complaints of a group of citizens, led by Caesar Kaskel of Paducah, Ky., Lincoln abrogated the ruling.[45]

Nowhere does Wolf indicate that he personally met with the delegation from Paducah.[46] Yet Washington was still too provincial a town and its prominent Jews too few in number for him not to have been aware of the prestigious assignment those visiting dignitaries had undertaken—revoking an order issued by the High Command in wartime. The entire affair took place only six months after Wolf had reached the capital. If immediate circumstances may have prevented him from actively joining in the work of Kaskel and his followers, then Wolf took the next best course. In 1863, he challenged the anti-Semitic descriptions of Jews as smugglers that had appeared in the *Washington Chronicle*. He had only harsh words for displays of past prejudices and condemned the paper for seeking to justify the purpose of Order No. 11. He thundered that the order itself marked a precedent, where "still less conscientious commanders can unscrupulously hurl forth their bulls against an unoffending and unnecessarily despised race. . . ."[47]

Even after the order was nullified, the racist atmosphere in which it flourished did not abate. In the spring of 1864, General Benjamin F. Butler, in command at Fortress Monroe, outside Washington, issued a dispatch that compared the capture of "359 rebels" to that of "90 mules, 60 contraband (Negroes) and 5 Jews." As in the matter of Order No. 11, Jewish spokesmen once again protested, not this time against incriminating an entire class of people, but rather at the general's peculiar powers of association. Given Wolf's propensity for political involvement and Lincoln's easy availability to a host of callers, there is no reason to doubt Wolf's word: once Lincoln heard about the incident, he granted Wolf a pass to the general's headquarters. There Butler protested his innocence, and claimed that a subordinate, using officially authorized forms, filed the statement. Yet the same commander did not disavow his own responsibility in the matter, when he sent an explanation of its ugly language to Myer S. Isaacs, secretary of the Board Delegates of

American Israelites. Butler coupled his apology to Isaacs with the observation that Jews, known for their predilection for banking and trade, constituted a separatist group, whose loyalties to the Union cause sometimes appeared dubious.[48]

Wolf accepted Butler's version of the affair, placing the responsibility for the crude remark upon an underling. Yet like those of Order No. 11, its implications were too offensive for Wolf to have completely ignored them. "Waving the banner of honest citizenship, he now took up the cudgels for law and liberty." On 20 November 1864, he wrote an impassioned letter to William Cullen Bryant, the editor of the *New York Evening Post*. There, Wolf accused the press in this country of catering to anti-Semitism. He contended that newspapers accused Jews of being blockade runners, or called them "Democrats," unwilling to bear the sacrifices of war. In this way, Wolf continued, contemporary journals obscured the "achievements" of the Jews, "who gave mankind its noblest religion, laws, poetry, and music." Wolf's rhetoric paralleled the exaggerated statements he so deplored in his opponents. Yet his references to bigoted editorials were factual enough. He wondered why it was newsworthy to cite the religion of every Jew indicted for a criminal act, but immaterial to cite the faith of non-Jews brought to trial.

> Several parties have been lately arrested . . . for an attempt to sell goods contraband of war. . . . Fortunately, there were some Christians among the number or else the Press would have teemed with abuse, and the telegraph would have lighted its startling news, of 'another batch of Jew blockade runners caught.' As it is the journals have been coy as doves; only when a Christian firm has been released or tried, it was officially announced as such; but when some unlucky son of Israel shared the same fate, it was chronicled as a *Jew released*.

In his eagerness to counteract such tendencies, Wolf detailed many instances of bravery by Jewish soldiers on the battlefield.

Responding to his protest, the *New York Evening Post* refused to believe that journalists would engage in deliberate malice. Instead, the newspaper complimented itself for publishing a reader's opinion which "demanded equal and exact justice for all men."[49]

The real turning point in Wolf's career was not such a plea for tolerance as he had just espoused, and to which he would return periodically. Rather it was his conviction, sprung to full bloom by the events of 1868, that here was an opportunity to fulfill himself politically and socially. Thousands had suffered from the dislocations imposed by Reconstruction, but Wolf would ultimately benefit by adjusting to the changes it wrought.

Momentous political contests between moderate and Radical Republicans characterized the incumbency of President Andrew Johnson. Ostensibly, the

battle lines were drawn in terms of reconstructing the South. More realistically, Radicals in Congress wanted to control the executive branch. This
they tried to accomplish by passing the Tenure-of-Office Act. Its terms
allowed them successfully to challenge the president's right to remove his
secretary of war, Edwin M. Stanton. General Grant, who originally sided
with President Johnson in the dispute, willingly replaced Stanton on an
interim basis. However, once the Senate affirmed that Stanton could not be
forced to leave his post, Grant relinquished the office. While the Radicals
rejoiced that the military hero of the day had joined their camp, the president charged Grant with acting deceptively. Johnson insisted that Grant had
promised either to remain in the Cabinet until the Supreme Court decided
the constitutionality of the entire procedure, or until a replacement could be
found, before the matter came to trial. Grant denied ever having made such
a pledge. Once the president questioned his honor, Grant accused Johnson
of character assassination. The break between them was complete. At last,
other Republican politicians, with the Radicals in the lead, were able to
unite behind Grant. He would become their standard bearer in the upcom-
ing elections.[50]

Earlier, his military victories had made Grant the most popular leader in
the North and West. Practical politicians banded together to commit themselves to him. Wealthy conservatives in New York, and local party workers in
Massachusetts declared themselves for the general. On the state level,
delegates to the Republican National Convention were instructed to vote for
Grant. Prestigious contenders for the Republican presidential nomination,
such as Chief Justice Salmon P. Chase and General Benjamin F. Butler, had
to withdraw in favor of Grant. Shortly before the Republican National
Convention, soldiers and sailors, assembled at Chicago, saw the general as
the ideal veteran destined to lead their country to greatness.[51]

Wolf seized upon this situation to promote his own fortunes.[52] He plainly
said as much in his *Presidents I Have Known*. Having come to Washington to
serve his country as best he could, he was also determined that his government would see him as an advocate of the "best and purest in life." Just then
that meant reinterpreting Order No. 11 of 1862 so that it would no longer
sully Grant's reputation.

Evidence suggests that he had to act quickly. In a speech, delivered on 18
March 1868 before a B'nai B'rith Lodge in Washington, Wolf was still able to
sympathize with the late Rev. Isaac Leeser for the way in which Christians
"tolerated the infamous Order of a celebrated General, which banished free
Americans from loyal ground."[53] Five days later, moreover, when impeach-
ment proceedings against President Johnson began, Wolf had only sympathy
for the chief executive, and scorn for his accusers. Seated in the Senate
gallery, Wolf watched the trial uninterruptedly. He saw no legal justification
for trying the president on charges of violating the Tenure-of-Office Act and
other laws.[54] Yet in the very same month of March when he bewailed

Johnson's lot and chastised Grant, Wolf was prepared to disassociate the general from the negative consequences of Order No. 11. In trying to pinpoint the responsibility for issuing that dispatch Wolf went directly to the source. He heard from Adam Badeau, an aide to Grant, that the general would issue no statement concerning the order. Were he to do so, the public might misconstrue his motives. Later, with consummate tact, Wolf would turn such inarticulateness to Grant's advantage. By refusing to shed light on the possible origins of the directive, or identify its author, the general would not be party to any unjust accusations against some innocent bystander. Now, however, Wolf must have realized that such moralizing carried little weight in the battle for political victory. He had to know, almost at once as it were, where the next presidential candidate stood in the matter of Order No. 11. By 14 April 1868, Wolf wrote once more to Badeau. Blatantly disregarding the original text of the order, Wolf asked whether the directive "proscribed the Jews as a class," or had been intended for "evil-designing persons," whose religion was immaterial to the problem. To clear Grant's reputation, Badeau had only to respond affirmatively to Wolf's stacked question. He agreed with Wolf that no "religious slur" had ever been implied, but that when the order was issued, the "guilty parties" were "Israelites exclusively." Though contemporary accounts of smuggling in the Department of the Tennessee disproved Badeau's observation, his response pleased Wolf. For Badeau made certain to add that Order No. 11 would have been equally stringent in its condemnation of "any other class of individuals, religious, political, or commercial," had it too been involved in crimes of this sort.

Previously, Wolf had gone to great lengths to "defend (his) race" "against cruel aspersions and uncalled for prejudice." This time, however, he saw no reason to protest Badeau's claim that Jews alone were the culprits. Instead, in a letter to the *Boston Transcript*, Wolf insisted that "the Order never hurt anyone, except those illegal traders, some of whom were Jews." "Having lived in Washington, for the past six years," he "knew how many of our people were indifferent to the cause, and how many cared only for the spoils." He then proceeded to detail their activities near the battlefields. Presumably, the "many who infested the camps," were "spies, blockade-runners, and others, who, owing no allegiance to the government, having ever a passport near, endangered the army, laughed at regulations and orders, and when caught attempted to bribe their way to freedom."

What compelled Wolf to add such pejorative comments when he ought to have been content with his earlier declaration that the order "never harmed anyone, not even in thought, except those *whom we as Jews despise and hold in contempt?*"[55] The answer may be found in his desperate desire for fame. Of course, his protests against anti-Semitism were still genuine, and would continue to be so. But at this stage in his career, he had decided that his future reputation meant more than the good name of his coreligionists.

Wolf wrote this sweeping condemnation of fellow Jews before the results of a parallel inquiry into the origins of Order No. 11 became public knowledge. Wolf had asked Adolph Moses to join in a defense of Grant. But Moses, angered by Grant's "violation of liberties," refused. Thereupon, Congressman Isaac Newton Morris of Illinois, urged Moses to write directly to Grant. Responding instead to Morris, on condition that the information remain confidential until after the election, Grant claimed that he issued the order. He did so, however, only after he had been rebuked by his superiors in Washington. They reprimanded him for allowing Jews to trade at will across the battle lines. Grant admitted that he had posted his directive hastily, and had given no thought to its consequences. He never intended to offend anyone's faith and wanted Morris to reassure Moses on that score.[56]

Both the Grant-Morris correspondence and Wolf's exoneration of Grant took place in August, at the height of the presidential campaign. Grant's reticence at the time made it possible for Wolf's view to sound authentic. In the midst of such secrecy, Badeau's reply that Grant never intended any malice acquired the trappings of an official document. It had come from the general's own headquarters. Meanwhile, Wolf's letter to the *Boston Transcript*, whitewashing Grant and detailing the criminal activities of some Jews, the *"Lazzaroni* who [swarmed about] the camps," was copied far and wide.[57]

It is not known how many Jews voted for Grant, who received 53% of the popular vote.[58] But the flowering of Grant sentiment in the general community apparently found no parallels among Jews. Only one Hebrew Grant and Colfax club was formed, and that was located in New York City.[59] Wolf himself indicated that he had never "fostered clubs of a political nature."[60] While there are other evidences that he did campaign for Grant in 1868 and again in 1872, there are no official Republican party records before 1900 to attest to specific activities by local workers.[61] Furthermore, in 1868, Jewish editors warned their readers against voting a straight party line. The Jewish public was asked to use its conscience as a guide at the polling booth.[62] These reasons make it difficult to estimate the extent of Wolf's influence on Grant's behalf. Yet by 1868, Wolf was already well known both in Washington and in the American Jewish community at large. The perception that his efforts were effective carried weight with professional Republicans.

Grant had let it be known that minor appointments to office were to be made through his cabinet members, who in turn were to consult congressmen as to qualified candidates.[63] Originally, John A. Rawlins, as Grant's assistant adjutant general, had countersigned Order No. 11. Then, he was part of a coterie of military leaders who obviously believed the command was justified. Now, however, in the winter of 1868, as secretary of war, he was prepared to support Wolf for a post specifically created for him. Rawlins nominated Wolf to be the recorder of deeds for the District of Columbia. Thereupon, Albert Gallatin Riddle, an Ohio congressman, wrote a letter testifying to Wolf's integrity. Apparently, in 1864, Riddle and Wolf, acting as joint attorneys before a military tribunal, represented several clients involved in the sale of goods. When one of the defendants turned state's witness, Wolf withdrew from the case. Riddle thought such action was highly commendable, adding immeasurably to Wolf's stature.[64]

While Wolf's nomination to the federal post was still pending, he began a weekly column in the newly published B'nai B'rith journal, the *Jewish Times*. In some of its columns Wolf protected President Grant against charges of nepotism, and compared the "shabby, seedy, greedy, office seekers" to "dogs, hanging about . . . expecting a bone." Wolf had a ready wit and imagined there could be nothing more stupid than enacting an unwritten law that would disqualify the president's relatives from holding office. These were strong words, when Washington chatter was full of the ways in which Grant chose his cabinet members and other federal officials. But Wolf laughed it off, by quoting his legendary friend, Sophronibus, that the only reason he longed for White House favors was to dispose of his kin. Those, for example, who "could not pick wet stamps off letters," Sophronibus would remove from the post office. The remainder he would send as consuls to Africa's East Coast, and present them each with "a ready-made coffin."[65] But Wolf was no longer so arch and coy when he sided with President Grant and the House of Representatives in hoping that the Senate would agree to a repeal of the Tenure-of-Office Act.[66] It was all well and good for Wolf to feel this way now, when he was awaiting a presidential appointment as recorder of deeds. Ironically, it was only in the previous year that a legal decision to retain the Tenure Bill had led to President Johnson's downfall, catapulted Grant into the presidency, and ultimately benefited Wolf in his quest for public recognition.

For a short while, in the spring of 1869, that goal still eluded him. In his memoirs Wolf pretended that he was an unwilling candidate, but decided to fight for his recorder-of-deeds office only after some "prejudiced legislators" were prepared to deny him the position. The fact is, no reluctant aspirant would ever have gone to such lengths to denounce Jews as criminals in terms of Order No. 11, as he had, were there not some vision of high office to entice him. To prove that he would succeed, he appeared before the Senate Committee of the District of Columbia, whose chairman was Hannibal Hamlin.[67] Congressman Riddle of Ohio came to Wolf's aid once more and in a note to Hamlin called Wolf a "Republican of the most ardent school, who did much to overcome the reluctance of the Israelites" in supporting Grant. Toward this purpose, he "wrote much, made many speeches and spent a good deal of money."[68] On 30 April 1869 the Senate ratified the Wolf appointment.[69] He assumed office on May 15 of that year.[70]

2

Recorder of Deeds

A Taste of Power

Shortly after Wolf became recorder of deeds, Grant said to him:

> You have been so highly recommended by General Rawlins, whose judgment is infallible, that I rely on you never to decieve him. I learn that you represent your coreligionists, that you also stand well with the German-American element. I may want to see you and consult you often; when I can no longer trust you, I shall ask for your resignation.[1]

Wolf kept his post as recorder of deeds during the entire period of the Grant administration. The president never asked for his resignation. Instead, the two men developed a close personal relationship. With the exception of his own family, and cabinet members, Grant saw Wolf more frequently than any other individual.[2] As President of the Scheutzenverein, a German-American society, Wolf regularly invited Grant to share in its festivities, which sometimes took place in its own twelve-acre park. Devoted to target practice and other forms of recreation, members of the Scheutzenverein frequently extolled the virtues of good fellowship, American patriotism, and loyalty to their common ethnic background. In fact, the president was once so taken with a Tyrolean concert presented at the Scheutzen Park, that he asked Wolf and his wife to a concert at the White House so that Julia Grant might also hear the musicians.[3] When, in January 1869, Wolf's son was born, not only did Adam Badeau represent the president at the circumcision ceremony at Wolf's home, but the child was named after Grant. This was Adolph Grant Wolf, who later became an associate justice of the Supreme Court of Puerto Rico.[4]

On other occasions, Grant himself was present at programs where Wolf presided: a German-American fair to aid wounded Prussian soliders; the dedication of the Baron Von Steuben Monument in Anacostia, Md.; and the consecration of Adas Israel, then an Orthodox Congregation in Washington, D.C. For his part, the president paid close attention to the highlights of Wolf's public career and carefully acknowledged his communal and literary achievements. He commended Wolf for his lecture "The Influence of the Jews on the Progress of the World," praised him for his chairmanship of the B'nai B'rith Convention in 1874, and two years later welcomed him and his fellow delegates of the newly formed Union of American Hebrew Congregations to the White House. During the same period, Grant praised Wolf for having been instrumental in commissioning the Statue of Religious Liberty in Fairmount Park, Philadelphia, to celebrate America's centennial.[5]

Socially and politically, Wolf had reached his goal. He had become an advisor in a president's court, and he took full advantage of his new position. Because he was directly responsible to the president alone, Wolf succeeded in obtaining pardons for one hundred people who had been convicted of crimes. He recorded two such occasions. Once, a blind girl asked that her father, accused of selling washed revenue stamps, be released from jail. At another time, a woman from Chicago brought a petition to Wolf, bearing thousands of signatures of leading citizens, which declared that her husband, a city editor of the *Chicago Tribune*, had been unjustly indicted in a financial conspiracy. On Wolf's authority, the president freed both men.[6] When a poor Jew in Jerusalem, requesting a dowry for his daughter, wrote a letter in "jargon" [Yiddish] to Henry Gersoni, a Jewish journalist, asking that he see the "king of the Jews," Wolf showed the message to the president. Grant complied and mailed a check for $25.00.[7] This story has a rather fanciful ending. During a visit to Jerusalem, in the course of their world tour, the Grants presumably found this same Jew praying at the Wailing Wall.[8]

So secure was Wolf in his position as recorder of deeds, that when Grant asked him during the 1872 campaign to stump two doubtful states, Ohio and Indiana, Wolf did so. Before 1900, individualized accounts of Republican party activity are spotty, or nonexistent. Yet in this instance, there is no reason to doubt Wolf's word. In a letter to Grant's successor, Rutherford B. Hayes, Wolf was to refer to his efforts in 1872 on behalf of the Republican party. Then he had been the president of its German National Committee.[9]

Wolf openly relished the power that came with public office. Not only did he derive an income from witnessing official documents, but avenues of patronage once closed to him now became open: that he succeeded in placing some fifty friends and acquaintances, both Jews and Christians, in governmental posts,[10] ought to occasion no surprise. In their respective bailiwicks, powerful senators and other legislators openly appointed their favorite subordinates to lucrative positions. The president placed few restraints on the patterns that congressional leaders followed in dispensing political rewards.[11] He could scarcely have acted differently with Wolf, who had no national personalities to compete with, no significant pressures to withstand, and no electorate to answer to. For this was an era when agreements depended on whispered understandings, promises spoken in private, and choices casually offered to candidates for government service. In such an atmosphere it was simple enough for Wolf to sharpen his skills at personal contact so that his generosity was to extend primarily to German-Americans, and to some of his fellow Jews.[12]

To his chagrin, however, Wolf would quickly learn that even the friendship of a chief executive cannot alter the policies of foreign states, or secure the approval of fellow citizens. Wolf had hoped, originally, in the fall of 1869, to entertain the readers of his columns in the *Jewish Times* with local chit chat and gossip,[13] and he almost would have succeeded with an amusing reference to the impending wedding of a local butcher's widow and a Catholic, "who had been abbreviated into the bosom of Abraham." Yet gaiety was not his forte. Not only had personal tragedy in his recalling the death of his six-year-old son made it impossible for him to be witty,[14] but the calamities that befell Russian Jewry forced him to forego all clever humorous comments. In matters of international moment, he could no longer sign his weekly observations with campy terms, such as "Lupus" [Wolf] or "Showmar" [Watchdog, or Guard]. For news reached America that Jews living along the westernmost outposts of Russia were being exiled to its interior. In November 1869, Russian authorities had revived an obsolete, forty-four-year-old decree, or ukase, preventing Jews from living within seven miles of the border. Earlier conditions of cholera and famine, worsened by economic, civil, and political restrictions, made life for these people tenuous at best. The reimposed edict affected some 30,000 Jewish families. Forced to leave Bessarabia, they were punished if they spoke Polish, while their wives and children were whipped.[15] Finally, they were "placed on carts and wagons and transported to the interior to a place sufficiently removed from the border; there they [were] taken off and left on the road to shift for themselves [as best they could.]"[16]

On Sunday, 28 November 1869, Wolf, as president of his B'nai B'rith lodge, asked a fellow member, and a correspondent for the *American Israelite*, Lewis Abrahams, to speak on the Jewish situation in Russia. The result was a petition addressed to President Grant that emphasized that such banishments and expulsions in the dead of winter were "offenses against humanity," and were therefore to be considered "infractions against the law of nations." The petitioners requested the president to use whatever influence he could "within the limits of diplomatic duty," to have the decree revoked or modified, and to instruct the American consul at St. Petersburg, Andrew G. Curtin, accordingly.[17]

Ten days later, President Grant received a "delegation of Israelites," led by Wolf and Adolphus Solomons, a well-known community figure and art dealer of the period. Secretary of the Treasury George S. Boutwell, introduced them to the president, who promised to request a revocation of the edict and to "lay their appeal before the Cabinet today for its consideration."[18]

Sometime during these same days, Wolf, Solomons, and several of their colleagues wrote a letter to the *New York Herald* in which they detailed the truth of the forced migrations and denied the allegations of the Russian minister to this country, M. Catacazy, that the whole story was an exaggerated rumor.[19] To Wolf's distress, Secretary of State Hamilton Fish, with no further investigation, agreed with the Russian point of view. Wolf thereupon cabled Adolph Crémieux, member of the French Chamber of Deputies and president of the Alliance Israelite Universelle, an organization devoted to fostering civil and religious rights for Jews on the continent and in Asia. To Wolf's question of 14 December 1869, "Are expatriations in Russia cabled days since correct?" Crémieux replied that these expulsions were in effect and would continue until the spring.[20]

Wolf fumed publicly and vowed to see whether ". . . positive instructions to the Secretary of State . . . can be postponed, if not altogether laid aside . . . at the mere request of a foreigner [M. Cataczy.]" He promised to have the "outrage ventilated" in the Senate, unless he received "satisfactory evidence of why we have been so cavalierly treated."[21]

The "we" of Wolf's complaint referred to his own protests, undertaken at the request of the Board of Delegates of American Israelites, situated in New York City, and to those of his B'nai B'rith colleagues against the apparent indifference of the State Department. When, at last, Wolf discovered why he and his peers had been so "cavalierly treated," there was precious little he could have done about the matter. Secretary Fish did instruct Ambassador Curtin to investigate further. Curtin's memorandum, based on the findings of the U.S. consul at Revel, Eugene Schuyler, confirmed the official Russian conclusion that Jews had engaged in smuggling and had monopolized all trade. They therefore had only themselves to blame for the shrewdness of their business dealings and the carelessness of their clients, who were both nobles and peasants. For this reason the Jews were now "distressed and ruined." Improvements in their condition would depend on limiting their acquisition of real estate and restricting their economic activities. However, Jewish professionals, merchants, and veterans were to be exempted from the new impositions.

The memorandum also noted that families could be given the privilege of waiting until the spring to leave; only single men were obliged to depart at once. This information was hailed as a signal victory for Wolf, the more so since Secretary Fish added a sympathetic note to Curtin's dispatch.

> The Russian government will find it consistent with its policy to grant additional privileges contemplated   . Our experience shows that the

removal of restriction elsewhere elevates the class and advances the common good and social organization.

Ambassador Curtin knew better. His private message to Secretary Fish noted that no action on the part of the United States could change the policy of the Russian government toward its Jews. At all times, forced expulsions, forced conversions, forced conscriptions, forced taxation, and forced attempts to destroy the inner structure of the Russian Jewish community were the continuing order of the day.[22]

Either Wolf was unaware of this, or pretended that he knew of no such Russian policy. For domestic reasons, he stood ten feet tall; his political clout had helped modify a Russian ukase.[23] The B'nai B'rith lodge, which first alerted the president to the expulsions, now presented him with a beautifully engraved resolution, thanking him for his efforts on behalf of Russian Jewry. Wolf attended the reception, which abounded in good fellowship, the one predictable response to this affair.

American establishment Jewry had cheered Wolf for attempting to involve its country's diplomacy in the mysterious art of altering czarist policy. For him personally, indulging in the social graces and being close to the sources of executive power was indeed exhilarating. But Crémieux and his colleagues saw such victories in another light. Would Wolf be prepared to organize welcoming committees in the United States for the reception, distribution, and resettlement of European Jewish refugees? The Alliance Israelite Universelle was certain that Wolf himself wanted to discuss the emigration of Polish Jews to America, for they could not live in the land of their birth and were subject to famine.[24]

Wolf did not immediately inform the readers of the *Jewish Times* of the radical perspectives Crémieux and his colleagues shared. Yet the Alliance's concern with repatriation in America indicates that it too, like immigrant agencies abroad, was aware of how high the fever for newcomers ran in this land.

As a burgeoning industrial state, as a country whose untapped wilderness had yet to be tamed, and whose agricultural lands in the South were laid waste by the ravages of the Civil War, America needed all the willing labor it could absorb. When, in 1868 and 1869, the leaders of the French and German committees of the Alliance looked to Eastern Europe and saw the suffering of their coreligionists and looked to the new world and realized its potentials, they knew that emigration to the United States might well spell the difference between life and death for the victims of Russian oppression. After numerous conferences and endless debates as to whether resettlement in the interior of the Russian Empire or emigration abroad were the best course to pursue, French and German representatives of the Alliance opted for removal from Russia. For the record, Crémieux included Western Europe as a possible outlet for Russian refugees, but it was obvious that he had all along intended for them to leave the Continent. [25]

What had Wolf promised that so filled his European recipients with the hope and certainty of settlement in America? Judging by their telegram to him, they had literally leaped at the notion of shipping their displaced brethren to America. Crémieux and his colleagues were all distinguished citizens of their respective countries; they would not have dreamed of emigration had they merely Wolf's query posed in a cablegram concerning an old law dealing with quixotically revived expulsions to the Russian interior. It is more likely that the specifics of a plan for Jewish immigration, contained in correspondence between Wolf and members of the Alliance, has been lost. [26]

What is known, however, is that in the winter of 1869, Wolf had gone west to Washington Territory, where he visited his friend, Edward S. Salomon, then governor general of the area. Wolf himself, as recorder of deeds, was responsible for Salomon's appointment. Eager to populate the West with "industrious artisans," Salomon told Wolf that here was open territory begging to be cultivated. At the same time, a real estate promoter in the region, Elwood Evans, was urging liberty-minded aliens to come to those western shores. Such a combination of circumstances could easily have led Wolf to couple his request for information about Russian decrees with promises of settlement in Washington Territory. For in March 1870, Crémieux thanked Wolf for having secured Salomon's cooperation in the immigration scheme, while other members of the Alliance viewed the intended project as an incentive for greater accomplishment. They were thoroughly convinced that a Jewish agricultural colony in Washington Territory would soon attract other settlers and lead to the eventual formation of a flourishing society. Certain of success, the French leaders went so far as to contemplate a similar undertaking in Canada. To cap it all, a subcommittee of the Alliance, the Koenigsberg Central Frontier Committee, then informed Wolf that it had shipped a contingent of immigrants, consisting of 114 adults and 22 children, on the *Prinz Albert* from Hamburg. They were due to reach New York on 20 April 1870. [27]

Such news became an embarrassment for Wolf. He had been unable to set up welcoming committees for the newcomers, because other American Jews had not cooperated. He was convinced that their lack of interest in this matter guaranteed his failure. [28] In conjunction with Governor Salomon he had even devised a plan to "secure half-fare" for the emigrants, but had to delay his response to the "noble" Crémieux. First, Wolf wanted to know what Moritz Ellinger and other leaders of B'nai B'rith in the East were prepared to do. He would not proceed without "some authority from New York and Philadelphia." [29]

This begged the question, since Crémieux and his followers had already told Wolf that neither the Philadelphia branch of the Alliance, nor the Board of Delegates of American Israelites in New York would receive the new-comers. American establishment Jewry, voicing its opinions in the pages of the *Jewish Messenger* for the Board of Delegates, and in the *Jewish Times* for B'nai B'rith, feared an influx of alien Jewish poor to this country. Here, leaders simply refused to believe that their West European counterparts were sending young people, "who either [knew] a trade or [were] able to adapt themselves to agricultural pursuits."[30]

Such anti-immigrant sentiments were the conscious reflection of a society whose own adjustment to a new land and a new way of life was still pre-carious. "Making it" in America remained a hazardous venture for these German-American Jews, the majority of whom were foreign born. Beyond their own sense of insecurity, there loomed the fear of interorganizational rivalry. Which Jewish-sponsored institution ought to retain the privilege of representing the Jews of America to the rest of the country, or even to the world at large? Later, this gnawing problem of spokesmanship would arise to plague Wolf during his declining years. Now, however, Wolf's friend from his Cleveland days, Benjamin Franklin Peixotto, inadvertently sparked that inherent jealousy between the American-sponsored B'nai B'rith organization and the European-based Alliance Israelite Universelle.

Writing from California, Peixotto informed the editors of the *Jewish Times* that a committee of private individuals in San Francisco had already raised $700 for immigrant relief and settlement. All that was needed to implement the program was to form active branches of the Alliance in the United States.[31]

Ellinger and other members of the *Times's* staff were furious with Peixotto. They feared that his scheme would enlarge the influence of the Alliance at the expense of B'nai B'rith. In no uncertain terms, they reminded Peixotto that charity ought to begin at home, and found a rationale for denying a welcome to the Russian immigrants. They observed that those East Euro-pean Jews, with their outlandish garb and ritualistic religious habits were the enemies of civilization itself.[32]

In the swelling chorus of hate and distrust for settling aliens here, other journals latched on to the Wolf-Crémieux venture; one of those called it a "premature experiment," designed to send unemployable, impoverished strangers here.[33] It was left to the *Jewish Messenger* to deliver the final blow. The paper insisted that Crémieux need not have supposed "that because the Governor of Washington Territory is a Jew, [the] promised land is in the Northwest border of the Union."[34] Though the words were intended of-ficially for the French statesman, their impact was not lost on Wolf. It was he who had taken note of the appointment of David Eckstein as vice-consul in Vancouver, and mused that perhaps Jerusalem was really in the Far West.[35]

At an executive meeting of the Board of Delegates, held late in the spring of 1870, Wolf exploded. "I have been wrongfully assailed," he declared. All he ever wanted, he contended, was to "rescue a small number of single, male, industrious immigrants," who might easily adjust to the demands of the new world.[36] What he did not say was that Peixotto's injudiciousness in urging the expansion and enhancement of a European Jewish charity may well have been the decisive factor allowing American Jewish institutions to close ranks against the immigrants.

Ironically, only the imminent arrival of those selected few on the *Prinz Albert* mitigated the harshness of such American rejections. Faced with a fait accompli beyond their control, the Board of Delegates and B'nai B'rith rallied to help the newcomers; funds were raised and prospective employers solicited.[37] But there was no mistaking the intent of such activities. Representatives of the American Jewish community warned their European colleagues about keeping all those lost and wandering souls locked up in the old world. Nor were there to be any further temptations such as had stirred Wolf's imagination. B'nai B'rith argued for retaining all funds raised for the immigrants within the confines of this country. Motivated by the same impulse, the Board of Delegates took the opposite approach; it was convinced that shipping monies to Europe would effectively keep the would-be newcomers there.[38]

Wolf had now to choose betwen rescuing fellow Jews whose lives were imperiled, or defying the collective voice of Jewish community leaders here in the United States. By listening to his colleagues, Wolf selected that course which suited him best. He had read the handwriting on the wall. It was not that he lacked either that singular grace or foolhardiness with which to defy his peers. It was merely that he could not have been expected to champion a cause deemed unpopular with those to whom he first swore loyalty. From his earliest days in the capital, he had been associated with B'nai B'rith. All he could do now would be to bide his time if those with whom he worked rejected any notions of encouraging Jewish settlement in this land. For by the beginning of 1870, because his political fortunes were rising, his stature in the general community expanding, and his efforts on behalf of his persecuted brethren abroad duly recorded, the most he could hope for would be a return to an old-fashioned diplomacy. This meant quiet negotiation based on the art of personal contact, cautiously worded messages, and even skillfully manipulated confrontations with federal officials.[39]

Dabbling in Diplomacy

Wolf did not have to wait too long to try his persuasive powers in the halls of government. Less than three months after his Washington Territory scheme collapsed, he heard through the press that thousands of Jewish men,

women, and children in Romania had been butchered in a massacre whose
magnitude "dwarfed the horrors of the Sicilian Vespers and St. Bar-
tholomew's Day." Angry citizens from St. Louis, Chicago, and New Orleans
telegraphed to Wolf, urging him to intervene. He openly admitted that the
position he now occupied in Grant's administration gave him access to the
sources of power.

> I rejoiced that Providence and our honored President had permitted me
> to occupy such a position here to be of benefit to Israel and vindicate in
> person the great principles of truth and justice so horribly outraged in
> the Danube.

Not minimizing its responsibilities, Wolf obviously relished the sense of
self-worth such a mission on behalf of Romania's Jews could impart. On
Thursday, 3 June 1870, he called on Secretary of State Fish, who, having
been "shocked," hoped the report would prove false, and promised to do "all
he could consistently and cheerfully." The secretary was all for implementing
a congressional resolution condemning the massacre. Wolf then wrote a
letter of appeal to Senator Charles Sumner, that former fire-eating aboli-
tionist, and now chairman of the Senate Foreign Relations Committee. In his
communication, Wolf observed that in the past America had "extended
legislative sympathy to other peoples suffering from miscarriages of justice in
Greece, Ireland, and Cuba." Wolf now "wanted the same compassion shown
for the oppressed in Rumania." Five times during the evening of 2 June,
Wolf tried unsuccessfully to reach Sumner in person. Finally, late at night,
he delivered the letter personally and left it on the senator's doorstep. Either
the impact of the note, or the interest evinced by Secretary Fish brought
results. By eleven o'clock the following morning, every member of Congress
had a copy of Wolf's appeal on his desk. In the Senate Chamber he met
Sumner, who was "horribly indignant," and had expected Secretary Fish to
have telegraphed various European capitals for confirmation of the news.
Senators Carl Schurz, Hannibal Hamlin, and others expressed their sympa-
thies, while Senator John Sherman offered a resolution expressing concern
and asking for a verification of the event. In the House, Congressmen
Godlove Stein Orth, Norman Judd, Benjamin Butler, and William Moore
wanted to pass the Sumner resolution, but Senator William Sprague of
Rhode Island was convinced Romania's Jews had brought the suffering on
themselves, for they had, he insisted, "obtained possession of the whole of
the trade, a great portion of the lands and about all of the business connected
with the affairs of that people [the Romanians]." Sprague would have preferred had the Senate turned its attention to domestic affairs. The Senate
adopted the Sumner resolution, but in the House, Sprague's sentiments

prevailed and the resolution was submitted to the Committee on Foreign Affairs for further study.[40]

In complying with the request of the Sumner resolution, Secretary Fish received some information from the American Minister to Turkey. This was based on official Romanian ideology. Russia, in the interests of ultimate annexation, had instigated the migration of Jews to Romania to create chaos between the new arrivals and the older inhabitants.

Such an interpretation did not accord with the view that the anti-Semitic massacre was the result of Romanian neglect of its treaty obligations. The Western powers, eager to limit Russian hegemony over Moldavia and Wallachia, allowed these provinces to unite to form an independent Romania. In return for their newly found freedom, Romania's leaders had agreed to English and French demands granting political and religious rights to Romania's non-Christian population. At best, such promises were words on paper. The Romanian government treated its Jews, particularly those who had but recently arrived from Galicia and Russia, as stateless persons. From 1866 on, mob violence against these people, who were traders, innkeepers, and managers of rural estates for the landed gentry, intensified. By 1870, governmentally sanctioned excesses against them had become commonplace. What had engaged Wolf's attention was only the latest in a series of similar episodes.[41]

While diplomatic dispatches concerning Romania's treatment of its Jews continued to reach Washington, Secretary Fish consented to a joint proposal by Wolf and Myer Isaacs, secretary of the Board of Delegates of American Israelites, that Adolphe Buchner, a Jew then serving as secretary to the American Consulate in Bucharest, was to be named consul general to Romania. On the very same day when Wolf tried so desperately to reach Senator Sumner, he had also written a letter to Secretary Fish, asking that Buchner be appointed.[42] In fact, earlier in April 1870, Buchner had begun his own campaign, from Bucharest, to convince the Board of Delegates that he was the man for the post. He would have succeeded, were it not for the fact that Peixotto, as he had once before, intervened, and matters took a wholly different turn.

Earlier that season, in November 1869, Peixotto was still convinced that San Francisco was the "half-way house" of the world. There he was "resolved to settle, to lay the permanent foundations of name, fame, and fortune." There he was prepared to "rear [his] six children, to fight the good fight, and to win."[43]

For the moment, San Francisco had become Peixotto's land of golden opportunity. After a series of business failures, he had gone west, and like Wolf before him, was prepared to read law and be admitted to the bar. He begged Wolf for legal books and materials, "the laws of congress in the shape of Public Documents among others," and then complained that printed matter took long to reach San Francisco. He also protested loudly to Recorder Wolf, who could now dispense patronage, that it would be unseemly to accept any federal appointments. But after the Romanian story broke into print, Peixotto was prepared to abandon all for Bucharest.

What had prompted his sudden change of heart? The real reasons may forever be shrouded in mystery. What is known is that Hayim Zvi Sneersohn, a visiting Chasidic rabbi from Palestine, here on a mission to improve the lot of Syrian Jews, may well have been the catalyst who altered Peixotto's dream from leading the good life and rearing his six children in San Francisco, to visions of conquest, glory, and succor in an old world setting.[44] Rabbi Sneersohn had electrified American audiences with his speeches; he even managed a meeting with Grant. By the time the rabbi reached San Francisco, he had beomc Peixotto's "constant companion and adviser."[45] Sneersohn thought little of Buchner and did not hesitate to so inform the president. At the same time, Sneersohn may well have succeeded in persuading Peixotto to try his hand at diplomacy.[46] Gratefully, Peixotto now warmed to the task. He combined the visionary's dream of saving Romanian Jewry with an unshakable belief in his own invincibility.

Peixotto would go to Romania; he would become his people's redeemer. He was ready to sacrifice wife, family, livelihood, fortune, and even his future, for Bucharest. He was convinced he knew what had to be done. In particular, he would free Romania's impoverished Jews from their East European rituals. He would establish schools and societies to alert his charges to the beauties of western thought. And as he restructured Romanian Jewish society, he would also succeed, or so he claimed, in obtaining its political, social, civic, religious and legal rights. All that was necessary then would be for Wolf to secure the consulship and all its perquisites for him.[47]

Peixotto dispatched essentially the same message to Myer S. Isaacs, but made certain to add that while "[another one of their mutual friends,] Adolphus Solomons was a 'true man,' Wolf overestimates his influence at the White House."[48]

However, the key to the matter was that Wolf was at the nation's capital, while Isaacs was not. Since Wolf had made the official request to Fish, in accordance with the wishes of Isaacs and the Board of Delegates, it was Wolf who had now to initiate the process of seeking the consulship once again. He was incensed; his earlier achievement counted for nothing; for Peixotto had obtained the backing of the powerful Seligman banking family, and had placed great reliance upon Rabbi Sneersohn's judgment.[49]

From Peixotto's perspective, Wolf's abandonment amounted to a betrayal of their friendship. The two had met when they were both young men in Cleveland, and it is possible that Peixotto, who was on close terms with Stephen A. Douglas, may well have introduced Wolf to early politicking within the Democratic party, before the slavery issue made him a Republican.[50] But now, a decade later, Wolf at first refused to entertain any notions of Peixotto's mission to Romania. It was as though the favors of the Cleveland days, the warm letters sent by Peixotto from San Francisco to Wolf, simply would not keep. Wolf wrote to Peixotto, saying:

> Language fails to convey my astonishment at your request to be appointed Consul to Roumania [sic], and I deemed your telegram a mistake, and awaited your letter that has now come and fails to convince me in the least, but as you positively request it, I have very reluctantly given your name to the President (and withdrawn that of Mr. Buchner, who resides there.) I can . . . see the machinations of Rabbi Sneersohn, who is unpredictable and impractical. You can do no possible good, on the contrary, harm; for in your capacity as Consul you are restricted to Orders and rules of the Department, no matter how insignificant the Mission, the Principle holds good in all cases. As a Missionary, our Government can give you no protection whatsoever; and the whole matter, as there are no fees or salary, is barren of results. . . . Do not make yourself ridiculous before the World. . . . It would be wrong to ask our Government to assist us as Jews. . . . Dismiss the subject at once. . . .[51]

Wolf's plea fell on deaf ears. In spelling out the demands of the consulship, Peixotto wanted to know "if it's not possible to get the President or the Department of State to draw upon the Civil Service Fund towards at least providing an outfit or mileage for the position." Peixotto could not imagine that "our great Government [would] send its consuls wholly without provision to far distant countries or expect that they shall bear the whole burden of expense where there is no recompence whatsoever. . . ."[52]

Wolf finally relented. Not only did he succumb to the wishes of the Seligmans that Peixotto be nominated for the post but together with him canvassed B'nai B'rith lodges in Philadelphia and Baltimore, to raise funds for the Mission. In Washington, Wolf arranged a meeting for Peixotto with the president. Peixotto had come armed with a message from Senator William Stewart, requesting an autograph letter to Prince Charles of Romania.[53] This the president refused to grant, but did issue a circular outlining the essential aspects of Peixotto's assignment.

> The bearer of this letter, Hon. Ben. F. Peixotto, who has accepted the important though unremunerative post of U.S. Consul General to Roumania [sic], is commended to the good offices of all representatives of this government abroad
> Mr. Peixotto has undertaken the duties of his present office more as

Missionary work for the benefit of the people who are laboring under severe oppression than for any benefits to be accrued to himself. . . .

The United States, knowing no distinction of her own citizens on account of religion or nativity, naturally believes in a civilization the world over which secures the same universal liberal views.[54]

Such a statement was too much for Wolf to resist. Here was a plan, motivated only by the most altruistic of values, and seconded by the chief executive of a great nation. Its message was certainly good for Republican politics. Furthermore, its ultimate effect on the Romanian Jewish situation would undoubtedly prove beneficial. At the same time, it could only enhance Wolf's own Washington base as a potential source of power.

Without consulting Peixotto, Wolf promptly relayed the contents of the circular to the wire services. Immediately, the press roundly accused Peixotto of having overstepped the bounds of political and diplomatic propriety. Without prior authorization, he had divulged what amounted to a verbatim account of a conference with the president.[55]

Peixotto did not respond publicly to the scorn heaped upon him. Had he spoken up against such a "frenzied rush" to impart all to the world, he would not have been able to take "Wolf's delicate position" into account. Perhaps, thought Peixotto, Wolf's close relations with Grant warranted publicizing the story. Peixotto also reasoned that suppressing the news of the consular appointment might have been politically damaging to Grant.[56]

In his anger at the turn events had taken, Wolf showed no such consideration for Peixotto, much less for the niceties of the situation. Instead, in brusque tones for Secretary Fish's benefit, Wolf described Peixotto's mission as a "begging scheme" and detailed his own intense opposition to it. Wolf insisted that the Peixotto appointment had been secured on the basis of Senator Stewart's accompanying letter of endorsement.

"I am too diplomatic to be indiscreet," Wolf assured the secretary. "But knowing the temper of my co-religionists, I kept silent fearing to be misconstrued [in my opposition to the entire project.]"[57]

Secretary Fish cooled Wolf's wrath. Realistically, he wrote:

There is no idea entertained of withdrawing the appointment of Mr. Peixotto at present. I trust that if admitted to the discharge of the duties of the Consulate, he may exhibit a proper appreciation of its appropriate duties and limitations and of his own proper relations with the Department under which he is to act. He goes out as Consul, not as an Ambassador.[58]

The unsavory aspect of Wolf's role in this Romanian business was simply that he felt obliged to hold two diametrically opposite points of view at the same time. Privately, he was convinced that Peixotto was not the man for the job. Peixotto's flair for the dramatic, his grandiose aspirations for noteworthy diplomatic conquests, and his flamboyant methods for defending Romanian Jews, Wolf reasoned, were factors that militated against a successful consulship. Nor did Wolf see how Peixotto could overcome the greatest obstacle of all. He was a poor man who would be unable to maintain a diplomatic establishment on a lavish scale beyond his means.[59]

Publicly, though, whenever Wolf referred to the Bucharest story, he would enlarge upon his own essential role in securing the post for his friend. For posterity's sake, it was Wolf, who by scouring the B'nai B'rith lodges for funds, on three different occasions, managed to accumulate several thousand dollars to sustain the Mission. When in 1872, anti-Jewish riots surfaced in Ismail and Cahul, it was Wolf who officially protested against these mob actions. He even found encouragement in Secretary Fish's response to the tragic news—that Peixotto could base his remonstrance to the Romanian government on the American State Department's condemnation of all acts of persecution. Ultimately, Peixotto did manage to obtain a pardon from Prince Charles for five of the Jewish defendants who had been charged with instigating the riots. And in 1873, Peixotto effectively delayed the implementation of a law excluding Jews from the liquor trade. By the following year he was able to point with pride to the temporary grants of municipal rights, circumscribed though they were, to native Romanian Jews. Peixotto also established the Zion Society in Romania, a group dedicated to the furtherance of Jewish cultural and educational interests in that land. This later evolved into a B'nai B'rith organization. Looking back on it all from the perspective of almost half a century, Wolf, together with his friend Max Kohler, agreed that Peixotto's defense of Jewish rights in Romania paved the way for the Western powers to seek minority rights in Romania at the Congress of Berlin, held in 1878.[60]

Had these achievements been all there was to the Romanian Mission, Wolf could well have expanded on an accomplishment that was basically his to begin with—how Consul Peixotto had brought progress, civilization, and basic human rights to backward Romania. But the truth of the matter was that Peixotto had come to a country beset by economic ills, one riding high on the waves of Balkan nationalism and riddled with anti-Semitism. To add to these woes, Romania's more settled, wealthier Jewish population, who had lived there during Turkish rule, had little use for the new Jewish immigrants from Russia and Galicia. Romania's established Jewish society came to despise Peixotto for his attempts to change the status quo of those poor Jewish artisans and traders. It looked askance at his ventures, financed largely by a few West European and American Jewish philanthropists, to create Jewish cultural institutions, to emancipate Jews politically, and to foster their emigration from Romania.

Wolf knew this, but as one of Peixotto's official sponsors could not speak openly about it. If, for example, Consul Peixotto's methods for rescuing immigrant Jews irritated other consular agents, or his strident communications on the outrageously prejudical behavior of Romanian officialdom embarrassed the European diplomatic corps, Wolf had only to inquire of Secretary Fish as to how Peixotto was faring at the consulate. Was his "conduct approved and commended by the Department?"[61]

Unfortunately, Peixotto's task involved more than his being concerned with diplomatic etiquette. He wanted to rescue people, and in his forthright manner embarked on schemes that tarnished his image. The State Department charged him with soliciting funds from wealthy Europeans for his Mission. One of his fellow consuls, B. Kreisman, accused him of shipping Romanian Jewish immigrants to the American consulate at Berlin, to beg for financial aid.[62] Peixotto was thoroughly censured by community leaders on the American Jewish scene for registering 404 Jewish families in Romania as potential emigrées to this country. For that, however, the Romanian government thanked him heartily and issued passports gratis to Peixotto's charges. American Jews, who were finally constrained to accept upward of 150 of these people, were dismayed and accused Peixotto of dumping paupers on the shores of the new world.[63]

Beyond all the resentments he had encountered from his own coreligionists and colleagues in the diplomatic arena, Peixotto had always to confront his own poverty.[64] When the monies Wolf had amassed for the financially strapped Peixotto proved inadequate, Wolf asked Secretary Fish, at Peixotto's bidding, to raise the Mission to a consul generalship, still without a salary, but with the possibility of having fees attached for services rendered. But Peixotto, apparently had a sudden change of heart, and argued that by right Wolf's request to Fish should have originated with the Senate Foreign Relations Committee. As a matter of fact, Wolf sent Peixotto a copy of a consular bill, written in 1870, intended to turn the Mission into a full-fledged consulship.[65] This proved to be scant consolation for Peixotto. For it wasn't until 1874 that Wolf, as president of a B'nai B'rith convention, succeeded in having its delegates petition Congress to create a salaried post in Romania.[66] This was not to commence, however, before July 1875. Meanwhile, Wolf managed to obtain $500 for Peixotto's work from the Board of Delegates. Earlier he had observed that the niggardliness of those who "ought to have sustained Peixotto," only insured that he "starve at Bucharest."[67]

At last the Board was moved to compassion. Through its efforts and those of a London based charity, the Roumanian Committee, funds were sent to Peixotto. These enabled him, finally, after considerable delays on a variety of pretexts, to return home. By now, it was May 1876, and the impact of the Romanian Mission had begun to disintegrate. Earlier, half-hearted attempts by European Jewish leaders at the Brussels Conference to petition the

Romanian government for the enfranchisement of minorities met with limited success. But at the end, even these measures were nullified, when the old, restrictive economic laws against the Jews were revived.[68]

After the Romanian experience, Peixotto's stay in America proved temporary. Having sought Wolf's counsel as to lecturing here on his European venture and stumping Ohio for the presidential nominee, Rutherford B. Hayes, Peixotto performed both chores well.[69] However, insofar as Romania was concerned, he was no longer the man to do battle. His diplomatic experience had become an exercise in futility.

Like Wolf before him, who had tried to enhance Grant's reputation, now Peixotto, as a distinguished leader and skillful orator, threw himself into the fray on Hayes's behalf.[70] A consulship was in order. Backed by influential friends in Cleveland, Cincinnati, New York, and San Francisco, Peixotto was appointed consul general to St. Petersbrug, a position for which Wolf claimed sole credit.[71] But as matters turned out, the Russians refused to welcome Peixotto because of his avowed anti-Czarist sentiment expressed during his American lecture tour on Romania.[72] Lyons, France, was his second choice[73] a decision presumably made at Wolf's direction.[74]

Lyons proved to be a rather pedestrian spot, where Peixotto devoted his energies mostly to commercial matters, one of the prime duties of American consuls abroad.[75] Here there was none of the glamour associated with the political animosities and upheavals rampant in Bucharest.

Was Peixotto a visionary, prepared to sacrifice himself, as he declared in purple prose, in the battle for human rights?[76] Or did the romance and status attached to the foreign service so intrigue him that he overlooked all personal privations? Was Wolf, despite his keeness of mind, sagacity, and polish, equally careless? To begin with, he gravely doubted whether Peixotto was the best representative to be sent to Bucharest, to mitigate its harshly anti-Semitic economic and political restrictions. But entering the diplomatic service was just about the highest goal upper-class, assmiliated Jews in nineteenth-century America could aspire to. And though he protested privately, publicly Wolf supported the Romanian Mission. He even trusted Peixotto sufficiently to gather subscriptions on his behalf to launch Peixotto's intended volume on Romania.[77] It would appear that Peixotto had almost persuaded Wolf into believing that from its proceeds the two might retire in affluence on adjoining estates along the Hudson where they would enjoy the good life in the style of European country gentry.[78]

At other times, such musings seemed a pipedream. Months would elapse before Wolf would respond to Peixotto's letters. "Why do you neglect your old friend? Do you love me no more?" Peixotto would inquire. In the end, Wolf would reply, often with suggestions for raising funds for noble causes, or with instructions concerning proper diplomatic behavior, interspersed by items of family news.[79] On occasion, Peixotto's letters plumbed the depths of their personal relationship. Once Peixotto compared his own heartsickness over the plight of Romanian Jewry to Wolf's personal tragedy. In September 1871, Wolf and his wife, Caroline, lost a six-year-old son, and by the following January, Mrs. Wolf had grown quite ill. Such then were the ties that bound the men to each other. Peixotto liked to imagine that the two would grow old together. As the friend of his youth, Peixotto was certain Wolf was attracted to him by a "deeper sympathy," by the "congeniality of their tastes."[80]

That congeniality once had its lighter moments. In 1881, Wolf visited Peixotto at Lyons, during Christmas. The party was gay indeed, so full of frivolity that after Wolf left, a broken sofa leg had to be repaired. Peixotto declared he would not have been able to look at another feminine undergarment, until tying his "dear Mandie's sash" broke the spell.[81]

With the Republicans out of power in 1886, Peixotto lost the consulship and returned to New York, where he edited the B'nai B'rith magazine, *Menorah Monthly*. There he ran a serialized version of his Romanian experience.

In the few remaining years of life left to him—he died in 1890[83]—Peixotto tried unsuccessfully once again to enter the diplomatic service. In 1889, accompanied by Wolf, he sought out Secretary of State James G. Blaine, and begged to be appointed minister to Turkey.[84] In fact, one of Peixotto's supporters, writing to President Benjamin Harrison, suggested that Peixotto was the man to replace Oscar S. Straus at Constantinople, because the latter had done all in his power to promote Grover Cleveland's election.[85] With the Turkish option lost, Peixotto was prepared to accept consulships to Romania, Serbia, or Greece.[86] Shortly after Peixotto's death, his wife wrote a pitiful letter to Wolf. She reserved all her hatred for him, though she did not refrain from venting her rage at her husband's colleagues in the B'nai B'rith Order. She insisted that its leaders had betrayed Peixotto.

> You tell me to have courage, to let no stranger pity me! And why not: Why should the stranger not pity me? Are we not to be pitied . . . and strangers have been attentive, helpful to us . . . what did his friends(?) do for him . . .—his beloved Order, his brothers of the Covenant—did they not let him pine and go down. . . .

As she warmed to her topic, the distraught widow grew more virulent in her attack on Wolf.

> . . . even you were not his friend, you call him brother, had he been your brother, you would have said, "Frank . . . I will pay your passage to join your wife in Berlin—you can pay me back when you have it—Leave *The Menorah* for a month. . . . It will cure you. . . .
>
> Perhaps, had you said this . . . he would be alive today.[87]

These were bitter words with which to reproach a man who, when all was said and done, helped sustain the Romanian Mission and took an ongoing interest in Peixotto's diplomatic aspirations. A year or so after Mrs. Peixotto penned this vitrolic note, Wolf was to lose his own wife of thirty-four years, and while the Board of Governors of the Union of American Hebrew Congregations had a resolution of condolence spread upon the minutes,[88] this earlier message from Hannah Strauss Peixotto did nothing to sweeten his lot. At best, it symbolized a pathetic little reminder, a last gesture to seal Wolf's remembrance of his one-time Cleveland friend.

Friends and Enemies

Here at home, the estimates Wolf's business associates had of him were far different from those of Peixotto's widow.

> The Recorder of the District, Simon Wolf, has made himself extremely popular with the legal fraternity by the zeal and energy he has brought to his office. The records of the location of the seat of government, in the territory ceded by Maryland and Virginia, had been loosely and carelessly preserved; no proper reference had been made or kept. Mr. Wolf has had everything carefully indexed and had the books, plots and surveys that were falling into decay newly bound and overhauled The bar talk of giving him a substantial testimony of their appreciation.[89]

Wolf graciously returned such compliments. Frequently, he would host social gatherings at his home on 616 H Street in Northwest Washington, where the more notable politicians and legislators would meet. He valued good fellowship, and a proper regard for the social graces as the marks of the cultivated man. It ought to be remembered that Wolf lived long before the time the smoothly functioning public-relations agency had intruded upon the ways of government. To be effective, he had to foster a sense of personal warmth for all the shapers of federal policy he was likely to meet. What better way to place them in his debt than to have invited them as his personal guests to his home?

At the same time, Wolf was also fulfilling a newcomer's dream, to immerse himself in the sophisticated ambiance cosmopolitan cities ought to be able to offer.

> If Americans would only take more pride in their capital, we could soon have here what is common in Europe, a metropolis worthy of a great country; to succeed both elements of society [the Southerners characterized by] an indolence and a lack of energy, [and the Northerners full

of spirit] and enterprise [would have to] work in unison and harmony [and] forget their petty local differences to have a grand and beautiful Capital.[90]

Together with other German immigrants of all persuasions, Wolf measured that pursuit of educational excellence and culture which ought to be acquired in an urban environment by the continuous expansion of newer social lodges, varied religious groups, additional orders, and brotherhoods of all sorts. Wolf was a product of that German-American generation which wanted its institutions to justify themselves in terms of reason, faith, and social achievements. Such advancement implied an "innate love of culture and improvement . . ." "a sense of worldly refinement, learning, comfort, religion, charity and benevolence in all their phases."[91] It became inevitable that the worth of social organizations, religious orders, and cultural endeavors had always to be evaluated in terms of the progress set for them by their adherents. If Wolf and his fellow countrymen had brought their notions of a superior civilization from the land of their birth, from their adopted country they acquired a keen sense of individualism, of skepticism, sharpened by the frontier spirit of the age. This allowed them to criticize their own communal agencies. Democracy had imbued these naturalized citizens with an inviolate belief in the righteousness of their own consciences. Resulting differences of opinion accounted for the steady increase in the number of philanthropic, artistic, intellectual, and social organizations of all sorts.

Yet Wolf would not allow those variations in belief, or in methods for accomplishing set goals, to diminish the closeness he felt for all immigrants of German extraction. Using his recorder-of-deeds post to reward these people for their services to the president, to the Republican party, and to the Union cause, was central to Wolf's way of thinking. As already noted, like most of his colleagues from the Fatherland, he brought with him a strong sense of duty. In the New World this meant an ardent patriotism, and an abiding loyalty to persons and places associated with the old country. While in his speeches he may have railed against the abundant political, economic, and religious obstacles so prevalent in Germany, his ties to his ancestral home remained indissoluble.[92]

The pride he took in his Germanic roots was particularly obvious during the period of the Franco-Prussian War. He boasted shamelessly that at his suggestion Grant ordered a halt to the shipment of surplus arms to France. With Wolf in attendance, Grant's Cabinet supported that decision. Under the circumstances, Wolf was able to afford a certain degree of magnanimity, when, at an evening banquet in Grant's presence, an overenthusiastic German-American, William Pullman, proposed a toast to the president of the United States, "the friend of Germany." Officially, such exuberance was misplaced because of American neutrality, and French sensitivity. Wolf saved the day by publicly proclaiming,

> No, no, the President of the United States is the friend of all the governments of the world, but General Grant is our guest and our friend.

Wolf was heartily applauded for his extemporaneous remark.

He wrote candidly that at his suggestion Grant had appointed numerous Americans of German backgrounds and origins to federal posts. Wolf was particularly proud that he had secured a seat on the San Domingo Commission for his friend, Franz Sigel, a former Union general. Once that position was terminated, Sigel managed, through Grant's good offices, to obtain a post as a collector of internal revenue. According to Wolf,

> President Grant said to me time and again that no man has done more than [Sigel] to aid the Union cause in the Northwest, and especially in Missouri . . . and his name had contributed greatly towards rousing the patriotic spirit of German-Americans.

For that reason, Grant continued, Sigel deserved the gratitude of the "American poeple."

More noteworthy assignments followed for other aspirants. Wolf claimed sole credit, as seen, for Salomon's appointment as governor of Washington Territory. Wolf also stated that he was instrumental in having Grant name David Eckstein as consul to Vancouver, B.C., where he settled a boundary dispute between Washington Territory and Canada in favor of the United States. Of these positions, Eckstein's lasted for seven years, while Salomon's was exceedingly brief—no more than a year, at which time certain subordinates charged him with financial discrepancies in the Treasury accounts of that region.[93] Andreas Willman's sinecure, to collect the taxes for the Port of New York, was delayed for twelve months because the president was obliged to keep an earlier political promise. But when the time was ripe, Grant turned to Wolf and said, "why would this not be a fine opportunity to appoint Willman?"[94]

In this way, political plums fell to those who had kept faith with the chief executive. Dispensing patronage where he could, Wolf was merely following the patterns set by the Grant administration. At a time when the president of the United States placed loyalty to his friends above other considerations, Wolf could hardly have been expected to do less. Ironically, sometimes he found it difficult to reconcile his protestations of democracy and overriding considerations of meritorious service, not with political rewards handed out to the incapable, but with federal discriminations against Jewish nominees to governmental office.

In December 1870, Grant announced his policy of allocating the supervision of Indian agencies to various religious denominations, who would "undertake to Christianize and civilize the Indians. . . ." Upon Wolf's request, the president then appointed a Jewish surgeon from Albany, Dr. Hermann Bendell, as superintendent of Indian Affairs for Arizona. A legislator from that state, Richard C. McCormick, objected on the grounds that the appointment of an "Israelite" was inconsistent with the presidential policy of "Christianizing the Indians," while Senator Roscoe Conkling of New York refused to accede to the nomination since he had not been consulted. Wolf persuaded McCormick to change his views, but could do nothing with Conkling, who remained adamant in his opposition. "I made the fight before the Committee on Indian Affairs in the Senate and won," wrote Wolf. Bendell served at his post for several years. But a Christian Board of Missions, chaired by General Otis O. Howard, reviewed the various superintendencies, and found Bendell's position untenable. Personally, the members of the Board of Missions admired Bendell for his excellent administrative abilities. "Unfortunately [however], he [was] not a Christian."

In his eagerness to defend his friend, Wolf overstepped his bounds, and lost the battle.

> I finally told them that if anyone in the world ought to be appointed to supervise the affairs of the Indians and to elevate them in manhood and morale, he should . . . be an American citizen of the Jewish faith, especially of the medical profession, for the reports read at that meeting showed that three-fourths present . . . of the population were affected by diseases engendered by immoral practices and. . . . Dr. Bendell could not only *civilize* them, but also use his professional skill in converting them to the *tenets* of Judaism, a physical cleansing process as well as a soul elevation.

Some years later, Dr. Bendell resigned from his post. He was unable to withstand the rancor and bitterness that his appointment had produced.[95]

Apparently such failure of will was not common to Wolf's way of thinking. Despite his quarrels with other German-Americans, he never thought of leaving his recorder-of-deeds office. On the contrary, as shall soon be seen, he had literally to be forced to resign. Furthermore, such disagreements he may have had with those who shared his Teutonic backgrounds never stopped him from continuing his prodigious efforts on behalf of the land of his birth, and for the sake of his German-American compatriots.

Only twice in his career did he publicly complain about them: once in 1876, when he denied any personal involvement in the Belknap scandals, and second, in 1877, when he realized that his efforts in the Hayes presidential campaign had gone unrewarded.

The country had already had its fill of corruption so prevalent during the early years of Grant's presidency. The Credit Mobilier scandal associated with the building of the Union Pacific Railroad, Jay Gould's and Jim Fisk's cornering of the gold market, and the unscrupulous manipulations of the Whiskey Ring in St. Louis[96] had tarnished many a federal reputation. But when the secretary of war, William W. Belknap, was himself exposed in connection with the military sale of post traderships in the Indian Territories,[97] it seemed as though all moral commitments in government had collapsed.

In the 1870s, merchants who operated the military posts on Indian lands commanded a monopoly in prices. Mrs. Belknap, the secretary's first wife, convinced one such trader, John Evans, at Fort Sill, Okla., that to retain his position he would have to pay an annual fee of $12,000 to another contender for the position, Caleb S. Marsh, a close friend of the Belknaps. Presumably, the secretary himself had suggested that Evans and Marsh enter into such a partnership. By the time Heister Clymer, the chairman of the House Committee on Expenditures, investigated the matter, Marsh had already received $42,000, while Mrs. Belknap, until her death continued to benefit from a certain percentage of the profits. Thereafter the remaining sums continued to line the pockets of the second Mrs. Belknap, a sister to the deceased.[98]

Fraudulent practices in official circles were so monumental that the senators were unable to impeach Belknap. Since he resigned before an official inquiry was to take place, the lawmakers became involved in a legal quibble. Could Belknap be tried for malfeasance in office when he no longer held the post in question?[99]

Wolf, too, had come under the scrutiny of the Clymer Committee. His German-American colleagues, he insisted, saw ugly parallels between the ease with which he had obtained governmental favors for his personal acquaintances and the story that led to Belknap's disgrace.

In 1870, Wolf obtained an agreement from Belknap that one Mr. Friedlander of Texas be allowed to retain his post tradership, provided the congressman from that state, Edward Degener, approved. Insofar as Wolf was concerned, that was the end of the matter. But in testimony before the Clymer Committee, a certain Mr. Loeb swore that he paid both Friedlander and Wolf $3,000 apiece for the post in question. To compound the difficulty, another witness, James Trainor, maintained that "over the bar at the National Hotel" he gave Wolf $250 for the position in question. Trainor added that he accompanied Congressman Degener to Wolf's home, where they met Colonel A. C. Jackson, who joined them in the talks. Jackson denied the allegation, but had heard the story from Trainor. For his part, Degener rejected any notion of escorting Trainor to Wolf's residence, but could not recall whether he had ever introduced Wolf to Trainor. Thereupon, Loeb refuted his charges against Friedlander and Wolf. Jackson also admitted he had paid General Elliot Warren Rice $2,000 for a post tradership, but that Wolf never received any monies from the transaction. Convinced of Wolf's innocence, the Clymer Committee thought it unnecessary for him to testify. Nevertheless, he appeared before the investigative body to clear his reputation.[100]

Wolf was blameless, but the charges dismayed him. In a vituperative letter to a local editor, he inveighed against his German-American confréres, and attributed their motivations to anti-Semitic tendencies. He was furious that they had accused him both of defrauding the government and of enriching himself at the expense of one of their institutions, the Saengerbund-Aktion group. He emphasized that while Americans would know he was guiltless, the Germans would persist in the canard that he "as a Jew [was] incapable of higher motives than money." True though he had been to the "ideals and sentiments" of his German friends, they were prepared to "drag him down," for they were jealous of him. Such an emotion, he continued, had "distracted Germany for centuries" in its treatment of the Jew. "What has this Wolf done?" he wondered, that he "should suddenly disappear from the scene?" Wolf responded to his own question by listing a lengthy catalogue of his own virtues as a patriotic American citizen, a loyal Israelite, and an inheritor of a proud Germanic background. He had traveled widely at his own expense on behalf of the Republican Party, had secured the recorder-of-deeds office, and had never discriminated against anyone. Should his friends again ask him for favors, he would respond as always.[101]

Wolf kept his word. After the Republican Convention had met in June 1876 and nominated the governor of Ohio, Rutherford B. Hayes, as a favorite son candidate, Wolf gladly accepted an invitation to stump Ohio, Indiana, and New York for the presidential nominee. "I am an Ohio boy," he told Hayes, "and feel a pride in seeing you elected." Yet Wolf's personal wishes did not deter him from calling Hayes's attention to the needs of the German-American element in the United States. Wolf was distressed, that unlike its predecessor of 1872, the current Republican Platform Committee disregarded his pleas "for a liberal emigration and naturalization policy," formulated under his auspices at a convention of German Republicans in Cincinnati.

> "You know best," wrote Wolf, "how sensitive our Germans are, especially in the West. I find already in reading German papers that they charge you with being a strict temperance man [and automatically opposed to the German liquor and brewery interests in the Midwest.] Now then why could you not in accepting say in your letter . . . when alluding to the paragraph on Naturalization and Emigration that 'the

Republican Party owes a vast debt to a healthy, intelligent Emigration and that to the liberal protection and recognition of that Emigrant Citizen the Republican Party owes a debt which you at all times shall be pleased to exert.' Something of this kind will sweep like a wind. . . ."[102]

By September 1876, Wolf also warned Governor Hayes, during the heat of the campaign, against irreparable damage to their cause, were that powerful spokesman for German interests, Senator Carl Schurz of Missouri, to disassociate himself from the political battle.[103] Schurz's earlier disapproval of Grant's foreign and domestic policies had cost the Republican party substantial losses in the German ethnic vote. In 1876, party regulars were determined that this would not happen again. By regaining Schurz's support for their standard bearer, Hayes, Republican leaders had effectively recovered their German-speaking constituencies. As is well know, the price that was exacted of them was that henceforth all the party hacks would have to adhere to Schurz's philosophy of government: the old patronage system would have to be replaced by a civil service organization based on merit. With Schurz at his side, Hayes then went on to win the presidency by a hair's breadth, in a hotly contested election that, ironically, was itself riddled by chicanery.[104] When Schurz became secretary of the Interior, he made a determined effort to revamp the entire federal bureacracy by applying standards based on a new morality. The Bureau of Indian Affairs with its post traderships, the Patent Office, and several other agencies came under his jurisdiction; for all of them he insisted upon the separation of partisan politics and administrative matters.[105]

Though the recordership was independent, responsible only to the president, to Schurz and his followers, the entire governmental apparatus, centered as it was in the District of Columbia, was weighted with fraud, with Alexander R. Shephard, mayor and urban planner, its chief offender.[106] Moreover, much governmental patronage had been channeled Wolf's way. Yet he saw no connection between President Hayes's request for his resignation as recorder and the reformers' determination to clean house. At best, Wolf was convinced that the president's call for his dismissal was necessary to fulfill a pledge to some other spoilsman. He also attributed his fall from grace to Mrs. Hayes's support for a newly formed temperance association. As a leader in a German social club, given to the consumption of alcoholic beverages, Wolf believed the prohibitionists had initiated a campaign to have him removed from office. He received the news of his impending resignation at a private meeting with the president, but it did not materialize until a year later, In April 1878. When it did, Wolf lost much of his customary aplomb and wrote to the president with unbridled frankness. "I did, during the last campaign," said Wolf, "everything possible to have you elected, and I find it perfectly logical that I should be punished, for no doubt had I opposed you, I

might have been elected to the cabinet." Wolf was deeply hurt; he had
worked diligently on Hayes's behalf. When the outcome of the election was
in doubt, Wolf traveled to New York, where he met "over one thousand
people, merchants, bankers, etc. mostly Israelites and Germans, "who were
convinced there "would be no physical trouble" and that Hayes would be
"inaugurated." Now, however, that the recordership would end, Wolf could
not resist a snide allusion to Carl Schurz.[107] For when all was said and done,
Schurz had to be persuaded by the Republican stalwarts to remain in their
camp. In the future, Wolf was to refer to this painful period in his relations
with the Hayes administration as a moment of disarray that was finally healed
when Schurz eulogized Grant at the latter's funeral.

Prior to his forced resignation from his office, Wolf had refused to consider
a transfer to a diplomatic post offered to him by Schurz. Wouldn't it have
seemed odd, given Schurz's view of the governmental process, for him to
have dangled the lure of a diplomatic assignment to a disgruntled employee?
Fortunately, this problem was resolved simply because Wolf's pride matched
his ego. Unless it were to be a first-class consulate, he would not be satisfied.
Anything else, he affirmed, would not be in keeping with his current status.
He deeply resented the president's suggestion of "being provided for, perhaps abroad." Three years later, he would be forced to trim his sails and
accept a second-class consulate, but meanwhile such a notion seemed unap-
pealing. As he had protested to Hayes against the abruptness with which his
recordership was terminated, so too did he ask Schurz to delay the resignation until July 1878.[108] In any event, his daughter was to be married in June
of that year. Given Wolf's flair for publicity, this alone would have been
sufficient reason for him to urge postponing the inevitable. He failed.
However, by the middle of 1878, Schurz did name Wolf a judge of the
Municipal Court, then in the process of formation in the nation's capital. Yet
Wolf was so deeply wounded by the loss of the recordership—not only had it
dealth him a financial blow, so that he was "without clients and without
means"—but also warped his judgment to the degree that he was prepared to
refuse any governmental position. He was determined to reject the mag-
istracy, unless the president added his approval to the nomination. Hayes
did, without referring in any way to Wolf's petulant letter of resignation.[109]

Such then were the trials of that office which Wolf had accepted back in
1869. Yet there were other occasions during his incumbency when he had his
triumphs. Other than the remunerations the post had to offer, it was good to
know that he had been instrumental in securing certain distinctive appointments for friends and acquaintances. His interventions with the State Department on behalf of his persecuted brethren abroad and his involvement
with Peixotto's consulship at Bucharest brought him a measure of fame. Two
other noteworthy incidents marked this period of his career. One capped his

earlier efforts in B'nai B'rith, while the second compensated somewhat for his retirement to private life.

In 1874, Wolf served as chairman of a national B'nai B'rith convention, held in Chicago. Its sessions were marked by self-congratulatory resolutions on the moral stamina and financial solvency of the organization. Always adept at parliamentary procedure, Wolf managed to secure an amendment guaranteeing life insurance benefits to members' families, wherever that was feasible. Delegates to the conference thanked him for his warmth, tact, and patience, when some of the sessions were marked by factionalism, or petty passions. But for Wolf personally, the most important aspect of the convention was its sponsorship of a resolution to erect a monument to religious liberty in Fairmount Park, Philadelphia. Wolf's eyes were always on the future. The year 1876 would be America's centennial, and Wolf was prepared for it. By then, the next gathering of B'nai B'rith was scheduled for Philadelphia. What better way to celebrate this nation's hundredth birthday than to commission a statue characterizing America's unique contribution to the world, freedom of worship. Under Wolf's auspices, Moses Ezekiel, an American artist residing in Rome, accepted the assignment. Years later, he credited Wolf for having had the insight to shape this project.[110]

In June 1878, Wolf and his wife, Caroline, hosted the wedding of their daughter, Florence, to Frederick Gotthold, a New York merchant. The wedding itself attracted wide attention, primarily because of Wolf's prominent position in the Washington community. By modern standards it resembled a traditional Jewish wedding service. But for its day it marked a radical departure from the norm.

The synagogue was decorated much after the fashion of a Christian Church. The shrine of the law, festooned with flowers and the reader's place banked with them. There were four ushers, as there are at every wedding, but there the resemblance ceases. The bridal party was made up of Mr. Wolf and his daughter, Mrs. Wolf and the groom, and last, an uncle and a sister of the groom representing his father and mother, both of whom are dead. The ceremony was performed by the Rev. Mr. Stern, who wore the black velvet cap and long black robe and white scarf [prayer shawl] of a Rabbi. The bridal party took their places before him, her parents to the right, and the representatives of his to the left, while the choir sang the Hebrew chant, "Hail to the Bride," with its ancient blessing. There was a short address in English from the minister, some questions and responses in the same language, and the ceremony itself in Hebrew. Hands were joined, the wine was offered by the bride's parents and thrice tasted, the ring passed and repassed and at length placed upon the hand, and at the close another Hebrew anthem.

Christians were curious as to the nature of the ceremony and seemed impressed by its simplicity and solemnity.[111]

Three weeks after the wedding Wolf was appointed a magistrate for the district, his anger at the loss of his recordership obviously having cooled. For the next three years he remained in Washington, until a brief venture in diplomacy brought about a change in the daily pattern of his life.[112]

3
Building a Constituency

Wolf had openly boasted that he used his recorder-of-deeds post to advance the careers of his friends and to succor those of his coreligionists abroad who stood in peril of their lives. What was far more subtle was his ability to secure his minor governmental clerkship—that of a glorified notary public—as a base from which he would shape his own constituency. In due time, he would be able to speak with authority to the federal government on all issues concerning the American Jewish community. Nowhere in his papers does he reveal this grand purpose. Yet in a relatively brief number of years, from 1869 until 1878, Wolf managed to coopt the most significant unified body of that period, the Board of Delegates of American Israelites, into the newly formed Reform Jewish Movement. In 1869 the Board of Delegates was a traditional-minded group of spokesmen for several Jewish congregations in the New York and Philadelphia areas. For the previous decade it had regularly contacted the State Department whenever civil and religious rights for Jews both at home and abroad had been threatened. By 1878, Wolf had so adroitly changed the structure of the Board of Delegates that he assured its executive a controlling voice in the affairs of the newly emergent Union of American Hebrew Congregations.

Early on, at the beginning of the 1870s, a unique combination of circumstances made it possible for him to transform the Board to his own use. The first factor in his ascent to political and communal recognition by the American Jewish Community as a whole was his appointment in May 1870 to the executive of the board itself. Second, the disunity that was rampant among fellow Jews presented him with an opportunity toward shaping a united group whom he could represent. Once he became its chairman, his authority was not challenged until 1906. By then, he was a septuagenarian. For the better part of his life he had been able to enjoy the fruits of uncontested power.

Although the old Board of Delegates was originally based on congrega-

tional affiliations and had extended its membership to include individuals
from different institutions and agencies,[1] its welcome to Wolf was an ex-
traordinary occurrence. In the spring of 1869 he had been fulminating
against "ritual Judaism"; he had no use for orthodoxy. The Board itself, with
Myer S. Isaacs as its chairman, was traditional in its approach. Its motive,
then, in appointing Wolf arose from a practical necessity. Here was a young
attorney, one who was well-known in the District of Columbia for his earlier
defense of the Jews caught in the trade war between North and South during
the Rebellion. Furthermore, as a functionary in the Grant administration
who was responsible for erasing the effects of Order No. 11 from the voting
booths, Wolf might be able to intervene successfully for the causes the Board
of Delegates held dear. He had already fought against Russian shipment of its
Jews into the backwashes of the empire and had his friend Peixotto stationed
at Bucharest to battle against anti-Jewish excesses in Romania. Such contacts
with the State Department as he was able to maintain were based not only on
his past experiences as the B'nai B'rith representative in the Nation's capital,
but also because of the power he might be able to wield in his new role as
recorder of deeds. In that capacity the pronouncements Wolf made concerning Jews and the international situation were duly reported in the Anglo-
Jewish journals of the day.[2] He had begun to speak with the voice of
authority. The Board obviously thought that it made a wise decision in
appointing him to its executive.

Wolf's German-American friends recognized the honor tendered him by
the Board and held a banquet to mark the occasion. Five hundred forty
people were present at the fete, including General Franz Sigel and ex-
Governor Edward Salomon of Washington Territory. Sigel expressed the high
regard in which they all held the Wolf, and spoke of his government service.[3]
Dr. Max Lilienthal, a Reform rabbi but recently arrived from Russia, and a
personal friend of Wolf's, went further. He extolled Wolf, calling him in a
letter a "god-sent messenger" whose appointment as recorder of deeds was
indeed providential. It had enabled Wolf not only to secure Peixotto's position as consul at Bucharest, but also to render invaluable service on behalf of
the persecuted in Russia and Romania.[4]

These were heady words indeed, intended for a young man seeking
distinction in life. With such compliments on all sides, Wolf could only
believe that his reputation had expanded miraculously. His correspondence
with Grant and Crémieux had catapulted him to new heights of leadership,
so that his membership on the executive of the Board of Delegates ought to
have signaled a more definitive recognition of his abilities.

But all was not well. The Board represented only a minority voice in
Jewish public opinion. There was a profusion of religious, social, fraternal,
and cultural establishments that engaged the interests of the many German-
Jewish immigrants who came to these shores during and immediately after

the Civil War. There was no single body to claim responsibility for the entire Jewish community, much less to order its internal priorities in terms of its own heritage. What were to be the standards for educating the rabbis and the laity? Who would decide what was proper decorum in a house of worship? Which portions of the liturgy were to be included and which excised? Who in the community was to have the authority to determine the appropriate methods for arbitrating disputes involving such complicated areas of Jewish law as marriage and property settlement, or congregational claims in matters of disputed wills and inheritances? The quarrels that these questions engendered were made more bitter by the keen sense of individualism that prevailed, sharpened by the recognition that here was a new land where variations upon traditional social and religious mores might in time become the norm. As with all other immigrants, democracy had worked its will. It imbued them with an inviolate belief in the legitimacy of their own religious interpretations. No matter how far such views had veered from accepted faith and practice, which had taken centuries to evolve, many German Jews in this country were determined to reshape their Judaism.

To overcome such disparate tendencies, some of Wolf's older colleagues had recognized the need for unity long before he was old enough to be concerned with this problem. Beginning in 1843, radical, liberal, and traditional theologians such as Dr. David Einhorn, Rabbi Isaac Mayer Wise, and the Rev. Isaac Leeser had attempted, at various times, to rally the Jewish people to congregational life and service. It was hoped that the Jews' lack of concern for their cultural roots would be reversed, their apathy halted, and their assimilation into Christian modes of worship reversed. Rabbi Wise of Cincinnati, then still a moderate reformer, and the Rev. Leeser of Philadelphia, a more traditionally minded clergyman, trusted that an informed laity would both insure the future of the Jews as a group in this land and reaffirm the basic ties between Judaism and American democracy.

From 1855 until 1871 all such intentions ended in failure. Wise's contemporaries in Reform Judaism accused him of submitting to an orthodox ecclesiastical yoke, while Leeser's more traditional associates charged him with acquiescing silently to Wise's suggestions for change in Jewish belief and ritual. By 1868, Lesser was dead. The Orthodox had withdrawn from further attempts at uniting with the Reform group, and Wise himself was involved in a vicious war of words with the more radical reformers, such as Einhorn, Dr. Samuel Adler, and Dr. Samuel Hirsch. The *Jewish Times* of New York, that same B'nai B'rith journal which had just begun to carry Wolf's observations from Washington, supported Einhorn and his followers, and fulminated against Wise, calling him a heretic.[5]

At first, Wolf was new to the fray, and admired the reformers under

Einhorn's tutelage. They preached in the vernacular, rejected ideas of personal immortality and resurrection, and looked askance at practices based on talmudic authority. Such men, Wolf was certain, would be "hailed as the prophets of the new dispensation of intelligent and rational Judaism."[6]

Such pronouncements were expected. Wolf had no profound intellectual insights; he lacked any truly deep theological convictions. As a moderately well-informed layman, he could hardly have been faulted for failing to distinguish between the seeming relevancies and irrelevancies in the Talmud and the prayerbook. For centuries, Jews far more learned than he had struggled over issues of priesthood and concepts of sacrifice. Others had long ago wrestled also with the social implications of messianic themes. Such thoughts were beyond Wolf's range. All he had ever wanted, in essence, was to worship his rational god, in what he imagined was a civilized fashion. To be united in an enlightened service with fellow Jews was his fondest wish. Only then, in his terms, would American Jews achieve equal status with the most "progressive" people of the day.

> "I know nothing," wrote Wolf, "of true Reform and enlightened unity, until the various congregations are represented by impartial, common sense members, who as a jury have to decide the future of ritual Judaism, while the Rabbis as advisers may be heeded and their knowledge made useful. The Rabbis have too many private hates, too many hair-splitting differences. . . . We as a group both commercially and politically have become a power; our status should be well defined, in all matters of public comment."[7]

A scant eight months after he had so warmly praised these radical reform leaders in Judaism, Wolf met Rabbi Isaac Mayer Wise. The latter had come to lecture before the Washington Hebrew Congregation. Wolf, together with two other congregants, Joseph Kauffman and B. Herzberg, formed the welcoming committee for the preacher from the West. What Wolf heard that night seemed platitudinous; Wise declared the object of Judaism to be the perfectability of human love.[8] Yet his talk mesmerized Wolf, who now forgot his admiration for Dr. Einhorn and his followers. Instead, in Wise, Wolf discovered a kindred spirit, eager to restructure American Judaism, away from its "ritual basis," and, in the process, to shape the American Jewish community into one grand union.

In several ways the two men were similar: both were pragmatists spurred on by a belief in their own ability to shape a new religious environment for Jews in this land. In this connection Wolf ignored the philosophical and theological differences Wise had with other leaders of Reform Judaism in the East, who took their cues for altering religious practice from certain rabbis in Germany.[9] As a layman, Wolf readily admitted that he could not care less for the fine points of intellectual discourse that disturbed Wise and his opponents.[10] In Wise, Wolf thought he recognized a winner. Therefore, in 1871, when at a meeting in Cincinnati Wise laid the foundations for Reform Judaism in America, Wolf cheered him on. At that momentous conference, Wise saw to the passage of resolutions establishing a Hebrew Union College to train rabbis, inaugurating the Union of American Hebrew Congregations to unite the laity, and establishing a Sabbath School Union to educate the young. Provisions were also made for circuit riding preachers for isolated congregations. The success of the program would depend upon its enrolling the first twenty congregations whose membership totaled 2,000 adult males. These societies would then form a national synod. By urging a union of synagogues in the South and West, Wise had effectively upstaged his competitors. Throughout the years of their quarrel with Wise, Einhorn and Adler and their followers persisted in their acrimonious evaluations of Wise's theological understanding of Judaism. More to the point, the Eastern Rabbis continued to denigrate Wise because he looked to middle America, and beyond, as the source for his Congregational Union.[11]

Discounting such criticism, Wolf, in 1873, as president of the Washington Hebrew Congregation, led his temple into the Union. For this he was rebuked in the editorials of the *Jewish Times*. The paper snorted that his latest effort to strengthen Wise's Congregational Union was but an ill-fated attempt to retrieve a modicum of success from his earlier failures as the Washington representative of the American Jewish Community. The charge cut him to the quick, for it meant that Wolf had not succeeded either in the earlier 1869 immigration scheme to rescue Russian Jewish refugees, or in the matter of improving the Jewish situation in Romania. The *Times* reminded him that he would never learn—he was of that "class which gathers wisdom only from experience." Accordingly, he would soon discover "to his sorrow . . . that the new Union will be as barren of results, if not more so, as the Board of Delegates which a few years ago he took great price in representing at the seat of government."[12]

Wolf, deeply angered, shot back,

> I shall go to Buffalo [the site of the ensuing convention of the Union of American Hebrew Congregations] not to aid any man be he Wise or otherwise, but, if possible, to do something for the general Jewish community. To me Dr. Wise and all the rest of the American rabbis are simply individuals, who [innocently enough] in [their] doctrinal prejudice are working for what they conceive to be proper, but in so doing have divided, not united Israel. Now if we laymen can bring about union, why not try it? If it fails, what harm? I am not going to be carried off by a flood of abuse from one direction against everything that Wise has attempted. I know that the people will control the union and not the rabbis and hence no humbug can be made.[13]

His next retort showed less prejudice and did not sound quite so sim-
plistic. He ridiculed the notion of the *Times* that he was leaving the Board to
try his luck at the Union, and cited his past activites as proof of his concern
for all Jews.

> Who tells you that I have gone back on the Board of Delegates? I shall
> cheerfully cooperate with either or both, or half a dozen schemes, until
> something practicable and enduring is evolved. I have nothing to do
> with your feelings against persons. Years ago when I first joined the
> Board, you ridiculed the idea because there were so many orthodox in
> it. I said then as I say now. I only know Jews and have nothing to do with
> petty quarrels or rituals. I am not the defender of Wise nor the accuser
> of anyone. My hope and wish is to contribute to the sublime tenets of
> intellectual and progressive Judaism. I know no East nor West; I only
> know that we are divided and we ought to be united.[14]

Seen in retrospect, these were more than idealistic, pious wishes. To wield
power effectively in the emerging Union, Wolf would have to develop a new
association, one that would reflect his own special abilities, involving his
representations to the federal government. Early in his Washington sojourn
he had grown accustomed to reinforcing the suggestions of Myer B. Isaacs
and other leaders of the old Board of Delegates to members of the Grant
administration.[15] Whether he had planned as early as 1870 radically to
change the nature of the Board of Delegates is unknown. Yet his first motion,
spread upon the minutes of the Board in May 1870, was "that any individual
Israelite in good standing" be allowed to join it.[16] At first glance such a
suggestion would seem to be a logical extension of the Board's decision to
expand its operations. It had moved away from its initial program, designed
in 1859, of representing religious congregations, to coopting delegates from
various institutions and agencies. But the Board was still too conservative in
its makeup to allow any one person to present issues in his own name. Had
Wolf's resolution carried, he could have handily modified the original structure of the Board just as soon as he was named to its executive. But his
motion lost, and Wolf had to bide his time.

Although the Board was not prepared for any radical alterations that might
have flowed from Wolf's plan, it was concerned with criticism leveled against
it. It was considered elitist and narrow-minded in its perception of the
American Jewish community. The *Jewish Times* had in effect accused it of
being a useless appendage.[17] Sensitive to such charges, the Board was eager
to revitalize its public image. In 1874 it named Wolf, by then a vice-
president, chairman of its new Popularization Committee. This group took
note of the Board's declining power in domestic matters, and optimistically
imagined that a growing liberal spirit abroad would obviate the need to
concentrate on European affairs. Primarily, the Popularization Committee

wanted to overcome the lassitude displayed by American Jewry here at home. With this in mind, Wolf suggested that the Board of Delegates provide educational stipends for deserving young people. Judge Mayer Sulzberger went further, requesting the Board's aid in forming a "united religious body" of Jews. But Ellinger of *Jewish Times's* fame, urged the Board to keep to its original intent. It was not to meddle in congregational or religious issues. For the record, the Board did accept Wolf's plea that it foster young, intellectual talent. However, Ellinger viewed this as a means of enticing Jewish youths to enter the Hebrew Union College by way of the back door, and as still another building block in Wise's projected Union.[19]

Wolf remained undaunted. To a Board of Delegates divided on the merits of "a united religious body," and chagrined that its school, Maimonides College, established in Philadelphia in 1867, was languishing for want of funds,[20] Wolf was able to offer the possibility of both a national union and a national rabbinic school. Instead of leaving the Board of Delegates to join forces with Wise, Wolf would lead the Board, as he had his own Washington Hebrew Congregation into the Union.

The path he took exemplied his own conviction that victory could always be achieved though conciliation and compromise. To reach his goal, he would have to balance three different concerns at the same time: the unpopularity of the Union of American Hebrew Congregations in the East, the issue of creating a viable Hebrew College, and his own uninterrupted representations of the Board of Delegates to the federal government. By 1876, it seemed as though several different events had conspired to assure Wolf a measure of success on all three counts. At that time, a group of congregations in the East, eager to establish its own Hebrew seminary, was about to issue invitations to a conference to be known as the New York College Convention. Wise's Union had already summoned all Jewish communities to become part of his growing movement and support its newly established rabbinical school. Wolf thereupon persuaded the Board of Delegates to appoint its own select group for the purpose of conferring with representatives both from Wise's Union and from the eastern congregations. To do this he overcame Ellinger's opposition and the conviction of other members that such negotiations were still premature.[21]

Meanwhile, the council of the Union of American Hebrew Congregations, meeting in Washington in the summer of 1876, and presided over by Wolf, received a letter from the Board of Delegates, signed by Wolf and Sulzberger. The note had gone beyond the mere mention of joint meetings contemplating the creation of a Hebrew college. Instead, the Board of Delegates' resolution now invited members of the Union to confer quickly with Board representatives and with spokesmen for the New York College Convention, "to bring about as speedily as possible a complete union of all Hebrew Congregations in the United States."[22] For the moment, Wolf's enthusiasm may have carried him too far. In urging a nationwide coalition of all Jewish institutions under the aegis of the Union, he declared that the "turf would first have to grow over the graves" of several die-hard opponents before the plan became a reality.[23] This caused a considerable stir, but Wolf soon recovered his usually discreet approach. At a Union meeting he urged that in place of helping to fashion a New York Hebrew College, all members ought to work for one Union. For the record, Sol Levi, Josiah Cohen, and Dr. Samuel Wolfenstein were selected to represent the Union in all future negotiations.[24] As chairman of the Washington meeting of the council of the Union, and as spokesman for the Board of Delegates, Wolf then wielded the necessary power to achieve his objective.

That goal seemed even closer when members of the New York College Convention refused to be drawn into any discussions because their next convention would not take place before October 1876.[25] But representative of the Board of Delegates and the Union would now meet, and Wolf would be able to speak authoritatively for both groups. Victory lay within his grasp.

Though some differences between the Board and the Union had developed at the very outset, these were not monumental, and Wolf managed to overcome them. Wolfenstein and Levi of the Union objected to certain aspects of the proposed reorganization suggested by Sulzberger of the Board of Delegates. Sulzberger wanted "to effect a good understanding between the constituent congregations themselves," while the Union's spokesmen wanted a "union of two organizations representing congregations." Wolf mitigated Sulzberger's fears that the Board of Delegates would be completely subjected to the centralizing power of the Union. So secure was Wolf in the knowledge that he would win the struggle, that he promised to "obtain the most trusted leaders in the East," who would thereby free the Union from charges of aggrandizement, and indicate to congregations still affiliated with the Board of Delegates, the "propriety of selecting the Union of American Hebrew Congregations as the best organization for carrying . . . [the merger] into effect." Though several spokesmen from Wolf's own Board of Delegates were still unable to accept this gesture,[26] representatives of the Union urged Wolf to persist in his efforts at unity, and added two more negotiators who, like Wolf, were determined to force the supremacy of the Union.[27] By the summer of 1877, Wolf's views had prevailed. The report of the joint conference between the Union and the Board of Delegates noted the complementary purposes of both institutions with the Union engaged in promoting education and fostering Jewish religious life, and the Board of Delegates dedicated to the furtherance of rights for Jews both at home and abroad. Were the Union to extend its activities to include relief for Jews overseas and concern itself with the legal protection of American citizens, the original Board of Delegates would cease to exist. In place of the now-defunct organization, the Union was to elect a nine-member board, devoted to matters of civil and religious rights. Three of its members were also to serve on the executive of the Union.[28]

Wolf's victory would shortly be complete; he had now only to tie up the loose ends. That he did by submitting a resolution to a Committee on Conference of the Union vesting the power of the Union in a thirty-man executive, half of whom were to come from the East. This was the evolution of that very body which in Wolf's original scheme was to guarantee representation to a newly created nine-member group, supplanting the old Board of Delegates. Now, the new Board of Delegates would not only speak for the Union, but also be able to influence its governing arm. Like Wise before him, Wolf resorted to the magic number of 2,000 adult males. Their inclusion, from congregations in the East, would signal the formal dissolution of the original, New York-based Board of Delegates of American Israelites.[29] Wolf thereby assured the Union of American Hebrew Congregations wide representation for its activities and disarmed his former critics, who feared the Union's hierarchical tendencies.[30] By the following summer of 1878, the Fifth Council of the Union happily counted the additional 2,000 members on its rolls and acknowledged Wolf's congratulatory telegram on its "progress toward Union."[31] The Fifth Council then revised the composition of its new Board of Delegates, now called "The Committee on Civil and Religious Rights of the Union," so that nine rather than three of its members served on the Union's executive, while eight additional representatives-at-large from the Union expanded the Committee to a total of seventeen delegates.[32]

Along the way, the staff of the *Jewish Times* read the handwriting on the wall. It editorialized that the (new) Board of Delegates would become the "medium for understanding between Eastern congregations and those in the West . . . under the auspices of a . . . Union of congregations.[33] But the *Times*'s writers were not gifted with sufficient foresight to realize the extent of Wolf's victory. With the passing years, the very existence of the Board would justify his representations to federal officials on behalf of the Jewish community. Wolf had created his own institution, which endowed him with all the authority to petition the government whenever the need arose. As the Committee on Civil and Religious Rights of the Union (or the Board of Delegates, as it was later called) presumably spoke for a significant section of the American community, so Wolf, in time, came to speak for the Committee. He did not however, become its chairman at once. Though there was to be a hiatus of thirteen years before that occurred, Wolf had secured the basis for his life's work. He would become the voice of his people.[34]

Of course, his resignation as Washington's first recorder of deeds, in the very year when he finally transformed the nature of the old Board of Delegates, marred the sweetness of this victory.

4
Egyptian Interlude

The Temperance movement and political pressures had combined to force Wolf from his recorder-of-deeds post. One can recall how he was peeved with President Hayes for having suggested the diplomatic service as an alternative career. He would not, Wolf declared, have wanted to be sent abroad to soothe his vanity.[1] But now, after three uneventful years of service as a magistrate in the District of Columbia, Wolf gladly accepted an appointment as consul general to Egypt. He received his commission from President Garfield one day before the chief executive was to fall mortally wounded from an assassin's bullet. Garfield's last words to Wolf were:

> Well, my dear boy, this is singular; I am placing my name on your Commission; there is still a God in Israel; I hope you will have a good time; be strengthened in mind and body; and pluck the mystery out of Egypt. . . .[2]

The truth of the matter was that Wolf had indeed been angling after a diplomatic post since 1869; less than a first-class consulate, however, he was not prepared to accept. But up until now, in 1881, his request had not been heeded.[3] In spite of all his efforts to have Grant elected president, Wolf had not been included among those few other prominent Jewish leaders, such as David Eckstein, Edward S. Salomon, and Benjamin F. Peixotto, whom Grant had commissioned for the foreign service. Why the president chose to withhold such an appointment from Wolf is unknown. Despite his protestations to Hayes, the glamour of a diplomatic post seems to have appealed to Wolf. Once the Cairo post had been secured, he was content to be compared to the biblical Joseph, so that in line with the president's comment concerning the Egyptian enigma, one journalist had gone so far as to ask Wolf to solve the "riddle of sphinxed Egypt."[4]

If one is to take his own account of the Egyptian adventure as the most authentic source, then Wolf came to the shores of the Nile not by dint of hard, calculated appeals to the highest authorities in government, but rather as the result of an informal conversation. By 1881, Wolf was a middle-aged man; his health was failing, and he desperately wanted a vacation. He was eager to visit Egypt, and said as much to Senator Carl Schurz, who promised to do what he could to obtain the appointment.[5] Cairo, now, would apparently do as well as any first-class consulate.[6] In its own way it did, though Wolf was later to complain about its meager salary. The compensation was to be $4,000 a year, with an additional sum of $500 to cover such perquisites as monies paid to guards, translators, and secretaries at the legation.[7]

At least in the beginning, Wolf's Egyptian sojourn fulfilled some of his expectations. Despite the unsettled conditions he would be encountering once he reached Egypt, his stay there would provide him with weeks of recreation, opportunities for socializing with European and American upper-class society, and an unparalleled chance to refurbish his image for his family and friends whom he had left behind in America.

It took Wolf two months to reach his post. He spent some time with his friend Peixotto, who now was the American consul at Lyons, France. Because he took ill with malaria, Wolf then left for a German spa, and from there revisited his birthplace, Hinzweiller, in Rhenish Bavaria. But for him, as a Jew, all that was left of his home turned out to be the cemetery.

Standing at the ancestral grave, he was overcome by the feelings of kinship he had always had for his people.

> A peculiar feeling came over me . . . as I stood near the crumbling stones, moss-covered with their lettering almost indistinct, when I remembered the days of my childhood, and the standing of the Jews in Germany then and now.

The Jews, of course, had all departed from Hinzweiller. The only person Wolf recognized was an old school chum, by then a married woman who insisted that she had earlier predicted his greatness. In gestures that were reminiscent of that past, Wolf proceeded to distribute coins to the children of the villages bordering on Hinzweiller, listened dutifully to speeches by its mayor and other local officials, and appreciated the music offered up in his honor by several church choirs.[8]

Wolf reached Cairo on 9 September 1881, the very day on which Moslem nationalists chose to rebel against their Turkish overlords, who had bowed to the English and French economic controllers. Egypt was already bank-rupted by European creditors, who having earlier taken control of its Ministries of Finance and Public Works, were determined that all surplus monies in the budget be used solely for lowering the country's public debt. Twice during Wolf's consulship, a Moslem officer, Arabi Bey, led a group of revolutionaries who overthrew the European directors and forced the Khedive to install one of their own followers, Mahmoud Sami, as minister of war.

As the representative of the most powerful of neutral nations in that part of the world, Wolf had to convince the nationalists of America's concern for their country's sovereignty. He had also to sympathize with the English and French representatives in the land. One of Wolf's vice-consuls, Baron Behar de Menasce at Alexandria, was the spokesman for the Rothschild banking interests in France. Their sizable Egyptian investments were not to be jeopardized by the rebels. At the same time, Wolf had to acknowledge Turkish suzerainty over Egypt. Accordingly, in dispatches to the State Department, Wolf warned of the consequences of Egyptian xenophobia, and foresaw the disaster that would ensue were England to lose control of the Suez Canal.[9]

For this reason, in several conversations with Arabi Bey, Wolf detailed the awesomeness of English and French military might, and trotted out the usual solution in such situations. Arabi Bey had better civilize his followers before they were to be allowed to taste the fruits of independence. In return the Bey promised to remain loyal to the khedive, but warned that unless the small army of European civil servants, administrators, and technicians were removed, he would institute another rebellion.[10]

Ever the optimist, Wolf chose to ignore that comment; he declared that as a result of his first interview with the leader of the nationalists open conflict had been avoided. The truth of the matter was that Arabi Bey, convinced that Egypt was powerless in the face of English and French determination, did not immediately act upon his threat. Instead, he comforted Wolf with verbal pleasantries, and compared Egypt to the Arab so badly beated by his wife, he could not stand up.[11]

By the time the inevitable arrived, with Arabi Bey at last "standing up" for his third rebellion against Tewfik Pasha, Wolf had left the country. It was then, in June 1882, that anti-Western riots shook Alexandria, while the terror in Cairo forced all Americans with the exception of one family to flee the city. The American legation there was in a shambles, with consular records destroyed or misplaced. It was also reported that not a Christian was left alive in the interior of the country. Arab mobs massacred all nonbelievers.

Months earlier, Wolf, in his naïveté, imagined that his conversations with Arabi Bey had prevented an uprising from occurring. But now in the summer of 1882, with Wolf gone from the scene, the revolution dragged on. Only after the British (the French having refused to participate) bombarded Alexandria did the war end. At last, in September of that year, Arabi Bey was banished from the country.

Looking back on the entire affair, Wolf grew suspicious, and wondered whether the khedive himself had not put Arabi Bey and his officers up to the scheme. Wolf surmised that perhaps Tewfik Pasha was "another Richelieu." Historians have also suggested that even Ismaîl, Tewfik Pasha's father, likewise employed military men to overthrow his consitutional ministry.[12]

Perhaps this sort of diplomatic chicanery was more commonplace than frank expressions in the consular game, which brought Wolf only trouble in their wake. As early as November 1881, Wolf was embroiled in an Egyptian-French fiasco, in which a French journalist, Laffon, maligned Islam and its founders. So incensed were the Pashas and the Beys that they clamored for the editor's execution, while the Council of Ministers ordered the paper in which the damaging article had appeared, *L'Egypte,* to cease publication. Religious leaders then urged that the offending writer be expelled from the country; otherwise they feared he would be assassinated.

Wolf viewed either of these alternatives to the writer's fate as a prelude to foreign interference, with its concomitant native rebellion and ensuing massacre of Europeans in Egypt. To avoid such dire consequences, he suggested that Laffon stop demanding his rights to a free press and leave the country voluntarily. Had Wolf stopped there, his meddling in the affiar might not have been taken amiss. He went ahead to suggest, however, that had an American in "enlightened Germany" libeled Catholicism, as the French jounralist in Egypt had slandered Islam, calling Osman, whom he blamed for burning the library at Alexandria, "the fanatical inheritor of a false prophet," the effect for the American "would have been the same or worse." Wolf imagined that in Egypt they would expel a man for such a crime, but in Germany they would jail him. [13]

Wolf's statement showed little thinking and less tact. That the journalist erred was beside the point—Osman was the third caliph in Mohammedan history, nor had he captured Alexandria, much less burned its library. What vexed Secretary of State James G. Blaine, however, were Wolf's observations, now deemed irksome and possibly dangerous. Blaine cautioned Wolf against judging Germany's behavior in "a hypothetical case," and worried over 'grave misunderstandings if government officials so speak of the internal affairs of nations to which they are not accredited." Wolf would have to learn to conduct himself in such a way as to "offend no parties in Egypt whether secular or religious, either in expression of opinion, in action, or in any other way." [14]

Shortly thereafter Wolf encountered a far more troublesome situation that not only threatened his self-esteem as a consul, but also limited the nature of his office. Originally, the Egyptian minister of foreign affairs, Fahmy Pasha, had appointed Wolf's predecessor, Elbert E. Farman, a voting delegate to the International Commission for the Revision of the Organization of the Mixed Courts. Wolf was distressed. He informed the State Department that from an official Egyptian perspective it was only proper for the consul general to be the accredited representative to the international tribunal. To make matters worse, however, the khedive had already named Farman to a judgeship on the same body. Beside himself with anger, Wolf inquired of Farman whether it was just for him to be both jurist and delegate. Farman responded by showing Wolf the proper State Department credentials confirming his appointment to the bench. Wolf grew even more chagrined when he realized that an earlier appointee to the Commission, Judge George Batcheller, continued to serve as a voting delegate even when Farman was the U. S. consul general. Wolf could not comprehend how as the senior American representative in Egypt he would not be granted the privilege formally allowed to Farman, to Batcheller, and to spokesmen for other foreign powers in Egypt. By serving as delegates to the Commission, they would be administering civil justice, involving Egyptian affairs, but he would not.

The State Department responded to his complaint with the suggestion that he too might be counted as a third representative, along with Batcheller and Farman, if the Egyptian government agreed. Since the Commission itself had been postponed for a year because of the political upheavals in the country, Wolf would have ample time to seek a solution to the problem.[15]

As matters turned out, he had no time. Wolf managed to spend twenty-one weeks in Egypt, from 9 September 1881 to 29 November of that year, and from 1 February to 27 March in 1882. Absences for medical reasons and a vacation accounted for the intervening periods. But the bloody upheavals in Egypt's political future, which Wolf predicted in confidential messages to the State Department, came true after he left the country. Consequently, he had no further opportunities to pursue the problem of his representation on the Commission of Mixed Courts.[16]

Such, then, were the frustrations to which service at a second-class consulate sometimes led. These disappointments were intensified by Wolf's inability to fulfill one of the primary tasks of a consul, to promote the exchange of goods and services between his native land and his host country. Wolf had always to contend with a British monopoly in cotton trading and other items, with British control of shipping in the Suez Canal, and with primitive methods of agriculture, all of which militated against trade with America. Wolf also rebuked his own government for its indifference to his attempts to develop a market in Egypt for American imports. One bizarre footnote to Wolf's unhappy commercial experiences was his observation that the lone American businessman in Alexandria, engaged in the illegal importation of pork to a Moslem country, received no help from the United States.[17]

Thus, the yardstick for measuring Wolf's achievements in Egypt is not to be found in his diplomatic skill, but rather in the contacts he made and in the influence he exerted on the people he met. All the social interaction of which he was a part reinforced the impression that he was a gregarious, charming man who thoroughly enjoyed mingling with the rich and the privileged.

Wolf was always taken with splendor and ostentation. His reception as consul general by the khedive was indeed a royal welcome. Accompanied by

Twefik Pasha's chamberlain, Wolf reached the palace "in a gilded coach (driven by) white Arab horses." As the carriage passed through the streets, soldiers lining the thoroughfares presented arms. When the entourage arrived at its destination, a band played "The Star Spangled Banner" and Wolf received a twenty-one gun salute.

Standing at the head of the stairway, the khedive welcomed Wolf, who was then led to an adjoining room where he was introduced to all the cabinet ministers. Unlike other consuls general, Wolf departed from tradition; he did not read his letters of credence. Instead, he gave an impromptu talk, alluding to the death of President Garfield and urging closer ties between Egypt and the United States. Meanwhile, recalling Joseph of old, Jews in the synagogues of Egypt offered prayers on Wolf's behalf.

Such honors were more than he could bear. He was "scarcely able to refrain from tears" when he heard the American national anthem being played to mark the occasion. Throughout the entire ceremony he thought constantly of his "dear mother," of the "struggles" they had had in the land of his birth. He was "overwhelmed to think that now (he) was the accredited representative of the Great Republic of the West to the land of his forefathers." So struck was Wolf by the awesomeness of his position that in this connection he remembered the phrase once used by Secretary of State John Hay and later repeated by President Garfield that the "God of Israel never sleeps nor slumbers."

Perhaps, Wolf's reception at the khedive's palace had proved to be too splendid after all. His host presented Wolf with an Arabian horse and a sword. He returned the animal, but mistakenly kept the sword. This time, the State Department lectured him on the niceties of diplomatic protocol. Citizens of the United States were prevented by law from accepting gifts or titles from a foreign government. Wolf protested that he had merely been following precedent. Other American consuls had now and then accepted tokens from the country to which they had been accredited. To solve the crisis, without offending the khedive who offered the present in the first place, the State Department ordered the sword be deposited in the National Museum in Washington. As a final compromise, it was placed in Wolf's own library, where it remained a highly prized memento.[18]

On another occasion Wolf had been invited to break the fast after the Day of Atonement at the home of Baron Cattaue, the representative in Egypt of Nathan Meyer, Baron Rothschild of London. Wolf was overawed by the wealth of the baron's mansion.

> It was an immense drawing room, one hundred people were standing in line, awaiting the drawing of the curtain, when the host appeared in his Turkish robes, his wife at his side. Prayer was offered, and we were seated, I next to the Baron.[19]

At a banquet in honor of Washington's birthday, which Wolf tendered the following February, he reciprocated in kind. Leading residents of Cairo, all the Americans then in Egypt, and members of the diplomatic community were invited to enjoy the most lavish of social functions. Wolf recalled that the affair had cost him $5,000 when his total salary as consul was only $4,000.

This constantly limiting sense of dining and wining with the privileged made Wolf appear rather patronizing when he considered the lives of fellow Jews in Palestine. Once, at Ismailia, he observed:

> Here I am only twenty-four hours from Jerusalem by boat and land and it annoys me greatly at the idea of not seeing it. I may finally get there yet, but am uncertain. I know there is nothing to see there except ruins, and to pay tribute not only to a sentiment, but to *Schnorrer* [beggars], but it is something to have been there.[20]

In the course of his career as consul general, Wolf saw much of the Egyptian countryside. The country's director of railroads placed a car at his disposal. Wolf and his friends also took a journey by ship up the Nile to Luxor.[21] Delighted with the accommodations, and armed with letters of introduction to all the different provincial governors, Wolf and his party of friends were treated as visiting potentates. These journeys gave him an opportunity to characterize his traveling companions. He was particularly impressed by Leopold Sonnemann, editor of the *Frankfurter Zeitung* and a member of the German Reichstag. Wolf admired Sonnemann for his common sense and clever mind, but had little use for a "parvenu Jew" whose predilections for Egyptian dancing girls so enraged that man's wife that she locked him out of their cabin for one night. Generous host that he was, Wolf then allowed the man to share in some makeshift sleeping arrangements. Such domestic quarrels Wolf viewed with equanimity, as he did the common-law marriage of an American dentist, an aquaintance of his then living in Cairo. As long as the couple had no children, Wolf saw nothing wrong with the relationship.[22] Such an attitude was scarcely in keeping with the Victorian customs of the day.

Wolf's composite view of the women passengers on that same trip indicates that he admired strong, free-thinking types, who nevertheless possessed all those "feminine" charms which accompany "quiet refinement." He became a confidante of the Princess Nazli, the sultan's cousin, who found her native custom of restricting woman to the harem, confining. Once some of her relatives were seen unveiled at the theater. For having broken this social and religious code, they were ordered to remain indoors. Princess Nazli then begged Wolf to intercede with the khedive for these women. Wolf promised to do so, and was as good as his word. The ladies were pardoned. Thereafter, when Wolf had an opportunity to meet the princess once again, he was told to come alone. This set him to musing on the biblical parallel of Joseph and Potiphar's wife. Gallantly, Wolf observed that "the difference the Princess Nazli and the woman who tempted Joseph was decidedly marked."[23]

Wolf was also taken by those signs of "long-patient suffering" which he imagined some of the women whom he had met in Egypt had to endure. In his diary, which he made part of his *Reminiscences*, he recalls a "Mrs. S." (a mother accompanying a Cleveland couple) as "a person not aged by time, but far more likely by trials, which she had concealed from her outward countenance. . . . Matronly and good she looks with a kind and intelligent face, truly religious and yet liberal. . . . Her very presence disarms the scoffer. I never look upon her but what I think of my dear wife. I never hear her speak but what it seems I hear the words of that dear good mother, whose homely sayings have been beneficial texts, from which I have discoursed and profited. I do not wonder, although others may, that I have had some success in the struggles of life, with such a wife and mother; I indeed would be a dullard were it otherwise."

It was at such moments that Wolf revealed his inner self. He longed for his wife and home; he was lonely, so lonely that at one point he moved into the living quarters of the consulate, rather than remain in a hotel room. Once, when he had waited a week and received no mail from the States, he was determined to accept the deterministic attitude of the Arabs. "I never mind trifles, and pray God grant me better luck next time." This, he assured himself, was "the only philosophy that will prevent a hole from wearing through my heart." Sometimes, however, the hole began to show. His mind, he was convinced,

> teemed with a thousand coruscating diamonds, [but with] no brow to set them in. [For] the brow that should wear it, the heart that should beat in responsive throbs, the soul that would elevate, the eye that would reflect the heaven that men aspire to [was] over the sea.[24]

Such romantic fancies seemed to corroborate Wolf's self-evaluations that he possessed a "restless and nervous temperament," given to impulsive action. However, his contacts with others show him to have been a complete extrovert, cordial, suave, and calculating whenever the need arose. Once, such a sophisticated approach saved him from becoming the foil to another's wit. When he and William Walter Phelps, the American minister to Austria, were visiting the Tomb of the Caliphs, Phelps observed that Wolf was the first Jew he'd ever met whom he "could respect." Wolf replied that under the circumstances Phelps must previously have "been in poor company indeed." Sometimes such facile verbal exchanges led to hilarious results. When Congressman Samuel Cox of New York and Wolf went to view the mummy of Rameses II, believed to be the Pharaoh of the Expulsion, Cox asked Wolf to "speak to the old duffer." Without a moment's hesitation, Wolf answered, "My dear Sam, you are a college man, and as you are versed in dead languages and I am not, you speak to him."[25]

Wolf's retorts were clever and pointed. In his *Reminiscences* he includes a description of Egyptian snake charmers. On the supposition that those "who drink Bourbon see snakes," for him these performers conjured up visions of Americans imbibing whiskey. Like all true humorists Wolf did not fear being laughed at.

The khedive had offered him the scarab that graced the neck of that same pharoah that Cox wanted him to converse with. Wolf accepted the gift. On the way back to the States a British official offered him a good deal of money for it. Wolf refused to part with the object. His father-in-law, hearing of the business arrangement, then declared there were two fools that day, he who made the offer, and he who rejected it.[26]

In the midst of his social junkets, Wolf did manage to protect Christian missionaries from being maltreated by Moslems. For this, these Christian workers were most grateful. Though they had at first been chagrined at the appointment of a Jew to the Egyptian post, they now informed their church convention that Wolf did more for their missions than all the other consuls general who had been his predecessors.[27]

He was not as successful in preventing a blood libel directed against an Egyptian Jewish family that was then deported to Corfu, where it was imprisoned and maltreated. By January 1882, the family was freed by a governmental tribunal; Wolf claimed his intercession with the Greek pope helped secure the family's release. Wolf may have put forth his best efforts to reverse the effects of this ritual murder accusation, but to date no details of his participation in the matter have come to light.[28]

The reasons for Wolf's brief sojourn in Egypt may be attributed to his poor health, the dangerous political situation in which the country found itself, and his failure at reviving Egyptian-American commercial relations. As a parting gesture, Wolf stressed that the poor remuneration given the consul general was the decisive factor in forcing his resignation.[29] There was no reaction from the State Department, except to disallow his first request for payment for the excess travel time it took for him to reach his post. However, a note from George Pomeroy, Wolf's successor in Egypt, indicates that Wolf received a letter of recall. The State Department apparently gave him the privilege of resigning.[30]

What remained with him of that time spent abroad was not only the Egyptian experience, but the distinction of having served in the U. S. Diplomatic Corps.

5

Champion of the Immigrant

Wolf's return from Egypt coincided with a series of large-scale East-European Jewish migrations to this land, movements of people that would ultimately fashion new values for American society, alter the nature of the older established American-Jewish community, and basically shape the remainder of Wolf's career. In time he would emerge as the defender of his people. Though challenged in the intervening years until his death in 1923, that title was to remain uniquely his.

Formally, Wolf had resumed his legal practice when he came home. Had he merely developed his skills as a successful advocate, his life would not have merited any detailed consideration. But he had returned to the nation's capital, armed by almost two decades of successful lobbying for his own causes. He knew the right people in Washington, was on personal terms with hosts of legislators, and had long ago fallen into the habit of contacting the State Department every time trouble was brewing abroad for foreign Jews.

Wolf had left Egypt for America in May 1882. What awaited him here in terms of international Jewish problems quickly propelled him to center stage. In the czarist empire, Alexander II had been assassinated by a nihilist on 13 March 1881. The Russian government used this occasion to refurbish its long-standing anti-Semitic policies. Everywhere the peasants had been informed that they were the victims of economic exploitation at the hands of the Jews. Pogroms broke out in many different localities. Jews were murdered indiscriminately, their women ravished, their children killed, and their property destroyed. Larger cities in the empire with sizable Jewish populations were the scenes of extensive anti-Semitic riots. One year later, in May 1881, Russia promulgated its infamous May laws. These ordinances expelled the Jews from the rural districts and villages in fifteen provinces of western Russia and drove them into overcrowded towns. These locations now constituted the Pale of Settlement. In the process, leases and mortgages held by Jews were canceled, their businesses liquidated, and their persons despoiled. Jews were no longer allowed to acquire or work the land. Contacts of any sort between Christians and Jews were fobidden. Because they were so sorely hedged about by economic and social restrictions, some 25,680 Russian Jews fled to America in the relatively short period between 1881 and 1882.[1]

In the early 1870s Wolf's attempts to pave the way for a handful of Russian Jewish immigrants were contemptuously dismissed by his own equals. Now, a decade later, fears were still rampant that these newcomers, with their "strange habits, shiftless ways and filthy customs," would once again imperil the social status achieved by their more affluent coreligionists. In fact, Wolf himself had lost his taste for his earlier heroics. While en route to his Cairo post, he made certain to suggest that prior to their arrival here, alien Jews ought to "prepare themselves for a proper understanding of American thoughts, customs, and habits of work."[2]

Wolf and his peers, leaders in the Reform movement in Judaism, and several spokesman for traditional institutions in the community may have felt threatened by this new development, yet something had to be done. The pattern of the seventies seemed to be repeating itself. Despite its protests, establishment Jewry organized a rescue effort on two fronts. Its success varied with time and circumstance.[3]

There was Wolf in Washington directing his campaign against Russian policy to the legislative and executive branches of government. He now spoke on behalf of the Committee on Civil and Religious Rights of the Union of American Hebrew Congregations, sometimes still referred to as the Board of Delegates.

At the same time, in New York City, charitable institutions, such as the short-lived Hebrew Emigrant Aid Society and its successor, the United Hebrew Charities, tried to meet the challenge encountered by the immediate problems of caring for the new arrivals.

On this occasion the record rung up by such institutions was not particularly laudable. These American Jewish welfare agencies first quarreled with their European counterparts as to the most effective methods for ridding themselves of the immigrant burden. Later, the United Hebrew Charities, working on the assumption that the immigrants were largely unemployables "lacking in diligence", instituted a program of repatriation that lasted through the 1880s. Such a determination to turn hundreds of East European Jews back to the lands of their oppression found its rationale in several factors. Funds for educating, training, and relocating the immigrants to areas of employment away from cities in the East were lacking. Fears that the very presence of thousands of newcomers would threaten the middle-class structure of established Jewry have already been alluded to. Specifically, German Jews in this country were convinced that a sudden influx of their poor cousins would stimulate the growth of anti-Semitism. To avert so dire a consequence, it was suggested that refugees from the Russian empire form a producer rather than a consumer class in American society.[4] Yet for themselves, German Jews remained perfectly content in pursuing such careers as stock-jobbing, merchandising, and factoring,[5] commercial practices that had long been the staple of economic activity for urban Jewish communities in Western Europe and England.

In urging the federal government to protest Russia's anti-Semitism, Wolf could not very well have voiced the fears of his German-Jewish compatriots. He could not have said publicly, in an official capacity as a spokesman for his community, that the presence of needy immigrants would pauperize the earlier Jewish settlers in this land, or effectively alter their standard of living, or raise the awesome specter of violent bigotry here. Instead, on behalf of the Board of Delegates, he contacted his old friend, Congressman Cox, a companion during the Egyptian interlude, to use his influence in high places. Perhaps then, Russian persecutions against the Jews would cease, and their migration here diminish accordingly. Conveniently, Cox now served as the Board's intermediary to President Chester A. Arthur. The chief executive not only informed Congress about the nature of Russia's proscriptive edicts, but also told the American minister at St. Petersburg that the American public wanted an end to such discrimination.[6]

All such overtures failed. Though the American minister to Russia, William Henry Hunt (1882–84), painted a confidential picture of the sorry plight of Russian Jewry for Secretary of State Frederick T. Freylinghuysen, the Presidential Message of 1883 minimized the gravity of the situation. For the time being, Wolf and his Board were kept in the dark as to the true nature of events in Russia. Having thus been lulled into silence, the Committee on Civil and Religious Rights saw no further reason to mention Russian anti-Semitism, or to urge the Council of the Union to take any new steps. The Committee's errors in judgment were compounded by the fact that fewer immigrants were arriving because of poor economic conditions here. This did not mean, however, that there was any improvement in the Russian matter. By the following year, in 1884, persecutions in Russia had not abated, while in Romania American diplomatic representatives displayed a callous indifference to the fate of European Jewry. Immigration had "become a necessity,"[7] but ironically enough, for the following four years, until the end of the decade, it seemed to be chaotic and disorganized.

During this period, from 1885 until 1889, approximately 80,000 Jews from Eastern Europe reached this country. The United Hebrew Charities continued its policy of repatriating jobless refugees and referring to their failure at industrial colonization. It made invidious comparisons between the Jewish immigrant, seemingly capable of work only in the garment industry or in retail merchandising, and other newcomers, eager to engage in all sorts of endeavors. Such limitations were in part the legacy of the Jewish aliens' earlier confinement to the Pale of Settlement, where restrictions on their businesses and recurrent pogroms had further reduced their ability to make a living in the New World. Yet at the same time, directors of the Charities did attempt to train immigrant youths in a variety of trades and technical callings.[8]

Earlier the Committee on Civil and Religious Rights had nothing to say about East European Jewish immigration either because economic factors made for fewer arrivals, or because it really knew little about the Russian state of affairs. Now, moreover, as the decade of the 1880s came to a close, other reasons may have accounted for the Committee's lack of interest. Many Jewish immigrants arrived here under private auspices. Second, the United Hebrew Charities took charge of all such matters. An equally cogent motive for the Committee's inarticulateness might well have been its attempt to reorganize.

In 1886, Wolf wrote a letter to the executive of the Union, suggesting that the seat of the Committee on Civil and Religious Rights be moved from New York to Washington. He was also prepared to change the name of the Committee to that of "The Board of Delegates on Civil and Religious Rights of the Union." As previously stated, in 1878, once Wolf had succeeded in merging the original Board of Delegates of American Israelites with the Union of American Hebrew Congregations, he had proposed such amendments to the Union's constitution as to allow his Committee on Civil and Religious Rights a share in controlling the Union's execuvite policy. At that time he apparently believed his scheme would suffice, were his Committee to consist of nine members of the executive board with eight others serving on an elected basis for one year. Now Wolf strengthened his own hand by requesting that the executive of the Union appoint all seventeen members to a two-year period. The *Proceedings of the Council of the Union* for 1886 show that its members accepted Wolf's changes in the form of amendments to the Union's constitution, and that the chairman of the Committee on Civil and Religious Rights, Myer S. Isaacs, a traditional Jew who led the original Board of Delegates of American Israelites, resigned his post. He was replaced by his brother, Dr. Abraham S. Isaacs.[10]

Records of the Committee, to be known once more as the Board of Delegates, do not reveal that Wolf sought Dr. Abraham S. Isaacs's post. In July 1889, however, at its Detroit meeting, the executive of the Union instructed its secretary on motion to have Wolf act as chairman of the newly renamed Committee.[11] Such a reordering of location to the nation's capital and a strengthening of the Board's central powers was in keeping with Wolf's objectives. He had for three decades been the spokesman for B'nai B'rith to the federal government. His contacts in the diplomatic field, with members of the Republican party, and with numerous local politicos had long ago been acknowledged. It became a matter of practical wisdom for services and activites on behalf of the Jewish community to be directed through one source and to be anchored in one locale. Thereafter, this argument that effective representation could only be had through officially sanctioned channels became Wolf's rallying cry.[12] It was ultimately to become his justification for the continued existence of the Board of Delegates of the Union, even when other Jewish defense and relief agencies tried to eclipse it.

More immediately, by 1890 the Council of the Union heard once more from the Board of Delegates on Civil and Religious Rights. This time, together with Lewis Abrahams and A. S. Solomons, Wolf signed the *Report*.[13] His appointment as chairman, made in 1890, could not have been more opportune. Though circumstances would be difficult, the situation was tailor made to Wolf's order. For a whole series of changes and new directions had so converged as to make it imperative that a spokesman be found for the immigrant Jew.

Wolf was forced to ask the federal government to modify its growing restrictionist stand on immigration precisely when the United States admitted losing faith in the blessings of open admission to this country. Paradoxically, throughout the 1870s and well into the next decade, while the United States was avidly seeking people to rebuild its devastated South, to man its factories, build its railroads, work its mines, and settle its homesteads, German-American Jewry, as noted, continually erected barriers to halt the arrival of Jewish immigrants.[14] Now, however, when Wolf and his peers, constrained by different circumstances, to seek admission for their poorer cousins, came with entreaties, opening the gates of America grew into a formidable task. For by August 1890, concern had already been expressed at the highest levels of government that repressive measures taken summarily against the Jews of the Russian empire would lead to unhealthy migrations to these shores. Such an influx, it was reasoned, might sorely tax the American system of individual enterprise and its labor market. This was the topic of numerous communications, continuing into 1891, that passed between Secretary of State James G. Blaine and American diplomatic consuls stationed in the larger cities of Russia, where there were noticeable Jewish populations.[15] Congress itself had been distressed by the prospect of renewed anti-Semitic oppression in the land of the czar, and asked President Benjamin Harrison to investigate the matter. For his part, Wolf had already appeared before the House Foreign Affairs Committee and urged it to communicate its displeasure with anti-Jewish persecutions in Russia, but the House Committee, fearing charges of interference in the domestic policies of a foreign regime, did not act.[16] Instead, in conjunction with the passage of its 1891 immigration bill, Congress did authorize a commission of immigrant inspectors to investigate the living conditions of potential immigrants abroad. Its *Report* confirmed the miserable living conditions eked out by thousands of Jews in various localities in the Russian empire, and included a summary of all the anti-Semitic proscriptions then in force in that land.[17]

Wolf had good reason to doubt the success of his appeal to the government. Not only was the battle for a humane immigration policy being lost on tactical grounds; it was also failing stragetically. For by 1891, immigrants no longer found open frontier lands on which to settle; farmers were plagued by foreclosures; manufacturers were suffering from the effects of a depression; and workers complained more vociferously than before against the perils of cheap, imported labor. The resultant tensions spilled over into multiplicities of distrust among different sectors of American society. Nativist groups, some of whom had survived intact since the Civil War, now grew stronger and spoke for a whole spectrum of public opinion. The one common denominator shared by the populist views of the native poor and the intellectual protests of the Boston Brahmins was that the alien, if unhampered in his entry here, would unravel the fabric of American existence.[18]

Reflecting such xenophobic fears, Congress, in 1891, passed an inclusive immigration bill. For the first time in America's history, the federal government was to have complete jurisdiction over matters of alien admission, while all assisted immigration was to be banned. Secretary of the Treasury Charles Foster, then in charge of the Immigration Bureau, wanted to apply this exclusionary policy to all persons coming from abroad who might have been helped to migrate here by friends and relatives in this country. This legal prohibition against assisted immigration occurred precisely when Russia had officially expelled thousands of Jewish artisans from the Moscow area.[19] The inescapable fact that untold numbers of Russian Jews would be flocking to these shores made it imperative that Jewish community representatives speak up against a newly forming federal attitude.

Wolf was neither a pioneer nor a radical, prepared to espouse unpopular causes. He had learned his lesson on immigration well, and would not have his motives impugned again, nor be hurt, as he had been in the early 1870s. Yet if events would force him to protest at an inopportune time, then at least the immigrants he would represent were no longer considered the ne'er-do-wells of the eighties. For the people now fleeing Russia were thought to be "frugal, patient, and industrious, skilled workers, adept at light manufactures."[20]

To be effective, such words of praise by representatives of the United Hebrew Charities had to be grounded in practicalities that went beyond the perceptions of some skilled social workers. The only feasible scheme that could move men and governments alike was to make huge funds available to American Jewish leaders for the care and distribution of newcomers. That plan crystallized with the formation of a trust fund, made possible through the generosity of a Paris-based philanthropist, Baron Maurice de Hirsch, eager to contribute "to the relief of [his] brethren in race."[21]

Fortified by positive estimates of the immigrants and encouraged in the knowledge that monies would be forthcoming, Wolf and Lewis Abrahams argued that persecuted Jews coming here under the aegis of welfare societies were, in effect, being brought over by independent, or private, means. On this occasion, a temporary association of Russian immigrants in Philadelphia, the Alliance, joined Wolf and Abrahams, who, as usual, spoke for B'nai B'rith and the Board of Delegates of the Union. In their letter to Secretary Foster, Wolf and Abrahams maintained that contributions from private charities to sustain the newcomers were not to be reckoned as public funds. Therefore, the immigrants were not to be regarded as public charges, reaching this country illegally.

Foster thought this a fragile argument. He observed that "private support of great numbers of dependent people still taxed the resources of the country." Nevertheless, he recognized that Jewish organizations discouraged the admission of destitute aliens, and were eager to insure quick employment for those who were deemed eligible to come here. Wolf stressed that such vocational placement involved the occupational retraining and immediate redistribution of the new arrivals, away from the crowded ghettos on the East Coast. Having accepted Wolf's interpretation of the "assisted immigrant" proviso, Foster then reshaped the entire matter in terms of a mutually acceptable equation. The United States, he informed Wolf, would meet his views "in other respects," if Jewish plans for refugee relocation were to prove successful.

For the remainder of his life, that phrase, "in other respects," involved Wolf and the Jewish community in a variety of schemes for shipping immigrants to distant cities, so that the seemingly excessive numbers of foreigners in any one area would not serve as signals for local tensions. At all costs Wolf was determined that the government's fear of an "excessive immigration . . . failing . . . to supply a real want in scattered communities . . . or interfering with . . . normal industrial conditions" would never materialize.[22]

The secretary's reply also vindicated Wolf's view that negotiations, like politics, meant compromising in good faith. Throughout his life, Wolf maintained the corollary to that policy. Potential adversaries were to be met midway and disarmed. As shall soon be seen, other men much younger than Wolf, who took up the gauntlet in defense of East European Jewry, seemed eager to appeal to legal principles whenever the occasion warranted. But Wolf always relied on the power of personal and social contacts to achieve his goals.[23] In addition, Foster's answer ultimately forced Wolf to become a legal expert in the domain of assisted immigration. The practicalities of any specific immigrant case impelled him to look for various shades of meaning that might remove the onus from any refugee's being deemed either a public charge or an assisted immigrant. As the years flew by, this became his métier. Others may have battled valiantly against the implications of literacy tests or over the difficulties to be encountered in achieving naturalization, but Wolf searched for ways to eliminate the terms "public charge," "assisted immigrant," and their related clauses, such as "low vitality, or poor physique,"[24] which served as code words for the restrictionists.

By 1893, the furor about swollen immigration from the Russian empire had subsided. The American depression and outbreaks of typhus aboard ships carrying the refugees accounted for a large decrease in the number of arrivals. But the restrictionists had already girded their loins for the approaching battle and were not to be dissuaded from their goal of shutting the doors of this country to all but a select group of white Protestants from northern and western Europe. Led by Senator Henry Cabot Lodge of Massachusetts, the antiimmigrationists lobbied and legislated against the newcomers, while Jewish groups tried unsuccessfully to distribute their "huddled masses" throughout the land.

Such relocation programs were closely tied to valiant efforts at vocational retraining. But only a few of the agricultural settlements designed to direct Jewish immigrants into farming succeeded. The record proved equally unproductive in terms of industrial reorientation. From 1891 until 1910, some 1,186,000 Jews came to this country.[25] Jewish social service agencies helped approximately 50,000 of these arrivals to settle in cities away from the Eastern seaboard.[26] Though this is not an inconsiderable number, Jewish officials viewed the figure with dismay. They understood full well that it was unusually difficult to persuade the immigrants to leave the ghettos where their own kin had earlier congregated, and where there were some assurances of employment, no matter how minimal the wages. But Wolf had struck a bargain with the federal government that had to be fulfilled. In this connection the Industrial Removal Bureau, created by B'nai B'rith in 1901, tried until 1922 to facilitate employment for immigrant Jews away from the urban centers. The established American Jewish community had taken Secretary Foster's quid pro quo arrangement with Wolf and Abrahams concerning "assisted immigrants" to heart. If the community had not measured up to its own expectations, it at least had put forth a valiant effort.[27]

In the short run, however, Foster's rejoinder provided Wolf with two advantages. First, by diminishing the number of accusations of illegality against Jewish immigrants, it allowed Wolf and his colleagues to press for reversal of deportation proceedings in specific instances. Second, it served Wolf as a tool in his arguments with the restrictionists.

In one such encounter with Senator William Chandler of New Hampshire, Wolf denied the legislator's accusation that President Cleveland had deliberately fostered a Jewish migration to this country, one which Baron de Hirsch himself had characterized as an influx of paupers. Chandler then wondered whether Wolf and John B. Weber, who was responsible for a federal report on emigrant conditions in Europe, were both on the baron's payroll. The senator surmised that Joseph Senner, a commissioner of immigration at Ellis Island, had to be a Jew because of his liberal views. Such snide allusions to ethnic designations or occupational choices were later to become decisive arguments in the nativist barrage against open immigration.[28] More immediately, Chandler was seeking a foolproof way to impose restrictionist demands. To close America's doors, he needed a more effective method than resorting to all those public-charge-assisted immigrant provisos whose terms, thanks to Wolf, were now subject to a latitude of interpretations.

Wolf would not be trapped into evaluating the merits of various beliefs or national origins. Instead he listed the national, religious, and occupational affiliations of the federal officials whom Chandler so heatedly denigrated. Taking umbrage at the senator's calling the immigration "Jewish," Wolf repeated the pledge he had made to Foster. By supervising, retraining, and redistributing its newcomers, the American Jewish community also controlled the nature and numbers of those people it was prepared to look after. At no time, Wolf continued, had such clients ever become a burden to the government.[29]

Wolf used this same argument in testimony before the Industrial Commission, created by Congress in 1898 to consider the economic, industrial, and agricultural state of American society. The commission duly recorded Wolf's views and those of several other witnesses that Jews look after their own coreligionists, who were among the more highly skilled of entering aliens. Yet it mattered little that "Russian Hebrews were now better equipped to earn a living" than their predecessors of the 1880s. Only adults, "with a tendency to pauperism," the commissioners insisted, would place their children in day schools, offering tuition-free education. Had such aid not been forthcoming, the parents would have been candidates for the poorhouse.[30] In fact, so determined were commissioners H. V. Schulteis and Terence V. Powderly to limit immigration that they were prepared to declare friends who came to the aid of new arrivals as being out of bounds.[31] Once again, the immigrants would be placed in the category of illegal aliens. Happily for Wolf, other members of the commission refused to ratify this last proposal. Had it been otherwise, then the work of many charitable agencies, including their main financial source, the Baron de Hirsch Fund, would have been invalidated. Jewish immigrants would then have been declared paupers, or public charges, and subject to deportation.

Except for Wolf's statements and those of Joseph Senner, who appeared as counsel for the Immigrants' Protective League,[32] the weight of the evidence presented by other witnesses favored the restrictionists. Statistics were marshaled to show that the children of the foreign born formed a larger percentage of the prison population than native offspring. Though there were far fewer Jews in jails than members of other ethnic groups, the general impression was established that, lumped together with other aliens, Jews also constituted part of the criminal class. Much was made of violations of the alien contract labor law that threatened the security of skilled native workers. The "Italian and Hebrew races" were singled out as the most "threatening aspect of unrestricted immigration," while manufacturers in the garment industry were the Simon Legrees of the new technology.[33] By commission accounts, the only calling that escaped the baleful effects of immigration was agriculture, where even Italians and Bohemians were included as being adept at intensive farming. But for Jews, who were regarded as the most urban of all incoming aliens, ventures in agriculture had to be bolstered by creating parallel industrial establishments. Wolf refuted this contention by emphasizing that in the Jewish agricultural colonies of Woodbine, Carmel, Alliance, and Rosenhayn in New Jersey, manufacturing enterprises merely augmented their financial incomes.[34] Judging by the overall tenor of the commission's *Report,* Wolf scored poorly on this issue.

The commission's tendency to distinguish between aliens arriving from Europe's northern tier and Jews and Italians from the southeastern portions of the continent occurred shortly after Romania, under Russian domination, had embarked upon a systematic campaign of restrictive civil and economic measures against its Jews. Though such laws were in violation of the Treaty of Berlin (1878), guaranteeing Romania's independence, these edicts were also accompanied by overt acts of anti-Semitic violence in scattered localities.[35] The result was a flood of Romanian Jews to this country.

Alarmed at the prospect, the federal government was determined to stop this immigration at its source. This was the gist of correspondence between Leo N. Levi, the B'nai B'rith president, and Wolf, now its vice-president. Levi urged Wolf to make Commissioner of Immigration Frank P. Sargent fully aware of B'nai B'rith's decision not to tolerate any infractions of American immigration law.[36]

This policy was in keeping with Secretary of State John Hay's wish to sign a naturalization convention with Romania. By its terms, Romanian Jews, accorded equal rights with other citizens, would be allowed the right of expatriation without the consent of the sovereign. Hay reasoned that under such circumstances, they would opt to remain in their country, since they would no longer be subject to legal, political, or economic restrictions there.[37] B'nai B'rith would then be relieved of its burden for securing the freedom of Romania's Jews, while their migration to the United States would greatly diminish.

Pending the outcome of Secretary Hay's appeal for a naturalization treaty, Wolf wanted to convene a conference in the matter of Romanian immigration to this country. At the same time, B'nai B'rith would be able to reassure the federal authorities of its determination to maintain a "law and order approach" to the subject. But Levi feared that Wolf's motives would be denigrated by "designing" (Democratic) "politicians" who might question the integrity of wealthy American Jews and their Republican allies. Such doubts might provide ample proof that affluent German Jews were still eager to bar the doors of this country to their poor coreligionists. Furthermore, there was the danger that Hay's call for a naturalization convention would alienate those Americans seeking a liberal immigration policy. They would claim that the Hay's request was at best a political trick to keep Romanian Jews in their homeland. B'nai B'rith might then find itself in an embarrassing situation: it was that very organization at whose instance the State Department had protested Romania's treatment of its Jews to the signatories to the Berlin Treaty.[38]

Nothing came of America' concern for Romanian anti-Semitism. Romania refused to accept Hay's offer of a naturalization convention. Henceforth, Americanized Jews of Romanian descent would not be welcome in their country of origin, and Romanian Jews, not being accorded the rights due them in their own land, would continue to flock to this country. For good measure, Romania, in rejecting the Hay message, also took note of the slight accorded its diplomatic representative here, who apparently had not been received with proper protocol.[39]

As chairman of the Board of Delegates, Wolf was invited to the State Department to read Romania's negative reply to Secretary Hay. In addition, several prominent Democratic Jewish leaders had prevailed upon Wolf to arrange a conference with President Roosevelt on the Romanian matter. Privately, Roosevelt chided Wolf for coming with all the others, so that meaningful discussions were not possible. Then Roosevelt asked his guests abruptly whether the Jews of the United States would have wanted him to make war against Russia and Romania because of their avowed anti-Semitic policies.[40]

Roosevelt was not one to let the matter of Romanian naturalization or the lack of it obstruct his political ambitions. Nor would he willingly disregard any potential immigrant vote. Accordingly, not long after commissioner of immigration at the Port of New York, William Williams, had embarked upon a more stringent admissions policy based on the presence or absence of cash on hand for certain aliens, Roosevelt quietly reminded him of the need to create an amicable working relationship between the Ellis Island administration and representatives of various ethnic groups. The president was concerned that certain prominant Jews, led by Representative Lucius N. Littauer of New York, had complained about the "star-chamber" nature of Williams's deportation procedures.[41] The president asked Williams that the immigrant be given every opportunity to present his case, and that spokesmen for the German, Italian, Irish, and Jewish immigrant agencies attend the hearings. More pointedly, Roosevelt reminded Williams that he too was engaged in a public calling, where he could ill afford to antagonize congressional leaders. In reply, the commissioner observed that several "Hebrew orders" had attacked him for "misdoings in office." Williams, aware that by law the public was to be excluded from hearings before boards of inquiry, was certain its "absence" would not have made "justice any less." Grudgingly, he was forced to accept the president's request.[42]

Unlike Williams, Sargent possessed a good deal of political prudence, and seemed more amenable to the president's wishes. At a 1903 Jewish Chautauqua Society meeting, presided over by the ubiquitous Wolf, Sargent assured his audience that any request by the Immigration Bureau to have the alien produce evidence of cash on his person was an illegal practice that had mistakenly crept into administrative procedures. It was thereupon abandoned. Sargent also denied that immigrant inspectors discriminated among different classes of aliens, such as the Romanians, the Russians, or the Italians. Any marked increase in the number of people being sent back to Europe, he contended, was still proportional to the "swarms of Italians and others flocking to these shores."[43]

Of the "Hebrew orders," only B'nai B'rith, with Levi and Wolf at its helm, accepted Sargent's explanations. Levi saw no anti-Semitic tendencies either in federal inclinations arbitrarily to impose regulations on the aliens that had not yet been written into law, or in the commissioner's obsession with ethnic distinctions.[44] Wolf wanted loyal Americans to cooperate with the government in preventing undesirable Jewish immigrants from landing here. His measuring rod for determining the acceptability of newcomers was the rapidity with which they would be absorbed into American life.[45] It would be difficult, however, to gage the extent to which Wolf's beneficent view concerning certain desirable arrivals was intended for public consumption, or to what degree his warnings against an unwanted influx were bound by the official pronouncements of B'nai B'rith, whose president he served so well.[46]

Roosevelt was more astute than both the commissioners and the advocates for the immigrants. He had now to intervene as he had earlier in his admonitions to Commissioner Williams. In the summer of 1903 he appointed an investigative commission to evaluate conditions at Ellis Island. Its *Report* was made public on 28 February 1904. In it the commission tried to effect a compromise among all elements concerned with immigration. Immigrants and transportation companies were to have the benefit of legal counsel. The commission questioned the wisdom of imposing excessive fines on steamship companies for the care of aliens detained for medical reasons. Instead, American labor contractors were to be charged with such expenses, while the immigrants would be kept there to serve as witnesses against such entrepreneurs. Were the charges against the contractors proved false, those immigrants would then be allowed to enter the United States. In certain instances, the commission was prepared to allow aliens to recover from illnesses at their own expense, in private hospitals. It was deemed expedient to appoint immigrant inspectors at points of embarkation to avoid costly travel for those who were certain to be deported. Accommodations at Ellis Island were to be improved. At the same time, the commission refuted any charges that Williams and his staff had engaged in abitrary decisions or overstepped their authority. Instead, the commission empowered Williams to hear appeals from the Board of Inquiry and reaffirmed its confidence in him.[47]

Wolf's testimony before the Ellis Island Commission was not earth-shaking. He dutifully recounted B'nai B'rith's efforts to absorb, educate, and redistribute the aliens, and restated the historic benefits that accrued to this country by virtue of a generous welcome to aliens. He did, however, complain that federal authorities misconstrued the public-charge feature of the law when they added the lack of a specific locale of immigrant settlement as ample warrant for deporting the immigrants.[48] Years later, however, two attorneys, Abram Elkus and Max J. Kohler, used this argument of the Ellis Island Commission, that the possibility of employment at some geographical location, rather than the alien's own possession of cash resources, ought to be the criterion for immigrant admission.[49]

In pleading his case before federal commissioners, Wolf had to be the pleasant, patient advocate. As a seasoned negotiator, he was afraid to risk what he had gained thus far. For the federal authorities to exclude Jews aided by private charities from the category of assisted immigrant was an achievement not to be lightly cast aside. Yet he was always constrained to remain adamant on the one issue he honestly believed was destructive of individual rights, and hence unconstitutional. That was the federal practice of tabulating Russian and Romanian Jews in terms of their religious affiliation. Wolf saw such action as an invidious intrusion by the state into the private domain, a process that also infringed on the doctrine of the separation of church and state.[50] This unconstitutional policy ultimately led to admitting aliens by quota, a system that Wolf was to protest to his dying day. In time, it would become part of his losing battle with those who were determined to shut America's doors to the immigrant.

6
Challenges to Power

Since that record-breaking moment in 1891, when Wolf spoke up on behalf of the immigrant, he had grown accustomed to being the representative of the American Jewish community to the federal government. His efforts on behalf of the Jewish immigrant persisted simply because certain European governments were not to be dissuaded from their anti-Semitic policies. The early years of the twentieth century bore witness to a constant stream of Russian and Romanian Jewish aliens to this land. Much as Wolf and his colleagues would have wished, they were unable to deflect this stream at its source. In 1903, Wolf had loudly trumpeted his role and that of other B'nai B'rith leaders in compiling a monumental protest against the Kishineff massacres with an accompanying petition to the czar, which bore the signatures of hundreds of influential Americans of all creeds. Since the czar had refused to accept the document, it had been deposited with due pomp and ceremony in the National Archives. There was nothing then, in all the circumstances attendant upon the petition or upon the protests and volumes written in the aftermath of Kishineff, that in any way altered Russia's policy toward its Jews, or narrowed the influx of those coming to these shores. Similarly, Romania's systematic economic and political anti-Jewish persecutions constituted insurmountable barriers[1] against which an attempt by Secretary of State John Hay to secure a naturalization treaty based on the equality of citizenship proved unavailing.[2] Romanian Jews continued to flock to this country, while B'nai B'rith, unable to check this exodus at its source as it had earlier hoped to do, had now, by 1904, to content itself with determined attempts at immigrant redistribution in America.[3]

This background, then, of forced migrations whose effects a secretary of state deemed injurious to the United States, and whose consequences American Jewry sought desperately to mitigate through rapid assimilation or relocation, might have made Wolf's concern with organizational pride and status appear picayune. But in 1904, upon the death of Leo N. Levi, Wolf inherited the presidential mantle of B'nai B'rith leadership. Eager at all costs to secure the standing of his institution, Wolf then took on Nissim Behar, a dynamic leader of the Alliance Israelite Universelle in America. Behar, a rather late arrival on the scene, tried locally to reinvigorate the battle against Russian inequalities practiced on its Jews, and much more celebratedly, to revitalize the longstanding issue with regard to czarist discrimination against American Jewish travelers in Russia. As is well known, this latter cause provided American Jewish spokesmen with a more immediate weapon to alter the course of Russian anti-Semitism than polite protests in the form of a petition to the czar against wanton massacres. For whenever American Jews were molested abroad, access was to be had to the State Department; where the lives of foreign Jews were at stake, their American coreligionists possessed no rules of universal legality on which to base their protests. In either event, both the issues of overt killings in Russia and Russian harassment of American Jewish commercial travelers were grist for the mill in America for the defense of human rights. Were Jewish spokesmen, such as the well-known banker-philanthropist, Jacob H. Schiff, or Louis Marshall, a prominent attorney, or Simon Wolf, to have succeeded in modifying the Russian treatment of American Jews abroad, then perhaps Russia's attitudes to her native Jews would likewise have been transformed, and fewer immigrants would come here. Above all, American Jewish representatives were determined that they alone, and no messengers from any European Jewish institution, were to claim credit for so welcome a change. The sheer jealousy of guarding one's institutional prerogatives no doubt was responsible for Wolf's rejection of Behar. Warning the French Alliance that Behar's work was rightly the jurisdiction of B'nai B'rith, Wolf demanded his dismissal.

> . . . we cannot for a moment allow the representative of a foreign corporation to meddle . . . in matters purely local or national in the United States. . . . What we do in this country we do as American citizens . . . to judge what is best in securing such legislation as is consistent with the object in hand. . . . We therefore, most respectfully ask that instructions be issued to Mr. Behar to place himself under the jurisdiction of the [B'nai B'rith] Order if possible, and to withdraw from active work for the Alliance, in matters of legislation affecting the interests of our citizens. . . .[4]

Wolf's request came after several suggestions from the Alliance Israelite Universelle that Behar steer clear of B'nai B'rith activities, and leave the United States. But Behar stayed on in this country, and persisted in "meddling," as Wolf would have called it.[5] In essence, Behar's presence neither helped nor hindered Wolf's frequent calls upon the State Department and other executive offices of this government. Wolf's interventions in no way altered the course of East European anti-Semitism,[6] so that immigration grew in direct proportion to increasing hardships abroad. Meanwhile, Wolf, having taken up the B'nai B'rith cause against Behar in the matter of countering Russian tactics, had once again to assert the priorities of leadership. This time, younger men than Wolf, some of whom came from his own Union of American Hebrew Congregations, rose to challenge the dominance of both B'nai B'rith and the Board of Delegates of the Union.[7]

Kishineff was but the prelude to further anti-Jewish excesses in Russia, whose effects not only intensified the immigrant flow but placed inequitable burdens of relief upon a few privileged individuals. Such concern for the weight of private financial contributions and for the safety of Jews overseas induced several leaders to seek the initiative in creating a new defense agency, devoted to the furtherance of civil and religious liberties whereever these were threatened. Oscar Straus, Louis Marshall, Cyrus Adler, Joseph Jacobs, and others spearheaded the new movement. By January 1906, Adler proposed the establishment of a national assembly to cooperate with other groups pursuing similar goals. There was, however, no mistaking Adler's intent: to date, he complained, no existing "body or committee" had effectively represented its constituents either at home or abroad. He implied that the responsibility of the Board of Delegates and B'nai B'rith would account only for a "very small number of Jews."

It took the new organization, the American Jewish Committee, three-quarters of a year to see the light of day. During this period, in 1906, none of the various proposals for its effective formulation, either on a democratic or more centralized basis, obscured the fact that its very existence would challenge the established authority of the Board of Delegates and B'nai B'rith.[8]

B'nai B'rith retaliated. Adolph Kraus, a Chicago attorney who succeeded Wolf as president of the organization, deemed it arrogant and improper for any one group to presume to speak for all of Jewry. B'nai B'rith, Kraus insisted, would go its own way.[9] More modestly, Wolf, having seen no need for any new institution, declared only that he would not actively oppose it.[10] In the jockeying for position that followed, and as a means of placating B'nai B'rith, Wolf was named to the executive of the American Jewish Committee, whose formation now constituted a compromise of various plans for effecting a truly representative body, capable of speaking authoritatively for the American Jewish community.[11]

Wolf's association on the executive of the American Jewish Committee endured only for half a year.[12] Good manners on the part of the Committee and the need to present a united front had accounted for Wolf's inclusion in its policy-making arm. But Wolf himself was unequal to overcoming entrenched individual and collective rights to power, spelled out in accumulated years of self-declared spokesmanship that were the hallmarks of B'nai

B'rith. A formal manifesto out of Chicago disassociating that fraternal body from the new organization was the result. As a B'nai B'rith leader, its immediate past president, and its Washington representative, Wolf had no choice but to append his signature to the document.[13] But he must have had his regrets; he sensed that battles that effectively cut all lines of communication sometimes serve only to dispense harm equally to all concerned. He therefore made certain that his personal letter of resignation from the Committee still left the door slightly ajar—for future contacts, however vague. He was prepared, he informed the Committee, to offer his cooperation, if solicited, in any future undertaking. He was, in fact, determined that such a request might ultimately come to pass; if B'nai B'rith were beyond the reach of his persuasive powers, there was always the Board of Delegates. And in 1908 an opportunity for joint action between the American Jewish commit tee and the Board of Delegates almost presented itself. It came about inadvertently and ultimately amounted to nothing at all. In the process, of course, Wolf tried privately to alter the route of his Board of Delegates, aligning it with a new force on the Jewish horizon. It began when Wolf rebuked Cyrus Adler, the true genius of the American Jewish Committee, for the deplorable way in which the Committee had bypassed the Board of Delegates and B'nai B'rith in matters of immigration and of safeguarding American travelers abroad from the caprices of Russian law.[14] Having absolved the Committee from any responsibility in failing to cooperate with other agencies, Adler then hinted broadly that there might have been a different scenario had the Union been prepared to abandon the Board of Delegates. Wolf leaped quickly to the fateful conclusion. Were the Board to become an independent institution, then he as its chairman would resign, affiliate himself with a reconstituted group, acting in liaison with the American Jewish Committee.[15] Currently, no further light has been shed on Wolf's intended change of direction. To the end of his days he continued to serve as chairman for his Board of Delegates, while the Committee's concerns with the defense of civic and human rights not only expanded in depth and scope throughout the same period, but burgeoned forth beyond all expectations in the decades following Wolf's death.

It was only in this context, then, of contending needs to speak for American Jewry, that the vituperative correspondence exchanged in the fall of 1908 between Judge Mayer Sulzberger, president of the American Jewish Committee, and Wolf is to be understood. These acerbic notes dealt with some alleged indignities a Jewish sailor suffered during a religious service. In this connection the *Boston Journal* published a story that one E. R. Williams, dressed in naval garb, had been denied admission to a synagogue during the High Holy Days in September 1908. The newspaper observed that there was a difference of opinion between two synagogue officials concerning the propriety of a sailor's appearing in uniform at worship.[16] The article also included an interview with Secretary of the Navy Victor H. Metcalf condemning those who discriminate against members of the armed forces. He noted that there had been instances when veterans were excluded from amusement centers, but this was the first time to his knowledge that a man in uniform had not been allowed in a synagogue.[17]

Wolf played a central role in this sorry episode. In his frenzy to protect the name of the Jew from any unwarranted assumptions concerning a lack of patriotism, he first alerted Secretary Metcalf to the story of the sailor and the synagogue, with the proviso that should it prove true, he would quickly remedy the situation. Second, having accepted the view of Isaac Rosnosky, the president of a [Reform] temple in Boston, that the tale was indeed authentic, Wolf then informed Secretary Metcalf that Jewish law prevented anyone from appearing in military dress at a worship service.[18]

What Wolf accomplished was to involve a federal official in a Jewish intracommunity affair and to invoke the anger of Orthodox Jews. They doubted the validity of the entire incident, disputed his view of Jewish law concerning the presence of uniformed men at prayer, and questioned his right to be their spokesman.

Judge Mayer Sulzberger took up the gauntlet for the disaffected. So astounded was he at the contention that Orthodox Jewry had "traditions and usages which forbid a Jew in uniform from participating in divine services," that he asked Wolf for the source of his authority. To compound the difficulty, not only did Sulzberger deny the accuracy of Rosnosky's statement (that the sailor was indeed denied admission), but accused Wolf of an "assault on Jewry large in numbers though deficient at present in wealth and influence. . . ." Sulzberger was certain that Wolf would not "wish it understood that the Board of Delegates entertains or fosters sentiments hostile to a section of the Jewish people."[19]

Under the direction of the American Jewish Committee, affidavits were taken from the persons involved, an explanatory letter from Pinhas Israeli, the rabbi of the synagogue in question, was sent to Judge Sulzberger, and Lee M. Friedman, a prominent Boston advocate and American Jewish historian, investigated the entire matter. Based on the various accounts he consulted, it appears that the sailor, merely looking for someone in the audience, had come to the services while the sermon was in progress. He thereupon left of his own accord, but went on to another congregation where the story was embellished to the point of fabrication. Once the *Boston Journal* got wind of the event, it telegraphed the secretary of the Navy, who asked Wolf to verify the report.[20]

The American Jewish Committee then informed Secretary Metcalf of the error; Cyrus Adler got President Roosevelt to look at all the papers in the case, while Wolf admitted his mistake to Secretary Metcalf. Petty though the entire incident may have been, it did not rest there. Sulzberger continued to

lecture Wolf as one would a schoolboy. "It was neither graceful nor necessary," Sulzberger wrote after the event, "[to assume the] voluntary role of
accuser," but that "guessing about a custom and imputing it to a large
number of Jews was even worse." Sulzberger had always thought Wolf's
function had been to "allay" prejudice [rather than] "increase [it]." Sulzberger completed his chastisement with the view that "Wolf's confession"
would never "undo wrong, . . . [it would be idle] to appeal to [his] record
. . . [since] good character cannot acquit where act is confessed." For these
reasons, the American Jewish Committee had assumed the duty of "protecting [the] Jewish name against unrighteous assaults in any quarter. . . ."
More important perhaps than the issue at stake and beyond Sulzberger's
wounding words lay Wolf's realization that he no longer played center stage
in the drama of Jewish concern for human rights.[21]

Wolf did not appropriate those new lobbying techniques which marked
the methods of his more notable peers, such as Max Kohler, Oscar Straus,
Louis Marshall, and other members of the American Jewish Committee.
These later leaders with Kohler and Marshall serving as liaisons to Wolf,
combined the tactics of nineteenth-century governmental advisors with the
modes of modern day advocates. Even a cursory reading of their correspondence during the first two decades of this century indicates that wherever
possible, they based their humanitarian demands for justice on what they
imagined were accurate interpretations of the law. When they thought the
situation warranted it, they even accused federal officials of deliberate misap-
plication and maladministration of the statutes. Wolf, too, as shall be seen,
was always concerned about extricating his clients from the "thickets" of the
law, but he did so in an old fashioned way, always relying on the good faith of
the bureaucrat he had to placate. Members of the American Jewish Committee, while resorting to legal prerogatives, might yet threaten and cajole
legislators and executives, but Wolf would operate from a different perspective. He would meet those he had to influence usually on the basis of a favor
granted for an obligation undertaken. Given this opportunity for functioning
in an open society, Wolf was able to contact the shapers and makers of
American domestic and foreign policy. Younger members of the American
Jewish Committee, who sometimes scoffed at his graciousness and called it
"palavering" with those on high levels of government, would on occasion
have to channel their need for tidbits of information through him. This was
particularly true in 1906–7, when the United States was about to reach an
agreement with Japan on immigration matters. At other times, however,
such men as Louis Marshall, Judge Mayer Sulzberger, and Herbert Friedenwald fretted that the news and rumors Wolf dispensed were deliberately
misleading, that his motives in such instances grew from a constant need for
self-gratification.[22]

As the second decade of the twentieth century sped by, Wolf now aging, was still cordially disliked by those of his own coreligionists who continued to battle for leadership in the American Jewish community. But his steady entrée to the power brokers in the nation's capital forced his competitors always to weigh the authenticity of his information, frequently obtained at the highest levels of government.

Even in the last decade of his life Wolf had become a sort of institution whom others, in their ascent to parleys with the near and the great, had always to acknowledge. As late as 1921, Marshall had to dissuade Wolf from appearing in any official capacity before a disarmament conference, lest such an event would negate the positive effects of the Minority Treaties signed at Versailles, which at least on paper guaranteed Jews in the emerging states of Eastern and Central Europe certain basic religious, political, social, and cultural rights.[23]

That Wolf's influence grew with the years despite new methods for approaching those in command should perhaps not be marveled at. Wolf himself was as practiced and skilled a negotiator as his younger peers. While they sought justification in constitutional law and sometimes irritated those in government whose support was needed, Wolf always stressed the human factor in any pourparlers.[24]

This sense of charm and ease, this ability to sustain an aura of friendship even on occasions when the results lent themselves to chilling effects, became the touchstone of his method for bargaining with those at the helm of government. He did so at a time when this country revealed increasingly xenophobic attitudes toward Jews and other strangers. It has been seen how his claim to leadership within this milieu found expression on several fronts: in the power play to wrest American Reform Judaism from its more radicalized proponents and to center it in Cincinnati, with his own Washington base as its pivot; in his personal struggle for acceptance on the local and national levels; and for diplomatic recognition on the international scene. For the remainder of his life, the other significant areas of his endeavors continued to be the pursuit of justice both for the native and for the alien, confrontations with Jew-baiting both at home and abroad, and intense if misdirected efforts toward downgrading the growing Zionist movement.

7
Justice for the Stranger

In the spring of 1906, Wolf was close to the biblical age of three score and ten. By right, he should have earned the rewards of a gracious retirement. But now he had begun to struggle in earnest with the results of an increasingly restrictive immigration policy. For it was then that organized labor, with its traditional antipathy to all aliens, had already found its political voice, while the professional and intellectual restrictionists under the guidance of Senator Henry Cabot Lodge of Massachusetts and Prescott Hall of the Immigration Restriction League were acquiring a new lease on life. The elite of the xenophobes introduced legislation in Congress that increased the head tax from two to four dollars, provided for an educational test, and initiated drastic changes in the administration of the law. Henceforth, the decision of medical examiners to deport such aliens as were of "poor physique," or possessed "low vitalities" sufficient to deem them unemployable, would be final. Williams's and Sargent's combined concerns with the physical appearance of the alien had at last borne fruit.[1]

Writing to Sargent, Wolf called the commissioner-general's attention to the perplexing problem that confronted Americans and American Jews in particular. What was to be done with those immigrants who, by virtue of inhuman conditions in Russia and proscriptions against resettlement in Germany, were being catapulted onto these shores? Wolf wondered whether America would be party to that pact of vindictiveness between Russia and Germany, where the one threw out its Jews and the other did not permit them to enter. Bluntly, he observed that there are occasions when, "owing to the great onrush of circumstances," the "technicalities of the law have to be swept aside." Wolf was now forced to spell out the facts with little circumspection. "Understand directly," he wrote to Sargent, "that no one, not myself, either personally, or as the representative of large Jewish organizations, desires the admission of any one who will prove a burden and public charge inimical to our institutions and who are distinctly barred by law. We are impelled by every feeling of patriotism in common with all our fellow citizens to uphold the government, its trusted officials and to strengthen every ligament of the body politic; but when a discretion is to be exercised, ought it not to be given to the immigrants coming from Russia?"

Wolf begged the commissioner general to understand that the rigors that Jewish aliens had to endure in the past would have made them appear deceptively weak physically, and obscure their true earning capacity. Wolf was especially fearful that an arduous ocean voyage, underscored by steerage conditions and meticulous adherence to a restrictive food regimen, inspired by the Jewish dietary laws, would only result in classifying these aliens as deportees due to "poor physique." Such a procedure, he insisted, was the "height of cruelty and inhumanity," meted out to people who came here "by stress of circumstances far transcending those of the Huguenots, the German, Irish or Romanians."

Sargent's rejoinder to Wolf's eloquent statement was cool but polite. The commissioner admitted it was not "a very pleasant task to make recommendations on the cases which constantly come before the Bureau and which affect the admission of aliens." Nevertheless, the commissioner did promise to "take into consideration the conditions under which Jewish immigrants came here" and assured Wolf that the Immigration Bureau would continue to "show a kindly disposition" in these matters.[2]

Wolf's exchange with Robert Watchorn, commissioner of immigration for the Port of New York, proved even less productive. Watchorn had long been regarded as one who pleaded the immigrants' cause. In 1900 he wrote a series of sympathetic accounts from Bucharest, Budapest, and Vienna, detailing the plight of Romanian Jews and analyzing the motives that impelled them to America. Now, however, in 1906, Wolf accused him of unwarranted harshness in pressing the public-charge issue against these aliens. Wolf observed that once Watchorn had decided upon deportation, the Department of Commerce and Labor was unlikely to reverse his orders, lest such a procedure demoralize the immigration "service." With a frankness rarely encountered in his correspondence with other government functionaries, Wolf wondered whether Watchorn's change in policy was not the result of top-echelon directives.

> . . . If you are acting under instructions from those above you—why that is another matter, and the sooner that fact be known, the better for the service and the cause I serve.

The cause he served, Wolf insisted, took precedence over everything else, including the wishes of Watchorn and his colleagues.[3]

Watchorn explained that he never fashioned policy, but merely executed the law. He further defined that law for Wolf's benefit. Since the recommendation to exercise wise discretion was merely a House amendment that the Senate did not pass, it was not a statute to be observed as Wolf would have wished. Defending himself, Watchorn insisted on his own personal sense of fairness and cited many instances when he had admitted immigrants in patent defiance of a law that justifiably called for their exclusion.

Petulantly, he challenged Wolf and asked,

> Why don't you write to the representative of the United Hebrew Charities at this station and ask him about the multiplicity of cases in which I exerted every energy to ascertain the facts concerning those who are attempting to enter the United States with such a terrible pressure behind them? If you do so, I think you will find it incumbent upon you to commend me for the many acts which your letters suggest you regard as meritorious, rather than condemn for the few cases which strike you as being out of harmony with your own views of the situation?[4]

The statistical increase in the number of public-charge accusations against Russian Jews, which the commissioner used to bolster his argument, were due both to the quickened tempo of anti-Semitic[5] persecutions abroad and to the stricter application of the public-charge law. Immigrants who still had relatives here to look after them were summarily deported. Upon the receipt of such news there was little that Wolf could do other than to complain of his own impending physical and mental collapse.[6] Had he been gifted with prophecy, he might have saved his despair for 1910 when deportations on the public charge began to mount exceedingly. Or better still, he might have contained his fury until the eve of the 1920s, when, for some minimal advantages, he went so far as to advocate a temporary cessation of all immigration.[7] But now, in 1906, his frustration with the new directives pursued by Sargent subsided momentarily, when an immigration bill more amenable to the aliens finally became law in the winter of 1907.

A combination of several historic factors granted Wolf a measure of success in two areas. Until 1910 he was able to postpone the bill's literacy requirement, a favorite tool of the restrictionists. He also managed to mitigate the effects of its "poor physique and low vitality clauses." These phrases, with their reliance on uncontested medical findings, would inevitably lead to public-charge accusations, directed in particular against Russian Jewish immigrants. On this occasion, however, Wolf and other spokesmen for the immigrant latched on to a foolproof method guaranteeing victory for their cause. That such an achievement was suited to this occasion alone was a matter beyond their control.

First, in addition to Wolf's constituencies, the Board of Delegates and B'nai B'rith, two other groups joined the fray as brothers-in-arms. The newly formed Liberal Immigration League now shared its plans and information with Wolf and his agencies, and with the American Jewish Committee. Moreover, the petty bickering[8] and animosities that marked Wolf's contacts with the Committee were set aside in the face of increasing pressure from the restrictionists. All might have gone well for the antialiens and their formidable allies, Senator Henry Cabot Lodge and his son-in-law, Augustus P. Gardner, and Senator William P. Dillingham of Vermont. But these men had to contend with the wishes of President Roosevelt and Secretary of State Elihu Root, and with the desires of the Speaker of the House, Joseph Gurney Cannon of Illinois. Cannon advocated open immigration to safeguard the interests of his electorate. Manufacturing and mining companies in the Midwest always needed cheap labor. At the same time, Roosevelt and Root wanted to eliminate any criticism charging the government with discriminating against Orientals in the Far West.[9]

All these factors then coalesced to insure the formulation of a moderately pro-immigrant bill. The key to is passage was to be found in Speaker Cannon's consummate political manuevering. He was prepared first to defeat the literacy provision of the bill, and barring that, to emasculate it once it reached the Senate-House Conference Committee. He achieved his first goal by prevailing upon the House Rules Committee to issue a special ruling that would have made it impossible to vote a separate yea or nay on the literacy proviso. When, however, it appeared likely that the measure would still pass, he walked onto the well of the floor and urged the legislators to defeat the amendment. This they did, while Representative Charles Grovesnor substituted a resolution calling for an investigative commission. Grovesnor's proposal passed.[10]

Having succeeded thus far, Cannon appointed two henchman Congressmen William Bennett and Jacob Ruppert of New York, to the joint Senate-House Conference Committee on the Immigration Bill. It was their job to keep the bill locked up in conference, until one amenable to Cannon emerged.[11] It was apparent that the entire bill, including its literacy proposal, which Senators Lodge and Dillingham had sponsored, and its strict clauses pertaining to the health of the aliens would be treated as one entity.[12] Therefore, its opponents, Wolf included, would be able to contend with all of its aspects at the same time.

This unified approach enabled Wolf to bring pressure to bear on removing the poor-physique and low-vitality clauses. He detected a discrepancy in their wording where one section of the statute made a medical decision to deport binding, with no recourse to appeal, while another allowed aliens with minor physical problems to post bonds. Basing himself on his long acquaintance with Commissioner Sargent, Wolf argued that such paradoxical rulings would only confuse the aliens and their advocates. Sargent advised him to consult Charles Earle, the counsel for the Department of Commerce.

While waiting for Earle, Wolf saw Representative Bennett in the corrodor, who assured him that in all situations bonds could be posted, even when medical inspectors on the line alluded to physical deficiencies.[13]

While the bill was still locked up in conference, members of the American Jewish Committee grew fearful that Ruppert, the second of Cannon's trusted appointees was wavering. He was prepared to strike out the educational test in return for retaining strict health requirements for the immigrants. Adler thereupon requested Wolf to speak with Ruppert. Currently, there is no record of their conversation, but Wolf responded by saying he had Cannon's promise that no bill would come out of the Conference.[14]

Five days after this exchange of information, on 28 January 1907, Adler, alerted by Bennett, again became anxious, since the bill was still locked in committee, and Lodge might create a furor on the floor of the Senate. Adler once more turned to Wolf for help. This time, Wolf, whose contacts with federal officials had continued for decades, and who was on friendly terms with Roosevelt, managed to speak to the president's secretary, William Loeb. The latter suggested that it would be wise for Wolf to write a letter to the president and request an Immigration Commission as a substitute for the literacy amendment.[15]

It would be presumptuous to assume that Wolf's charm, and more than a nodding acquaintance with those who manipulated the machinery of government, were the only factors that spelled success in eliminating unwanted legislation. His letter, requesting an immigration commission in place of a literacy bill, was but an additional endorsement of what Roosevelt and his secretary of state wanted all along. They were eager to avoid any confrontation with Japan, now chafing at discriminatory measures passed against Japanese pupils in the San Francisco school system and over anti-Japanese feeling in the West in general. In their agreement with the Mikado's government, Roosevelt and Root promised that Japanese children would no longer be subject to harassment, while Japan itself would voluntarily control any unwanted influx of its laboring classes to this country. Cannon was now ready to concur, but only on condition that an investigative immigration commission, whose findings would be made public by 1910, would be substituted for the literacy bill.[16]

Cannon had his way, and he informed Senator Lodge that it would be useless for him to continue his agitation on behalf of an educational test. Under the circumstances, it was easy for the president's secretary to suggest to Wolf that a letter requesting an investigative commission be sent to Roosevelt.

On 12 February 1907, Roosevelt and Root made an arrangement with Cannon and Lodge by which the low-vitality and poor-physique clauses were dropped and diseases of a noninfectious and nonloathsome nature made bondable; the educational test was waived, and a Japanese exclusion amendment together with an immigration-commission proposal were added to the bill.[17]

In practical terms far more immediate, if less provocative, challenges still awaited Wolf in attempts to reverse deportation proceedings based on well-worn public charge or assisted immigrant concerns. The 1907 Immigration Bill, for all its promises of liberality, in no wise altered those federal assumptions continuously entertained by inspectors on the line; if an alien arrived with what were deemed insufficient funds, or if he or she evidenced inadequate physical stamina, or manifested no immediate vocational prospects, or contrariwise, was about to be employed on the basis of a pledge made in violation of the alien contract labor law, his or her ultimate fate was always the same. Either the immigrant was destined for deportation, or he or she would be remanded to the poorhouse, in which case deportation would ensue. Time and again it had explicitly to be proved that the immigrant was not too weak to earn a living, that the alien was capable of occupational readjustment, and that welfare agencies were not heedlessly sending unemployables to this land to displace native workers. In this kind of context, for which exclusion appeared to be the only alternative, there would be little or no opportunity for recourse to abstract principles of justice and ethics.

For these reasons, Wolf's emphasis on the human factor stood him in good stead. Federal officials, after all, were first individuals and secondarily, had careers to pursue. They were not averse to flattery, nor did they seem to recall those instances when Wolf may have veered from his usual conciliatory stance. In fact, once in 1910, when testifying before the Immigration Commission, Wolf did become entangled in his own semantics. He deplored those draconian tendencies to which some federal immigration authorities resorted in executing the law, yet he was quick to admire the "wise discretion" that seemingly characterized official policy.[18] But he had so long grown accustomed to praising those in command that they apparently overlooked the contradiction. By 1911, a grateful secretary of commerce marked Wolf as the advocate par excellence, who, unlike any other spokesman for special interests, knew when he was defeated. His gracious acceptance of that fact always endeared him to officialdom.[19]

For this reason Wolf's *Annual Reports* to his Board of Delegates are replete with his constant praise for the government's impartial and effective ways of administering immigration law. It mattered not whether restrictionist tendencies were increasing, or by chance temporarily abating. From 1900 until 1910, Wolf's official statements dealing with immigrants and their problems sounded sympathetic to the federal point of view. His complaints and illustrations to the contrary were issued for private consumption, primarily to Kohler, who in time would become his heir apparent as chairman of the Board of Delegates. For the record, then, Wolf found the directors of the

Bureau of Immigration and its supervisory agency, the Department of Commerce, always "sensitive" to the cases that came before them. These insitutions, he insisted, gave "the benefit of the doubt" to those whose entrance here may have been questionable. As late as 1911, when most immigrant spokesmen realized they were fighting a losing battle, Wolf instructed his younger associate, Kohler, to tell the representatives at a Union meeting that the Board of Delegates had successfully reversed 85 percent of all deportation judgments brought to its attention.[20] For Wolf, this figure sounded all the more remarkable, because immigration statistics indicated a large upsurge in the number of aliens being accused of "public charge" or "poor physique." He took comfort from the fact that arriving Jews had a lower ratio of exclusions to admissions than other immigrants.[21]

It would be difficult to imagine that opinions such as these revealed Wolf's innermost judgments. Nor would a man, seasoned by more than half a century in the practice of law, have been so naïve as to detail the kindness and humanity of entire administrations for immigrant affairs, while he underscored his constant battle to devise happier fates for those aliens destined by federal fiat for deportation.[22] Certainly, he must have been aware that had justice prevailed, his Board of Delegates and his B'nai B'rith would not have had to strive that hard for success. While he himself did not say as much in so many words, he was party to precisely the same thought, expressed by the Board of Delegates, the B'nai B'rith, and the American Jewish Committee. They declared that they would not have had to be that concerned with public-charge matters, involving habeas corpus, the right to appeal, and bonding privileges, had legal ethics been the predominant motif.[23] But justice was not the overarching factor. Wolf knew this. All he had left then was to praise the fairness and consideration of those in charge, while he himself, with all his personal contacts and powers at his command, tried to change the course of administrative decisions. What had become a pattern of a lifetime for Wolf, in saving aliens by whatever means he had at his disposal, was not to be altered in old age.

Such lifelong habits never confined Wolf's younger peers whose goals of rescuing refugees were basically the same as his. Marshall, Adler, and Sulzberger of the American Jewish Committee or Abram Elkus, representing the Hebrew Immigrant Aid Society, and Max Kohler were free to resort to principle when the occasion required it, or to rely on Wolf's methods of personal contact when these suited their purposes.[24]

Principle appears to have won the upper hand in a brief prepared by Kohler and Elkus. The case merits special attention because in petitioning for their clients, these attorneys resorted to the 1891 ruling, originally obtained by Wolf from Secretary Foster. Aid extended to the aliens by private charities or friends freed the newcomers from public-charge accusations. The case involved four aliens who, led by Hersh Skuratowski, could have posted bonds against assisted immigrant violations, but were neverthe-less ordered deported. Kohler and Elkus thereupon accused Commissioner Williams, but recently reappointed as commissioner of immigration for the Port of New York, with an unwarranted abuse of executive power. Not only had he reinstituted a law already eliminated by Congress when he insisted that the aliens have an explicit amount of cash on their persons at the initial hearing, but he also declared that the proffered financial assistance of rela-tives was not to be recognized as legally admissible. Wolf then called on Solicitor Charles Earle of the Department of Commerce to reaffirm the legality of Foster's decision.[25]

While Earle's opinion signaled a victory for Wolf, in practical terms it amounted to little. The aliens were admitted later on grounds that work had been found for them. Such rights as they might have entertained under the law were abandoned, for they had gone unanswered. This was in conjunction with the Court's decision to grant a hearing on appeal only on condition that the habeas corpus proceedings would be quashed.[26]

By February 1910, Wolf was forced to pursue a course of action that, privately at least, ran counter to his published evaluations of the immigration establishment. He told Kohler that the Department of Commerce dis-regarded Solicitor Earle's opinion. There were no distinctions being made between public and private charities, so that the number of Jews classified as "assisted immigrants" soared. To compound the difficulties, hundreds of Jewish immigrants, shipped to Galveston, Tex., under the auspices of the Jewish Information Bureau, were regarded as fit subjects for public welfare. Federal authorities contended that these people were unemployable. On the other hand, if they had been promised jobs by immigrant agents abroad, they were now arriving in violation of the Alien Contract Labor Law. Were such criticisms validated, then the Galveston movement, to deflect the Jewish masses away from the eastern seaboard, would simply dissolve. Begun in 1907, with a grant from Jacob H. Schiff, this program was one of American Jewry's responses to the old arrangement set before it by Secretary Charles Foster, back in 1891. To the extent to which the American Jewish community would minimize the impact of new arrivals upon the social and economic sectors of large urban areas,[27] to that degree would the federal government respect the wishes of its Jewish citizens in immigration mat-ters.[28]

In seeking Kohler's aid to confirm the legality of the Galveston movement, Wolf was responding to a directive from the assistant secretary of commerce, Benjamin W. Cable. The latter was convinced that European Jews abroad were deliberately sending their brethren here, and wanted Wolf to prepare a brief on the matter. Wolf turned the problem over to Kohler, whose ensuing argument neither placated the authorities nor apologized for the activities of the Jewish Information Bureau. Kohler contended that Jews reaching Galveston were morally fit immigrants, needed to develop the resources of unsettled locations. Under no circumstances had they arrived as inadmissible contract laborers. In his brief Kohler maintained that the Jewish Information Bureau never resorted to inducements to recruit aliens abroad for special tasks here. To buttress his statement, however, Kohler did include an 1891 report by a congressional committee and a Supreme Court decision stressing the desirability of accepting those aliens who were helped financially by relatives or private institutions. This was the basis for Kohler's assumption that in determining whether a person were likely to become a public charge, *all* the people at his disposal, including those who were not legally bound to support him, were to be considered. To sum up, Kohler again referred to the Earle verdict on private and public aid obtained by Wolf the previous year in the Skuratowski case.[29]

Wolf sweetened the tone of Kohler's brief for Cable's benefit. Absolving himself from any personal complaints, Wolf reassured Cable as to the justice displayed at all times by federal officials in assisted-immigrant cases. Wolf even reported how he scorned those Anglo-Jewish journals which indulged in "hysterical judgments" heaped upon the Department of Commerce. Yet at the same time, Wolf reminded the secretary of the time-honored principles concerning Jewish aliens that Kohler referred to in his brief.

Cable was not impressed. He refused to commit himself to any legal interpretation of the assisted-immigrant, public-charge, or contract-labor aspects of the situation. Personally, he thought all of the eighty-two immigrants originally held for inquiry at Galveston had been induced to come here in violation of the law. Since fifty of these had already been admitted on appeal, the whole issue of whether or not "Jewish societies" had been trespassing on the law had not yet been decided. Until his suspicions were confirmed, the best he could do, Cable felt, was to inform Jewish representatives of his doubts.[30]

Prodded by Jacob H. Schiff, who upbraided him for his department's "unreasonable obstacles," Secretary of Commerce Charles Nagel eliminated Cable's doubts and voted in favor of the action taken by the Jewish Information Bureau. Attorney General George W. Wickersham seconded Nagel in confirming the legal course pursued by the Bureau. In this instance however, the victory secured by Schiff's wrath, Kohler's memorandum, and Wolf's honeyed words proved temporary. The hard-won concession, that certain mitigating circumstances were lawfully sufficient to deny the indiscriminate application of public charge, assisted immigrant, or contract laborer to incoming aliens, barely survived the year. It received casual treatment at the hands of Secretary Nagel. Defending his department before German-American critics, Nagel referred to the Galveston matter, as "an exceptional situation" where he had accepted the guarantees of the Jewish Information Bureau that it would find employment for those impoverished new arrivals

who came here under its auspices.[31] But principle was not built on exception. Nagel continued to insist that aliens had no judicial rights under
American law. In the years following the Galveston issue, Kohler complained
that immigration inspectors applied overly stringent standards of admission,
a process that resulted in illegal exclusions. Though he admitted that there
was nothing concrete in the record to bear out this contention, Kohler was
convinced that at Galveston petty immigration inspectors persisted in their
harsh policy of deportations fashioned from their strict application of immigration law.[32]

Here indeed was irony compounded. Kohler, who had always proceeded
upon principle in interpreting the law, had now to pay the price. Nagel may
have doubted whether aliens were to be accorded the same constitutional
privileges normally granted to citizens. On other occasions, the secretary
would warn Kohler that "immigration procedures (did not) flow from rational
precedents in law." Nagel would urge Kohler to realize the value of legal
judgments left unresolved. Matters of ethics and abstractions, the secretary
would sometimes emphasize, were not the issue. Like Wolf, Nagel was a man
of compromise, who, rather than battle for ideals, was prepared to cherish
the discretion employed by "broad-hearted" men in interpreting the law
kindly but judiciously. If, in the judgment of some, such applications were
still harsh and cruel (witness his observations on the Galveston matter), there
was always the possibility that on other occasions more humane decisions
might be forthcoming. On the other hand contending for exact justice,
implied in strict adherence to the law, might have frozen the options for
many a well-intentioned administrator.[33] This theme of Nagel's found its
echo in Wolf's frequent references to the "humane discretion and wisdom"
he found operating at all levels of Nagel's bureau.[34]

Kohler, however, took no comfort in Nagel's formula for relying on the
sound judgments of benignly disposed executives. What would become of
immigration policy once it became regulated by strict constructionists?

The secretary retaliated by distrusting Kohler even on those occasions
when the two were in agreement on any specific subject. Writing to Wolf,
Nagel could not refrain from taking note of that "irony of fate" by which
Kohler's "continual carping and criticism" threatened even the secretary's
efforts to invalidate a literacy clause that had been introduced in Congress.
Nagel himself was opposed to the requirement, but because he imagined
Kohler needled him, any thought of cooperation in search of a common goal
was out of the question.[35]

Wolf would not allow such differences to impair his friendship with the
secretary. Both in background and in methods of political approach the two
men had much in common. They came from German immigrant backgrounds and had absorbed much of that liberal thought basic to a European
tradition that rejected petty despotism. Moreover, both had ties to Jewry—

Wolf by virtue of his birth and Nagel through a short-lived marriage to the sister of Justice Louis D. Brandeis, which ended with her death.[36] Nagel steadfastly regarded Wolf as the true representative of Jewish interests in the United States. As seen, it was this attitude that once prompted Nagel to remark before a conference on immigration that Wolf was superior to all those other pleaders for special causes. He would never pressure federal officials beyond the limits of endurance.[37] Nagel had obviously found a man to suit his tastes.

Wolf repaid him with boundless loyalty. At all costs, Wolf was prepared to shield Nagel from any criticism intended either for the Department of Commerce and Labor or specifically aimed at Nagel's subordinates. For this reason, even Commissioner Williams, distrusted by a majority of immigrant spokesmen,[38] still received Wolf's support. In 1911, after a stormy session directed against the secretary, his department, and Commissioner Williams, mainly by Americans of German descent, Wolf refurbished Williams's image for the benefit of the German-American Alliance. Nagel was most grateful to Wolf for his help, especially in an age, when an "official had always to protect himself, against . . . groundless accusations." So excessive had Wolf's concern for Nagel become, that even President Taft tried to mitigate it. Assuring Wolf that Nagel was immune to adverse comments, the chief executive underscored them as mere examples of "Jewish muckraking."[39]

Ulysses S. Grant, U.S. President, 1869–1877.

Tewfik Pasha, Khedive, 1881–1882.

Arabi Bey, Secretary of War, Egypt, 1881–1882.

Consul General Simon Wolf and friends at the Temple of Luxor, Egypt, February 1882.

Princess Nazli, cousin to the sultan.

The laying of the cornerstone of the Jewish Temple on Eighth Street, 16 September 1897, at which President McKinley and the Cabinet were present.

Leo N. Levi, President of the I.O.B.B., 1900–1904.

Justice Wendell Philips Stafford, 1904–1931.

Joseph Gurney Cannon, Speaker of the House, 1910.

Simon Wolf and friends with President Taft, 1912.

To Simon Wolf, on His Seventieth Birthday, by Mr. Justice Wendell Philips Stafford

"Call no man blest till his last day is done,"
    The Theban counselled with uncovered head.
And if life's blessing be a cloudless sun,
    Which yet may be o'ercast 'twas wisely said.
But if our blessings of ourselves are born,
    And they that bless the world are ever blest,
The day may keep the splendor of the morn
    Whatever storms may gather in the West.
For thee, dear friend, who all thy life hast striven
    To blow aflame the love-enkindling spark,
If all the lamps be blotted out of heaven,
    Their going will not leave thee in the dark:
Thou shalt be lighted by the light thou givest,
And so we call thee blest while thanking God thou livest.

Stafford's verse to Wolf on his seventieth birthday.

To Simon Wolf
on his 85th birthday

"And Pharaoh said unto Jacob, How old art thou?
And Jacob said unto Pharaoh, The days of the years
of my pilgrimage are an hundred and thirty years:
few and evil have the days of the years of my
life been, and have not attained unto the days of
the years of the life of my fathers in the days of
their pilgrimage." Genesis XLVII, 8 and 9.

Many and good are the days of the years
    Of your life, O Simon the Wolf:
May all that remain to you be as their peers
    Till you cross the inscrutable gulf!

'Tis a one-way road, O Simon, my friend,
    As all of the sign-boards say;
But I reckon one need not have fears of the end
    Who has helped all the lame on the way.

You are Simon the Lamb in your kindness
    To the weak and the humble of birth: [and grace
You are Simon the Wolf to the foes of your race,
    And your race is, all men on the earth.

Stafford's verse to Wolf on his eighty-fifth birthday.

In Memoriam
SIMON WOLF

CHAIRMAN BOARD OF DELEGATES ON CIVIL RIGHTS
DIED JUNE 4, 1923

At the first convention of the Union of American Hebrew Congregations held since the passing of Simon Wolf from the scene of his earthly activities in June, 1923, the Delegates assembled from all parts of the country deem it a duty to make public record of their appreciation of his unforgetable services in the cause of Judaism and in behalf of the Jewish victims of oppression and persecution, although at the time of his death well nigh two years ago both the Executive Board of the Union and the Board of Delegates on Civil and Religious Rights gave fitting expression to their feeling of what he had done during the half century of his unselfish and devoted service.

A familiar figure at every Convention of the Union from the first held in Cincinnati in the year eighteen hundred and seventy three to the Jubilee Meeting celebrating the fiftieth anniversary held in the City of New York in January, 1923, a few months before his death, Simon Wolf occupied a distinguished place in the Councils of the Union and aided mightily in shaping its policy and carrying out its aims. For five decades he was the representative of the Union and its spokesman in the Capitol of the Nation. He fulfilled this exalted mission with singular fidelity and ability. He was untiring in his service and unremitting in his devotion. Loyal to his faith and to his country, he stood forth as a fine type of the American Jew.

Simon Wolf was a watchman on the tower of humanity. He was an illustrious son of the synagogue. He is numbered among the great in Israel in our United States. He shall never be forgotten. In the annals of the Union of American Hebrew Congregations his name shall ever be in the very forefront. He was among that select company who constantly and unreservedly upheld the hands of the great founder, Isaac M. Wise, to whom he was as a brother. He had a passion for service. He heeded to the full the call of the ancient prophet inasmuch as he did all in his power to make justice flow as water and righteousness as an unfailing stream. He was a friend to the needy in distress, a father to the fatherless, a helper of the helpless. Thousands arose during his life time and called him blessed. His name is written high in American Judaism's hall of fame.

As man, as American, as Jew, he was faithful in all his ways. He loved his fellowman, he served his God. The world was better for his having lived. He shall be held in loving and appreciative remembrance. He was among the chosen. Whenever the call came "Who will go for us?", he never failed to respond "Here am I, send me." He was a true servant of the Lord.

Twenty-ninth Council of the Union
of American Hebrew Congregations,

KARL M. VETSBURG, President.

Resolution honoring Wolf's memory.

8
In the Shadow of Restrictionism

By 1910 the very Immigration Commission whose creation Wolf had effectively helped to postpone now reflected the antiimmigrant tendencies that were rampant in the land. The atmosphere was rife with a jingoistic nationalism. Southern and eastern Europeans were scorned by indigenous Americans and held in low esteem. Jews in particular were regarded both as intellectuals and as workers. Even if such categories appeared mutually exclusive, their common denominator apparently was the negativism such factors inspired in the native born. As intellectuals, Jews were thought of as obviously contributing little to the American economy, or to improving their own material resources. As sweatshop operators and workers, they were regarded as sheer opportunists, taking advantage of the many social services offered to them by their coreligionists.[1]

Though Wolf's contacts with federal officials were usually marked by discretion, such palpable prejudice as was evidenced in this period forced him to speak up once again about an issue that had always obsessed him. That was the federal practice of classifying immigrants in discriminatory terms. Wolf viewed all questions concerning an individual's racial origins or his religious affirmation as infringements on the right to personal liberty.[2] What follows is a brief account of how at long last he was able to exercise his most significant option in registering his protest against classifying immigrants by race or religion. That he was destined to fail, given the milieu in which he operated, seemed a foregone conclusion, but at least he had the satisfaction of recording his opposition to such federal investigation.

Ever since he had assumed the chairmanship of the Board of Delegates in 1891, Wolf believed such classification violated the spirit of the U. S. Constitution. As early as 1898, at a private meeting with Commissioner of Immigration Terence V. Powderly and Commissioner Frank McSweeny of the Immigration Bureau, Powderly informed Wolf that inquiring after the stranger's faith or ethnic origins ran counter to American law. Dr. Lee K.

Frankel and Henry Rice of the United Hebrew Charities and Philip Cowen, editor of the *American Hebrew*, were also present at a later session at which Powderly agreed with Wolf that federal interest in immigrant statistics did not warrant any governmental disclosures as to the aliens' racial or religious orientations. In fact, Powderly acknowledged that such a process would allow prejudice to prevail.[3]

Powderly was an avowed restrictionist, who viewed the Jewish migration from Russia with hostility.[4] His concern therefore for libertarian principles did not indicate a change of heart; rather it was the attorney general's ruling that the Census Bureau might not inquire after the religious affiliations of the population in the United States. Wolf noted that for a while Powderly did abandon the system of tabulating Jewish immigrants as Hebrews.[5] Such benefits, however, did not long endure.[6] The Immigration Bureau justified its need to reveal the alien's race and nationality, rather than his religion, in the interest of securing a "more exact ethnology." Wolf hoped that the law limiting census inquiries would also apply to racial classifications, but this was not to be.[7] The fact was that the government continued to apply racial specifications to aliens, and labeled those of the Jewish faith as "Hebrew." Requests for racial identity on ships' manifests, which were in use from 1899 until 1902, were then sanctioned by law in 1903. When the measure was first debated in the Senate, Lodge stated that any additional questions concerning the race of the immigrant were inserted to make the bill conform to the actions of the Department of Commerce and Labor, which by then had charge of immigration matters.[8]

Wolf was now forced to admit that Sargent, Powderly's successor, "established the practice of registering Hebrews as a race." To Wolf's objection that even the oppressive czarist government identified Jewish aliens as Hebrews to prove that few Russians were emigrating to the United States, Sargent could only wonder why the Jews would normally not take pride in acknowledging their racial origins. In self-defense, Sargent added that he merely continued the process undertaken by his predecessors of publishing immigration statistics giving racial designations.[9]

In a final effort to circumvent such practices, Wolf had no choice but to contact Sargent's superior, Secretary of Commerce George Cortelyou. He reminded the secretary that in 1903, at a summer session of the Jewish Chautauqua, held at Atlantic City, Cortelyou agreed with him that "all immigrants landing at our seaports should be listed uniformly in matters of classification." That is, if Russian Jews were to be designated in terms of their faith, the same practice would have to apply to other Russian nationals. In addition, Wolf claimed that the Jew "has no nationality other than that to which he has sworn allegiance." Second, it would be inaccurate to label the immigrant Jews as "belonging to a race," since he "comes as a native of the country in which he was born." Third, if the purpose of classification were scientific or ethnological, its benefits ought to be extended to the "world at large." If, however, the intent of such tabulation were religious, it would run counter to the "spirit and genius" of American institutions, and would be proof that the government had undertaken an illegal administrative function, one that was religious, rather than political in nature.

Unhappily, Wolf learned from Cortelyou that the State Department delayed making a decision in the matter, since it believed that the Jews were a race, if not a nation. Nevertheless, Cortelyou had urged Wolf to gather sufficient evidence to disprove the State Department's contention. It was this request that led Wolf to canvas prominent people, whose opinions would prove that the Jews were neither race nor nation. His task was doomed from its inception. Some of his respondents disagreed completely with him. Others denied any scientific ascriptions to the term "race," but saw no harm in having Jewish aliens listed as "Hebrews." In addition, there were those who, like Wolf, felt that applying racial identification and revealing religious affiliations to all immigrants were the only ways of mitigating the evil effects of conferring such classification upon Jews alone.[10]

Such a multiplicity of responses only confirmed the State Department in its view that the "racial cohesion" of the Jewish people derived from its "ability to survive, . . . the vicissitudes of many centuries, . . . (despite) wide dispersion." However, in deference to the concept of the separation of church and state, the Department agreed with Wolf that the Russian practice of tabulating Jewish immigrants by faith was unjustified.[11]

By 1908, Wolf had an "extended conversation" with Assistant Secretary of Commerce Walter W. Husband, who informed him that the Immigration Commission, authorized by Congress the previous year, had avoided all references to religion in its investigations. The term "Jew" or "Hebrew" was meant to refer to race, and "nothing more."[12] The government had made the basis of race the justification for its ethnological observations of the immigrant.

It was but a small step from such inquiries to evaluating human intelligence in accordance with any one group's racial characteristics. Even so noted an anthropologist as Franz Boas was convinced that measuring heads would provide one means for predicting the success of the immigrant's adaptibility to his new environment.[13]

It was in such an atmosphere that Wolf, now burdened by age and the increasing responsibilities that overseeing immigration matters entailed, obtained the services of Max Kohler, whose *Brief in the Matter of Hersh Skuratowski* has already been referred to.[14] There, Kohler had cited the illegality of immigrant classification as prejudicial to his clients. He contended that the federal gathering of statistical and ethnological data had gone beyond the legal limit because it disclosed the immigrant's religious preference. The government, believing that Jewish aliens were Hebrew by race, countered by saying that it was not to be held responsible if in the process of its inquiries, it revealed the immigrant's faith. Kohler, however, admitted that if the alien were indeed Hebrew both by race and religion, then he would have to invoke the principle in law that of "two possible constructions of a statute, the one avoiding any serious constitutional question would have to be adopted." Since racial specification did lead to religious disclosure with reference to Jewish immigrants, the only solution was to abandon racial classification. To illustrate his thesis, Kohler cited Wolf's correspondence with prominent personalities on this topic, back in 1903. If the experts at that time were unable to reach a consensus, Kohler queried, as to whether the Jews were a race, then what was the purpose of the government's continued search for such information?[15]

Kohler's question went unanswered, because the hearing at which the brief was to have been presented never took place.[16] But fortunately, Wolf was able to avail himself of one more opportunity to state his and Kohler's objections to the federal practice of immigrant classification. This time, a Congressional Immigration Commission, whose decision-making powers Wolf had helped delay for three years, now, in December of 1909, invited him to present testimony on the problems of categorizing aliens in particular, and on matters of immigration in general. The American Jewish Committee, having learned that Wolf was scheduled to speak, managed to secure equal time at the hearing and sent Judge Julian W. Mack as its representative.[17]

An increasingly restrictionist and prejudicial atmosphere had forced these Jewish leaders to cooperate in presenting their testimony before Congress. The decision was made that Wolf and Mack would appear jointly before the Immigration Commission,[18] whose chairman was Senator William P. Dillingham. At the session, Wolf and Mack encountered a redoubtable opponent in Senator Henry Cabot Lodge of Massachusetts. Lodge led Wolf into a maze. Were Wolf to contend that the Jews were only a religious entity, how would he account for famous men born of Jewish parentage who had abandoned their faith? Wolf replied that in those instances, men such as Disraeli, or Heinrich Heine, ceased to be Jews religiously. However, Wolf found it difficult to respond in an unqualified manner to Lodge's overriding question: was a change in religion the equivalent of an alteration in one's race? Wolf was forced to acknowledge that Disraeli's or Heine's baptism did not eradicate their Jewish birth. They and others, who had made significant contributions to the world, were classified by the "Jewish people as having been born of their blood."[19]

This exchange had gone poorly for Wolf, so poorly that the senator dismissed the proffered evidence of a communiqué from the Committee on the lack of Jewish racialism as valueless. There was no justification whatsoever, Lodge insisted, to Wolf's complaint that the Immigration Bureau was classifying the Jews as a religious body. On the contrary, such tabulation had been racial from its very inception; indeed, Lodge felt it to be all the more pitiable that racial specifications had been stricken from the census. Lodge was convinced of the benefits of this kind of labeling; like the Irish and the Poles, the Jews were a race, though all three had neither country nor nationality. The senator further confused the matter when he insisted that in his system of tabulation, classification would proceed on the basis "of the historic races," rather than "by resorting to the broad, scientific divisions of mankind, such as the Mongol, the Negro . . ., the Aryan, the Semitic."[20]

To Mack's question concerning the possible worth of racial classification, the senator responded that all ethnology was imprecise, but continued throughout the hearing to insist that the Jews were a sharply defined race. Apparently, such contradictory thinking was contagious. Both Wolf and Mack were trained lawyers, but once Mack agreed that racial classification was acceptable for immigrants coming from multinational states, such as Turkey, Russia, and Austro-Hungary, the game was lost. Wolf and Mack now saw no objections to calling Jews arriving from these areas "Hebrews." But those coming from France, England, and Germany were to be designated as nationals of those countries. Wolf and Mack had been forced at last to accept Lodge's obsession "to serve the interests of a more exact ethnology." Thereupon, all of Wolf's protestations that the word "Jew" would further inflame an already intensified anti-Semitism abroad in the land, became an opportunity for Lodge to protest that the government had only racial classification in mind.[21]

Wolf's efforts to fight against federal tendencies to create ethnic and racial distinctions among immigrants were also weakened by the method he chose to defend the good name of his coreligionists. Dedicated to the premise that all men were created equal, and ought therefore to be accorded all those liberties with which their very humanity endowed them, Wolf nevertheless claimed that the Jews were an eternal people whose ethical teachings and moral sensitivities proved their superior nature. This thesis was implicit in his confrontation with Lodge. Geniuses such as "Heine, Borne, Disraeli, and others," Wolf insisted, were part of the Jewish people, "when they speak of persons who have accomplished something wonderful in the world."[22]

Wolf, however, was not to have the best of both worlds. He could not, on the one hand, have praised the contributions of the Jews as a people to the development of civilization, the very thrust of many of his written essays,[23] while he excoriated his critics for damning them as a group.[24] Had he not continually spoken about the Jews as the exemplars of family virtues, or as the originators and practitioners of humane legal and social service systems, or as contributors to the very foundation of morality,[25] his strictures against attempts by legislators and immigration officials to categorize Jewish arrivals by race and religion might have carried more weight.

The dilemma that confronted Wolf as to the most effective way for battling the bigots grew from the religious movement of which he was a part. Reform Judaism had been intended as a humanizing faith, striving for universal ideals while eliminating the particularistic in ritual. At the same time, however, the Jew, no longer ethnically identifiable, had yet to persist in Judaism's age-old mission, of teaching God's word to mankind. Wolf, then, was obligated throughout his life to fight prejudice by stressing the right of each individual to basic human freedoms, while furthering the values by which the Jewish group lived. One recalls his ringing protest against those who defamed the Jews in the collective sense during the Civil War years. Then Wolf, still considering the Jews as an identifiable entity, had asked whether "all blockade runners and refugees were the descendents of Abraham." He even questioned whether there were no "meek followers of Christ within the folds of Tammany."[26] Later, as a mature man, in 1896, he crystallized the attitude that perhaps Christians were also guilty of misconduct into its obverse: that Jews as a group were to be praised for their "morality, humanity, and true religious fervor." In his zeal as an advocate, dispelling prejudice, he had lost himself. He blamed the Christian majority for the presence of Jews and other minorities, specifically Negroes, who may have formed a criminal element in society. In placing upon his adversaries the onus of locating unsavory characters in any seemingly decent number of people, he may have resorted to a favorite device of seasoned debaters. However, all he accomplished in practical terms was to blame Christians in general for the anti-Semites among them, and to praise Jews for their intellectual keenness and humanity, while absolving them in the main from the misdeeds of any individual in their midst.[27] Such a lack of objectivity weakened the thesis of his book, *The American Jew as Patriot, Soldier, and Citizen,* whose intent was to verify the unalloyed patriotism of his coreligionists.[28] By the same reasoning, his harried defense of the Jewish barricades diminished the strength of his arguments in all those battles he waged for the separation of church and state. Eloquent though his speeches and testimony may have been in decrying attempts to make this a Christian country, or to introduce the Bible into the school curriculum,[29] he was never able to overcome his own emotional appeal with which he invested his defense of the Jew. Now, therefore, as an old man, fighting a losing battle against the restrictionists, he was not content merely to argue that inquiries into an alien's faith would lead to bigotry. Instead, he was unable to resist the fallacy of attributing racial uniqueness to qualities of genius. Had he been objective enough not to boast of any alleged Jewish superiority, Lodge might not have demolished his argument.[30]

In the long run, then, Wolf's desire to protect the Jewish image merely earned him the enmity of those who disagreed with him. Zionists were outraged by Wolf and Mack's decision to designate Jews coming from Eastern Europe as "Hebrews," while their remaining coreligionists, natives of Western Europe and England, were to be known as Jews by faith. One irate correspondent, in fact, complained that Wolf and Mack were not Jews at all: they had denied their racial and ethnic origins.[31]

So tense had the situation over the matter of immigrant classification become that it rekindled the petty quarreling that characterized Wolf's relationships with the Committee members. He was piqued that in publicizing the confrontation with Senator Lodge, the Committee omitted all references to him. In stepping in to heal the breach between Wolf and the Committee, Kohler acted on a suggestion by Abram Elkus that all Jewish representatives attend an immigration conference. There they would be able to reach a consensus on specific principles to be recommended to the Congressional Immigration Commission. Wolf, along with such other notables as Louis Marshall, Louis Barondess, Nathan Bijur, Judah L. Magnes, Leon Sanders, and Jacob Schiff, was present at the session. Kohler and Elkus signed their names to a list of proposals and accompanying legal arguments that, in slightly altered form, were finally used as the core of the written testimony for the Commission, scheduled to hold a final hearing in March 1910. At last, cooperation among B'nai B'rith, the Board of Delegates, and the American Jewish Committee was assured. Wolf and Adler would now confer on how to merge their forces in the hope of achieving a more effective presentation at the congressional hearing.[32]

Their working arrangement to insure the efficacy of a united presentation was simple enough. Both men bound their respective organizations to the promise that their representatives would appear jointly at any legislative hearings, and to the pledge of instant communication concerning any relevant material to be brought to the attention of the Immigration Commission or to the Committee on Immigration and Naturalization of the House of Representatives. Both Wolf and Adler were eager to arrange preliminary meetings with Judge Henry Goldfogle of New York and Congressman Adolph Sabath of Illinois, two members of the House Committee on Immigration noted for their liberal views.[33] That the Jewish representatives were heard on 10 March 1910 was due primarily to the successful back-door maneuvers of Representative Goldfogle. He made the time easily available to Wolf and Kohler as spokesmen for the Board of Delegates and B'nai B'rith; to a coterie of prominent men leading the American Jewish Committee; and to the Hebrew Immigrant Aid Society, represented by its president, Judge Leon Sanders.[34]

At that hearing before the Immigration Commission, all of the speakers, believing implicitly in the benefit to be derived from immigration, urged the need for a return to a national policy of welcome for the alien. But other than their shared belief in open admissions for immigrants, and a decision to appear jointly, individual speakers stressed their own understanding of the problems of immigration, and adhered closely to the motivations of the groups they represented. True to form, Wolf again extolled the "wise discre-tion" practiced by federal officials in executing the law. He cited his opposi-tion to the literacy bill, an increase in a head tax, and to the extension of time in which it would become feasible to deport an alien criminal, matters with which spokesmen for the American Jewish Committee were likewise highly concerned.[35] But aside from these specific criticisms, Wolf tried to soften the harshness of any censure he may have borne by lavishing praise on the Immigration Bureau's Division of Information for services rendered the aliens. In fact, for him courtesy was the watchword of the entire federal immigration apparatus. If on occasion, there had been "too liberal a con-struction . . . in the main, the law [nevertheless] had been justly observed." Personally, he had no complaints to make, because he had in the past, out of his vast experience, spoken to the proper authorities whenever the situation warranted.[36] No fairer self-estimate could have been offered.

In essence, Wolf had left the heart of the argument to friend Kohler. Always the pragmatist, Wolf saw no value in any recommendations that tried to define the nature or level of those authorities who were permitted to post bonds for immigrants. The law, he thought, had already taken care of such provisions. He also deemed it unwise to tamper with the decisions of medical inspectors whose findings might lead to public-charge accusations against the alien. Wolf believed it would be pointless to request that medical decisions be reviewable on appeal. Unlike Kohler and the others, who were eager to uproot the entire prepaid ticket provision, Wolf only wanted to make certain that relatives who paid the passage for their immigrant kin were not endangering their admission.[37]

Under Kohler's direction, Wolf's practical concern for reversing the hap-hazard application of public-charge provisos was elevated to the level of legal justice. For Kohler, the battle did not cease when, in any given instance deportation orders were withdrawn on the basis of personal pleas, or worthy assurances that the alien's name would not swell the charity lists. Instead, Kohler was prepared to convince the Immigration Commission that the entire federal immigration system, with its utter disregard for legal prece-dents based on reasonable interpretations, sometimes trespassed on certain rights due all individuals, both citizens and aliens alike. Before Senator Dillingham and his colleagues, Kohler argued that an administration lacking adequately written interpretations of the term "public charge," or using erroneous court determinations as to the implications of the "prepaid ticket" provisions, was flouting the law. More pertinently, by relying on the testi-mony of prejudiced officials, stringently classifying aliens as public charges, overlooking the admissibility of evidence on their behalf and denying them counsel, the Immigration Bureau indulged in the art of government by personality. Such a process wreaked havoc with the individual lives of those who came before it in judgment.[38]

The implications in Kohler's statement were clear. The Bureau of Immigration, by its maladministration and misinterpretation of the immigration laws, had abridged the alien's rights to habeas corpus, to due process, and to religious liberty. These complaints then became the basis for the corrective suggestions in the form of written recommendations submitted jointly by B'nai B'rith, the Board of Delegates, and the Jewish Committee in the latter half of 1910.[39] In September of that year Senator Dillingham invited Wolf to submit any additional testimony, and urged him to have all the necessary material in the hands of the Commission by 1 November.[40] Kohler promptly complied with this request for the Board of Delegates and submitted a draft for Wolf's consideration, while he informed the American Jewish Committee of the most recent turn of events.[41] Both Wolf and the Committee then accepted Kohler's proposals. In these memoranda many restrictions referred to previously were contested. They ran the gamut from impositions such as head tax, literacy qualficiations, money requirement, arduous physical examinations, and race and color classifications, to an indiscriminate inclusion of the term "moral turpitude" in connection with any past political activities and alien registration certificates. But the essence of the entire argument lay with the material introduced by Kohler the previous spring.[42] It was a tribute to Kohler's emphasis on the public charge matter that the three societies viewed its elimination as the one condition that would obviate the necessity for any other modifications. Were this goal achieved, these agencies contended, there would be no need to insist that aliens be granted other legal rights.[43] Under such circumstances, immigrant affairs would be administered in conjunction with laws carefully compiled at regular intervals and justly arrived at, rather than as the result of individual whim.[44]

The response of the Immigration Commission to this testimony was harsh. It merely enhanced the primary goal of the restrictionists, who hastened to fashion a highly selective admissions program as a prelude to exclusion. While the Commission had pinned its fondest hopes on a literacy test as a most effective excuse for limiting immigration, it also suggested increases in the head tax, condoned a money requirement, toyed with the introduction of a quota system for incoming aliens based on ethnic origins, and insisted on keeping public-charge provisions.[45] By paralleling such literacy and racial proposals with suggestions for making earlier restrictive legislation more effective, the Commission alerted the proponents of a full, untrammeled immigration to the dangers they were facing.

Now, once again, as they had done in the past, these spokesmen met these problems and later onslaughts with methods of attack that were the reflections of their own value judgments.[46] With his continued inclination for intellectual analysis, Marshall sought to undo the formulation of discriminatory statutes directed against the alien. When confronted with legislative proposals he thought transgressed basic human rights, Kohler invoked ab-

stract principles of justice. Wolf, instead, as was his habit, sought dispensations wherever the law itself appeared unyielding.[47] So important had his
ability to know the right people at the opportune moment become that he
would be appealed to in concert with prominent legislators to stem the
restrictionist tide. Twice at least, when House-originated literacy bills sponsored by Representatives Augustus P. Gardner of Massachusetts and John L.
Burnett of Alabama were to be introduced, Wolf, on instructions from the
American Jewish Committee, prevailed upon Speaker Cannon to prevent
the passage of such legislation.[48] Wolf's delaying tactics ultimately failed, not
from lack of ability on his part, but because by 1912, the Progressives in
Congress revolted and stripped Cannon, the protector of the immigrant, of
his parliamentary powers.[49]

Most of the rebels favored a highly restrictive system of immigration. In
January and February 1913 a combined Dillingham-Burnett Bill replete with
provisos for an educational requirement, for increasing the number of excluded classes of aliens and endowing the Federal Government with unprecedented powers in public charge matters[50] passed both Houses of
Congress. As matters finally turned out, only President Taft's action in
vetoing the bill saved the day for the immigrants and their spokesmen.
Undoubtedly, many factors had influenced the president's course of action,
including the demands of various minority groups, the price of political
expediency, representations by strong industrial interests, and Nagel's own
sincere opposition to the literacy test.[51] But from now on, Wolf and his
colleagues were to face a continuously upward climb in their battle against
restriction.

Of these beleagured proponents for a liberal immigration policy, Kohler
alone somehow remained undaunted. To all intents and purposes, he had
become Wolf's heir apparent in the work of the Board of Delegates. Soon,
the tenor of its *Reports* changed progressively from overoptimistic evaluations of events and suffusions of good will to demands made in the name of
principle. Whenever Kohler's influence was manifested, Wolf had to abandon that more cautious tone which had ever been his watchword. Yet when
the occasion presented itself, and Wolf was able to, he would cling to his
well-worn methods of gracious bargaining. Such moments, as the years sped
by, grew less and less frequent.

This stiffening of the liberal attitude toward immigration that now issued
forth under Kohler or Kohler and Wolf's auspices coincided with Nagel's
departure from office. For all that Nagel delighted in ambiguities, his going
left a void, not to be filled either by Wolf's continuous search for influence,
nor by Kohler's reliance on ideals. This happened not because Nagel
seemingly held forth a beacon of hope for the newly arrived, nor because, in
Wolf's romantic terms, the secretary's heart was "wrung time and again" at
injustice unrelieved by the efficacy of the law. It was rather that by the time

Nagel was removed from the immediate scene, the force of restrictionist sentiment had so enlarged as to diminish the chances for flexible application or interpretation of the law. Wolf was particularly distressed that immigration now became the concern of a new Department of Labor, manned by representatives who were the traditional foes of the immigrant. While publicly and in correspondence with officialdom he had nothing but praise for the humane attitude with which the new department disposed of its immigrant cases,[53] privately he warned Jacob H. Schiff, the directors of the Galveston movement, and Louis Marshall that no public-charge or assisted-immigrant accusations would be overlooked. The new Cabinet officer, Secretary William B. Wilson, was prepared to adhere to the letter of the law. Sadly, discreetly, Wolf admitted that his tried and reasoned methods of personal contact, of a favor granted for a favor given, were failing.[54]

9

Toward Racism: "An Expense of Energy"

With Speaker Cannon out of power, and Secretary of Labor Wilson en-
sconced in the Department of Labor, Wolf's access to the sources of power
had begun to slip away. All three Jewish organizations that had banded
together in one last effort to stave off the buffeting of the restrictionists were
now roundly trounced. Flexibility and "humane understanding" had flown
out the window. Wolf complained that the secretary of labor himself remained adamant, insisting upon deportation in situations that revealed the
most trivial of medical problems. Now Wolf busied himself with document-
ing official obstructionist policies in specific immigrant cases, so that his
accounts came to read like a litany of human suffering.[1] Meanwhile, Kohler,
in his capacity as a representative of the Board of Delegates, contended with
the passage of an ever-increasing number of restrictionist provisos. The fears
of both men, contingent upon antiimmigrant legislation proposed during
President Wilson's first term in office, were now confirmed. Committee
chairmanships in Congress, moreover, went to representatives from the
South and West, themselves conservative or populist restrictionists from
traditionally antialien areas. Rising unemployment and a heightened sense of
nationalism on the eve of the First World War made the task of the immigrant
spokesman all but improbable.[2] Features of the Taft-rejected Dillingham
Immigration Bill were revived in the new Burnett measure. Kohler was
particularly concerned that like its predecessor, the bill imposed judicial
penalties on hapless aliens through its continual denial of the right to counsel
on appeal. Furthermore, during one stage of its development, the resolution
declared that the mere accusation of a crime committed overseas, rather than
legal conviction, constituted sufficient grounds for exclusion.[3] Although in its
final form the Burnett bill omitted this particular clause, its other provisos
continued and expanded upon restrictive techniques inherent in earlier
legislation. Barring those ineligible for naturalization from entry to this
country was kept on the books. Prohibitions against alien contract laborers

were intensified to include menial workers; persons possessing "constitutional psychopathic inferiorities" were not to be admitted. The likelihood of
deportations after landing was extended to two more years beyond the
original three, while the possibility of becoming a public charge was made
tantamount to its probability. The new Burnett bill also contained a literacy
test from which only those escaping religious persecution would be exempt.[4]
Earlier, in their contentions against the original Dillingham bill, Kohler and
Wolf argued that it would be impossible for an alien always to prove that the
terror from which he was fleeing was purely religious, rather than social,
economic, or political in nature.[5] Through Marshall's personal efforts, several
congressmen tried to introduce amendments that would have justified
Kohler and Wolf's objections: that exempting religious refugees from the
literacy test was meaningless, unless all other immigrants, subject to overt
acts of discrimination, were likewise freed from the obligation of the education requirement.[6] But all of these amendments failed, and in February 1914
the Burnett bill, passed the House. The outbreak of war the following
summer and an impending election were sufficient to halt debate in the
Senate. After the presidential election, however, the bill passed the Senate.
Like Taft before him, Wilson vetoed the bill because of its literary proviso
and because it violated the historic right of asylum this country had always
granted the oppressed.[7]

Such an atmosphere was ripe for nurturing the soil of racism, whose seeds,
long planted, would soon grow to fruition. In his declining years, Wolf had
now to contend with two racist encounters. The first tested his age-old
defense of the Jew on an individual basis, and the second, which occurred six
months before his death, proved to be his last battle with the federal practice
of inquiring after immigrants' origins.

The onset of World War I in Europe had released a pent-up virulent
patriotism in America, intent on rejecting the alien and the naturalized
American alike. In terms of mass interest, both on the intellectual and the
populist level, the Jew became the pariah of society. Even that earlier
movement, inspired by progressive tendencies to help strangers adapt to
American ways, lost its humaneness. The decade-long effort from 1900 to
1910 at Americanization then deteriorated into antialien attitudes and led
ultimately to witch hunts against radicals. While urban American society
looked askance at the newcomer as the product of a hyphenated existence,
American populists had long nurtured such an approach to Jews, Italians,
and other immigrants. At long last, the poor farmer, the blue collar worker of
the South, the whites who lived on the edge of poverty in forsaken rural
hamlets of Georgia, found their most comprehensive expressions in the
statements of Tom Watson, a political agitator, whose hysterical rantings were
ultimately responsible for that well-known travesty of justice, the lynching of
Leo M. Frank. Frank's treatment, or rather the lack of it, at the bar of

American justice, was a reflection in miniature of Southern and rural disgust with the immigrant, the foreigner, and the exile who reached this country.[8]

Wolf always viewed himself as a public defender, and in this instance could have done no less when a Northern Jew, Leo M. Frank, transplanted to Atlanta, became his concern. On the basis of perjured testimony rendered by a drunken black, Jim Conley, the custodian of a factory managed by Frank, the latter was convicted of assaulting and murdering a fourteen-year-old worker, Mary Phagan. The local judge in the case, Leonard Roan, was never convinced of Frank's guilt, and later admitted that an innocent man may well have been condemned to death. Yet every one of the appeals instituted by Frank's attorney for a retrial, even at the Supreme Court level, was rejected because of technicalities in the law.

Frank had been denied due process because of the mob passions that prevailed in and around the courtroom, with openly voiced demands that he be judged guilty, because false evidence was accepted as testimony, and because the counsel for the defense waived Frank's right to be present when the verdict was read. Thereafter, all appeals to reverse judgment by securing a new trial on the basis of new evidence were rejected. Although witnesses for the prosecution had recanted their testimony, only to change it once again at the instigations of the state prosecutor, Hugh Dorsy, Frank's lawyers were not able to use this fact to defend their client. The court's argument continued to be that it was the obligation of defense attorneys to correct any original errors in law. Thus, they should have objected to the lack of due process when it first occurred, at the initial trial. Therefore Frank's decision not to be present at the verdict was a procedural, rather than a constitutional matter. On this basis two Supreme Court justices, Joseph R. Lamar and Oliver Wendell Holmes, refused to consider a writ of error on Frank's behalf. A writ of error is the method by which the court of record is directed to submit the account of the trial to an appellate court, to correct any mistakes in the original proceedings. However, Justices Lamar and Holmes did grant the petition by Frank's lawyers to hear the case before the Supreme Court. Once again, the appeal was denied, because a writ of habeas corpus does not take the place of a writ of error. Mistakes in law were deemed to be the jurisdiction of the local court. Furthermore, the Supreme Court reasoned that the right of the defendant to be present at the verdict was incidental to the right of trial by jury, a right that a state could [at that time], without infringing upon the Fourteenth Amendment, abolish at will. Under such circumstances, the Court deduced that Frank's absence from the courtroom was limited in its effect. Technically, there had been no need for a trial by jury. Finally, the governor of Georgia, John Slaton, convinced that the Frank case was a denial of justice, endangered his own political career by commuting the sentence to life imprisonment. In August 1915, however a mob broke into the prison farm at Milledgeville, Ga., forcibly removed Frank to an area close to the home of Mary Phagan, and there lynched him.[9]

Wolf, despite his age, became so completely involved in the Frank matter that he sent his son-in-law and partner, Meyer Cohen, down to Atlanta to speak with the prisoner. Convinced of Frank's innocence, Wolf and Cohen traveled to New York, at the express bidding of their "Atlanta friends" (Frank had been president of his B'nai B'rith lodge), to confer with Marshall. In addition, Wolf contacted a score of legal authorities for Frank's sake.[10] Against Marshall's advice,[11] he petitioned members in the Union of American Hebrew Congregations with suggestions that a campaign be mounted in the press, decrying the racial prejudice and the absence of a fair trial to which Frank had been subjected.[12] By the time the Supreme Court confirmed the guilty verdict, there were one million individuals, both Christians and Jews, who objected to the summary justice meted out to Frank, and who appealed for executive clemency.[13] In this connection, Wolf wrote to President Wilson, but he refused to consider the plea.[14] In trying to avert the inevitable, Wolf earlier suggested that it would have been better for Frank's attorneys to apply for a writ of error to Justice William Rufus Day of the Supreme Court rather than to Justice Holmes. Day had promised Wolf in the Frank matter to "do everything in his power," and "take the warmest interest" for Wolf's sake, who had been so "fearless . . . in advocating the rights of all men."[15] Yet the record shows that Judge Day voted with the majority in denying Frank a new trial. Only Justices Holmes and Charles Evans Hughes dissented; they were appalled at the evidence of mob terrorism surrounding the original proceedings, but they were in the minority.[16]

Racism in its popular form had prevailed in the Frank case. In its intellectual garb, however, such bigotry had a much longer history. From 1887 on, a noteworthy assortment of New England Brahmins and other intelletuals had shed an anti-Semitic aura over the entire immigration picture. Both in discreet and overt tones, this group poured forth a steady stream of racist propaganda against all aliens and Jews in particular. Strangely enough, in seemingly learned journals devoted to the study of heredity and eugenics, the overriding themes proved to be a negation of Darwin's classic principles. The fittest in any species would never survive, since lower racial types of the new immigrant variety would simply outbreed the native American stock, or more effectively assure its destruction through admixture and intermarriage. As early as 1870, Francis Walker, the director of the Census Bureau, who once asked William B. Hackenburg and Simon Wolf to provide a census of the Jewish population in the United States, was convinced that unrestricted immigration would lead to either American racial suicide or retrogression to a more primitive kind of human.[17] Henry Cabot Lodge paid more than lip service to the idea, though, as seen in his encounter with Wolf in 1910, he defended a concern with immigrant racial origins as a need for statistical information.[18]

By 1913, Senator Dillingham, as chairman of the Immigration Commission, attributed sufficient importance to racial distinctiveness to warrant immigrant admissions to this country on an ethnic basis.[19] Three years later, Madison Grant, a museum curator, gave a concrete illustration to Walker's notion of racial defilement. Grant insisted that in any crossbreeding arrangement between a member of a superior race and a Jew, the result would always produce a Jew.[20]

It was in a sense both ironic and fitting that Wolf should have been awarded public recognition for his defense of the immigrant in the very year that American racism had come of age. The year 1916 was indeed the appropriate time for the Hebrew Immigrant Aid Society to have taken the measure of Wolf's achievements in immigrant matters, not for the ostensible purpose that he reached his eightieth birthday, but rather because thereafter, any defenses of the alien that he would be able to muster would fall before the siege of racial implications. Such celebrations as the Jewish community afforded an old man were also tinged by the paradox that what he had gained through personal contacts, the reversal of over 100,000 deportations, would no longer constitute an overriding pattern of action.[21]

Once the Armistice was signed, nativists were able to feed the fires of racism with the fuel of industrial unrest and increasing unemployment, with labor agitation, and with an alleged Bolshevik menace purportedly brought here by Russian Jews who were deemed the catalysts of revolution. The director of consular service of the State Department, Wilbur J. Carr, sent negative evaluations of the migration of hundreds now fleeing East European religious persecution. Congressman Albert Johnson, a restrictionist from the West, was convinced of the benefits of a eugenically controlled society. He took comfort in Carr's views, and latched on to a bill suspending immigration for a period of one year.

In this connection, it is difficult to understand Wolf's agreement to halt immigration temporarily. For the moment, his rationale was that such a cessation would safeguard America's institutions from a Bolshevik menace, and diminish the number of unemployables reaching this country. However, he was prepared to request exemptions from the law only for relatives of American citizens.[22] By publicly tracing his concern over the results of an imported revolution, bent on destroying American democracy, and agonizing over a displaced native work force, Wolf jeopardized his role as champion of the immigrant. His private suggestions that such aliens who refuse to opt for citizenship be deported[23] were at variance with all those earlier calls of welcome for the stranger. Could it be that what drove him now was his

constant desire for peaceable accommodation rather than any inherent ac-
quiescence in a prevailing ideology? Yet his advice favoring alien expatriation
under certain circumstances ought not to be confused with the demands of
the superpatriots, for whom failures in naturalization became texts for excluding all foreigners. Rather, Wolf continually urged the immigrant Jew to
Americanize himself and obtain his citizenship papers as security against
deportation.[24]

For all their differences in intent from restrictionist purposes, Wolf's
ingratiating words did not turn the tables in favor of the immigrants and their
allies. Once again, as in the past, only the protests of American employers of
foreign labor, resident in industrial states, prevented the Senate from agreeing to an exclusionist policy.[25] Yet public opinion demanded that immigration be restricted, and Senator Dillingham, somewhat more moderate in his
views than Congressman Johnson, found the substitute in a bill that would
limit the number of immigrants of any nationality to 5% of the number of
foreign born persons of similar origins resident in the United States at the
time of the 1910 census. In the last months of his office, Wilson let the
Dillingham bill die by refusing to sign it. Under Harding's administration,
the measure was reintroduced in slightly altered fashion, and passed both
houses of Congress.[26]

As Wolf had echoed the sentiments against immigrants current in his day,
so too did he temper his criticism of the Quota Law. Though he acknowledged some of its harsh features, he was quick to refute the evidence on all
sides that the 1921 Immigration Law was designed primarily to exclude
Russian Jews. Instead, he took hope from the fact that at one point in its
progress through the legislature, the bill would not become applicable to
refugees fleeing religious persecution. Since there was no such provision in
its final form, Wolf soon found nothing more to say about the humaneness of
the Department of Commerce when it administered a whole series of
inequities that flowed from the terms of the law.[27]

Soon enough, Wolf realized that practical difficulties compounded the
problems associated with the new bill. How was the matter of an excess
monthly quota of immigrants, dumped here partly through the ignorance of
American consuls overseas, to be handled? Were those aliens to be charged
against the succeeding month's total, or to be deported? Frequently, such
issues were resolved not in terms of principles, but only through expediency.
In December 1921, because it was the Christmas season, Secretary of Labor
Davis freed some 1,000 Polish immigrants, tied up on a steamship in New
York harbor, from the onus of being counted as so much excess population.
They were not to be returned to their country of origin, nor would their
presence diminish the number of their compatriots due to land the following
month.[28] Kohler cautioned against the seeming liberality of the decision,

which he warned stemmed from an official desire "to prevent the judicial construction" of such deportation orders that might have violated treaty regulations with other countries.[29]

Wolf did not live to see the 1924 Immigration Bill, which merely intensified the effects of the Quota Law passed in 1921.[30] In March 1923, however, just a few months before his death, he managed to fire off one last salvo of righteous indignation against the general course restrictive immigration legislation had taken. Wolf's opposition to laws requiring the registration of aliens was now as forthright as his earlier anger at methods of immigrant classification.

For Wolf, the tragedy of such a restrictionist victory was compounded. The one principle for which he had always stood, the one ideal he would not cast aside in the interests of political accommodation, now eluded him. All his life he had resisted tabulating new arrivals in terms of racial or, more accurately from his perspective, religious backgrounds. In the end, he was defeated. As the insidious doctrine of racist thinking invaded all levels of the population, both the intellectual and the untutored, it also engulfed federal immigration inspectors and their superiors. In their eagerness to lend status to their restrictive techniques, they pursued a pseudoscientific approach, cloaking racial and religious inquiries in the garb of ethnological information.[31] The government did not question the justice of such investigations. However, Wolf's argument that such official prying into private matters of faith was unconstitutional because it abridged freedom of expression was not itself absolute. The federal government had not declared openly that aliens possessed the same constitutional guarantees that were accorded to citizens. Abolishing this distinction had been the burden of Kohler's criticism of the entire immigration apparatus.[32] Until the Department of Commerce and later its successor, that of Labor, were prepared to acknowledge the equality of all, Wolf would continue to encounter difficulties in his request that aliens also benefit from the Constitution.

Here then was the crux of what would become Wolf's last confrontation with federal authorities on immigrant matters. To Secretary of Labor, James Davis, Americanizing the alien who came here, and rigidly restricting the mass of immigrants from southern and eastern Europe seeking admission to this land, were the two most effective methods for insulating America's Anglo-Saxon world from becoming polluted by contact with peoples of so-called inferior races. Where limiting immigrant entry might have fallen short of this objective, forcibly assimilating the newcomer to the American way of life would at least diminish the effectiveness of foreign influences. Therefore, governmental registration of aliens in terms of age, marital status, occupation, race, and nationality would enable the immigration service forcibly to enroll the stranger in courses in English, history, and civics. Any failure to register would result in fines or deportations.[33] Obviously, immigration officials imagined asserting the rights of aliens in law a totally irrelevant issue, but for Wolf and his colleagues in the Union of American Hebrew Congregations the Alien Registration Bill was patterned on the Alien and Sedition Laws of 1798 (which either lapsed or later fell into disuse). Spokesmen for the immigrant were convinced that the Alien Registration Bill would extend the practice of excluding the Chinese to European aliens, would invite extortion and blackmail on an unprecedented scale, and would increase enormously the likelihood of deportation on purely technical grounds.[34]

Secretary Davis reacted personally to Wolf's opposition to the Alien Registration Bill and to that of the Union of American Hebrew Congregations, which Wolf represented. To say the least, the secretary's reply was carping.

> "It is hard to comprehend," wrote he, "that anyone of the racial groups in the United States should so vehemently oppose a program of assimilation, least of all a race which has received so much at the hands of this mation. . . ."

Convinced that doctrines of "anarchy and hate" were taking place in the immigrant community, Davis wondered whether Wolf's antagonism to the Alien Registration Bill arose not only from a desire to protect the "alien criminal," but also from "doubts as to the justice of the court system." The secretary believed wholeheartedly that the judiciary would quickly correct any inequities growing from the measure. Davis thought Wolf's fears, that the bill might imperil an alien's acquisition of citizenship or hasten the likelihood of deportation proceedings, groundless.

However, Wolf was not to be deflected from his purpose, this time for the last significant moment in his life. Having restated the Jewish community's avid pursuit of educational and acculturational programs for its newcomers, he then parried the secretary's main thrusts. For Wolf openly contended that the courts would be powerless to reverse any administrative procedures that were the natural outcomes of a harsh and unjust law. To add weight to his argument, he refused to believe that "doctrines of anarchy and hate" had become the measuring rods of immigrant society in America.[35]

After a lifetime of pleading and cajoling, Wolf had come round to Kohler's point of view in immigration matters. Like Kohler, he no longer sought to placate the Davises and others in positions of command. As the secretary appeared intransigent in his appraisal of the alien community,[36] so now too Wolf had nothing more to lose. Compromise appeared out of the question. What else was there to do but speak up for justice.

10

In the Russian Maze

Staggering as the dimensions of problems in Jewish immigration may have been, they paled in significance before the issues of freedom for Jews in the czarist Russia. If throughout these years Wolf had spoken up for his oppressed kin in Russia, or had tried continually to ease their entry to this country, he had not yet touched the heart of the matter.

Paradoxically, much of Russia's legal justification for its ill treatment of Jews arose from its interpretation of a commercial treaty shared with the United States since 1832. By one of its terms, Americans or Russians having commercial interests in either country were permitted to travel and sojourn at will in both lands. The same protection and security extended by each nation to its citizens was to be accorded to foreign travelers. These visitors, however, were at all times subject to the laws and ordinances prevailing in the territories they traversed. Such obedience to local law was specifically illustrated in the tenth article of the treaty: this proviso allowed individuals of either country to dispose of their goods in the other country, provided this process in no way denied the Russian prohibition against emigration of its nationals. Russia maintained the doctrine implicit in this proscription: no one born on its soil could voluntarily opt for citizenship in another country. By 1845, America had repudiated this point of view. Twenty-three years later the right of expatriation became American law; Russia continued to deny this privilege to those born within its borders. Consequently, after the Civil War, when naturalized American Jews of Russian origin returned to the country of their birth, either for personal or commercial reasons, they frequently were either imprisoned for having failed to comply with Russian law, or in being summarily expelled from the empire, were forced to abandon their mercantile establishments and property. From 1866 on, State Department dispatches refer to instances of diplomatic negotiations on behalf of American naturalized citizens abroad in the czar's domains. Sometimes the petitioners involved were either released from jail, or as a result of American diplomatic pressures were permitted to resume their occupations temporarily.[1] In no way, however, did such ad hoc arrangements modify prevailing Russian regulations.

At first glance it would seem a paltry matter if a few Jewish merchants, who were naturalized American citizens of Russian origin, temporarily residing in the empire, were first harassed and then, in conformity with the usual vagaries of Russian law, ultimately released. If, on occasion, Russian bureaucracy bestirred itself into creating yet another exception to the rule, then this too was to be explained as a unique administrative procedure. But the terms of the Russo-American Commercial Treaty raised a host of legal problems, whose resolution favorable to concepts of American democracy might have altered certain economic and social conditions in this country.

First, were Russia to abandon its doctrine of perpetual allegiance and allow those persons born on its soil the right of expatriation, then its persistent mistreatment of foreign, naturalized Jews in its territories would cease. Under the circumstances, the Russian government would not be able to maintain one set of libertarian policies for the relatively few foreigners temporarily resident or traveling in its lands, while yet persisting in the imposition of legal and economic restrictions upon its native Jews. Equality of citizenship for all would force the ghetto walls to crumble, and America would no longer be inundated with hundreds of thousands of East European Jews fleeing the effects of Russian persecution.

Second, the terms of the Russo-American Commercial Treaty effectively limited the freedoms of naturalized American Jews and perpetuated the concept of the inviolability of Russian law wherever it was applied. Yet the treaty was the one wedge American officials had in trying to pry loose Russia's entrenched policy of anti-Semitism without trespassing on the laws of international comity. It then became a matter of executive interpretation whether the internal policies of one country so adversely affected another as to warrant official criticism.

These two elements, of differing concepts of naturalization and the right for one nation to intervene in the internal affairs of another, because of special circumstances, formed the bases for American reactions to the terms of the 1832 Commercial Treaty.

Thus, in 1880, Wolf and Lewis Abrahams, representing the Board of Delegates of the Union, inquired of Secretary of State William Evarts whether this country could protest Russia's expulsion of its Jews into a specially restricted enclave, the Pale of Settlement, and not infringe upon that nation's sovereignty. In his response, Evarts complied with the letter of the law. Only where Russian regulations had violated the "natural rights" of American citizens, or "treaty obligations," or the provisions of "international law," did America have a right to criticize Russian policy.[2]

Ultimately, Evart's subordinate, John Foster, the American ambassador to

Russia, took a more radical point of view. In no uncertain terms, Foster told
the Russian foreign minister, Nicholas de Giers, that bureaucratic exceptions
to the law allowing wealthy naturalized American Jews to remain and do
business in the empire would not solve the matter. Foster asked that proscriptive edicts against all Jews, both native born and naturalized, be abol-
ished.[3]

Some American critics may have been bolder than others in their demands
that native Russian anti-Semitism cease. Diplomatic protocol, however, continued to demand that all such rebukes be coupled with statements of
concern over Russian mistreatment of naturalized Americans in the empire.

Throughout the 1880s, this was the pattern of American reaction to Russian anti-Jewish activities. Representative Samuel S. Cox, acting as an intermediary for the Board of Delegates at Wolf's behest, managed to introduce
congressional resolutions asking that Russian anti-Semitism against both
native-born and naturalized American Jews cease; he even alerted the president, who though he minimized the gravity of Russian excesses, did agree
with Cox.[4] Yet, despite his much vaunted entrée to federal circles, Wolf, and
his Board of Delegates were not privy to a secret State Department report
that validated the sorry plight of Russian Jewry. Once the Board realized the
extent and level of the persecutions, Wolf could only complain that American
diplomatic indifference merely compounded the difficulties for his Russian
coreligionsts.[5] Publicly however, secretaries of state would protest the harassment or expulsion of American citizens or urge that the United States
had better learn the truth about Russian persistence in interpreting the
treaty to its own advantage.[6]

During the last years of the decade, internal problems of reorganization
and changes in leadership had made it difficult for the Board of Delegates to
react to these latest State Department activities and pronouncements. Finally, by 1889, once Wolf had gained control, he alluded to the need for
shaping a more equitable commercial agreement between the two countries.
Yet he too was quick to realize the impossibility of asking Russia to adhere to
the principle of equal citizenship when, like other nations, it enjoyed the
privilege of extraterritorial jurisdiction.[7]

By 1891, however, Evart's successor, Secretary of State James G. Blaine,
added a third element to the issue of native Russian anti-Semitism and that
country's disregard for the rights of foreigners. In that year the sudden
expulsion of 10,000 Jewish artisans from Moscow and the prior arrival here of
more than 200,000 refugees from the czar's domains led Blaine to imply that
the United States could object to Russian internal policy when it resulted in
massive Jewish migrations to this country. The secretary agreed with Wolf's
complaint that the American minister to St. Petersburg, Charles Emory
Smith, had unfairly minimized the extent of the violence against Jews in
Russia; therefore Blaine urged Smith to warn Russia against the con-

sequences of a precipitous flight of its Jewish residents to this country.[8] In so doing, the secretary not only responded to Wolf as chairman of the Board of Delegates and as spokesman for the Jewish community, but also reinforced the view of secretary of the interior, Charles Foster, that any untoward Jewish migration to the United States would sorely tax this country's economic resources. One recalls how Foster cautioned Wolf and Abrahams. They were to monitor the American Jewish community lest it unwittingly aid paupers to reach these shores.[9]

While Blaine may have viewed the presence here of an additional 200,000 Jewish refugees from czarist oppression as just cause for America's condemnation of Russian anti-Semitic practice, both Wolf and the legislators before whom he testified were constrained to decry Russian governmental policy toward its Jews within the framework of problems encountered by American naturalized citizens inside the borders of the empire.[10] A decade earlier, in 1881, Ambassador Foster could have requested the abolition of all Russian proscriptive edicts when he communicated with the Russian foreign minister. Now, however, Wolf may have expressed his shock at the events that transpired against the Jews in Russia, their sudden expulsions, and renewed persecutions, but in his Board of Delegates report he had constantly to note that only through American concern for its nationals abroad would questions reflecting on the injustice of Russian law not be deemed an infringement of another nation's sovereignty. Therefore, when Senator Wilkinson Call of Florida introduced a resolution applying the principle of American freedom to all of Russia's inhabitants, he sadly enough insured the failure of the protest itself; his resolution died in committee. It, like its substitute, proposed by the Texas legislature, that the State Department communicate a sense of "horror and sorrow" at the Russian state of affairs to the czar, was abandoned lest it impinge upon internal Russian jurisdiction. The joint Senate-House Conference's final *Report*, upon which no action was taken, merely expressed the pious wish that "the enlightened spirit of the past [would] allow the Emperor to act again [in the spirit of humanity]."[11]

Shortly thereafter, matters took a turn for the worse when Russian consuls in American cities applied religious qualification tests on America soil to American naturalized citizens seeking entry visas to Russia. Though Secretaries Clifton R. Breckenridge and Richard Olney protested against such practices, oddly enough their underlings at the State Department saw nothing wrong in allowing foreign governments the right to determine the extent to which their accredited representatives might be permitted to act. With Russian consuls enjoying the widest of latitudes in issuing passports for American Jews, Wolf protested in vain that "there can be no revocation of the oppressive practices of that country with which we have laws of comity."[12]

This impasse between American and Russian perceptions concerning the allegiance due one's country forced the State Department to settle for the rescue of specific individuals with no regard to the principles involved. There was little left for Wolf to do in his role as chairman of the Board of Delegates, other than to enumerate his successes, significant though they were, in saving those unlucky Americans who for some reason or other found themselves trapped in the tangled web of Russian bureaucracy. Thus Wolf noted how in 1891 he saved one Hermann Kempinski, of the B'nai B'rith Abraham Lodge in Bridgeport, Conn. Kempinski, upon returning to Russia, was arrested for evading military service, and he was advised to renounce his American citizenship. He did so and was ordered exiled to Siberia. Wolf maintained that since Kempinski had severed his American connection, the State Department was powerless to act. But the Board of Delegates intervened, and the State Department secured his release by having the czar grant him clemency. [13] Years later, at a B'nai B'rith meeting in Bridgeport, on Sunday, 11 February 1917, Wolf recounted how a grateful Kempinski arose and thanked him publicly for having saved his life. [14]

In 1896, Wolf again reported that he was instrumental in preventing the deportation of three naturalized American Jews from Memel and Berlin to Russia. On this occasion, Wolf boasted that at his insistence the U. S. embassy in Germany instructed the Prussian government that these men were naturalized citizens who therefore could not be delivered to Russia. In the absence of a naturalization accord between Russia and Germany, Russia would be able to invoke severe penalties upon its former residents who had foresworn their allegiance to it. To have sent these men to Russia, Wolf warned, would have meant their exile or imprisonment or both. [15]

If earlier, the State Department had abandoned principle in the rescue of American nationals, now the obscurity of Russian law was at last matched by the ambiguity of American intentions. Despite its seeming concern for the equality of citizenship abroad, the U.S. Senate in 1887 ratified a secret extradition treaty with Russia that was not made public for five years. Not having obtained a copy of the convention until then, Wolf was at a loss to understand why Russia should have acquired such privileges while it could, with impunity, continue to disregard the passport rights of American citizens. Moreover, one of the most dangerous consequences of the extradition treaty, Wolf contended, was that it removed lesser crimes than those of killing chiefs of state or magistrates from the area of political offenses. This way, while "escaping assassins would be protected," anyone else, charged with revolutionary intent—and Russia was particularly keen in leveling such accusations against Jews—would be subject to arrest and extradition to the czar's lands. Chances are that once there, the prisoner would not necessarily receive a fair trial, but would be destined for exile. Wolf conveyed these fears to Senator John Sherman of the Senate Foreign Relations Committee. But the legislator told Wolf the treaty was "beyond [the Senate's] control, since it was ratified and in the hands of the President."

The treaty's legal validity gave Wolf even more cause for concern. Combined with the terms of the Russo-American Commercial Treaty, this new extradition agreement would now make it possible for Jewish immigrants to be returned to Russia to stand trial. It could also force naturalized American citizens of Russian origin, hitherto legally barred from entering the empire for commercial or personal reasons, to be "despoiled and imprisoned with the full benefit" of a law authorized by the United States.[16]

The very dangers posed by this new statute forced Wolf to add his name to a petition, sponsored by Congressman Isidor Rayner of Maryland, which asked the State Department to revoke the Russo-American Commercial Treaty. Wolf, Rayner, and the other signers were determined that unless equal treatment were accorded to every American citizen in the czar's lands, all diplomatic relations between the United States and Russia were to be severed.[17] More than a decade later, in 1908, this was to become the rallying cry of the American Jewish Committee. But now, fourteen years before, Wolf had already endorsed legislation demanding radical changes in Russo-American relations.

Such resoluteness of purpose on Wolf's part did not long endure, however. State Department approval of Russian dispensations allowing wealthy American Jews visitation and commercial rights in the empire weakened it.[18] And Secretary Hay's view, embodied in a communication from Assistant Secretary of State David H. Hill that the passport issue was a matter for local Russian jurisdiction, dealt it a mortal blow.

In effect, this was Hay's way of rejecting Wolf's request for a new nondiscriminatory trade treaty between Russia and America. What made Hill's communication sound even more ominous than those which preceded it was that, in years to come, it would be elevated to the level of standard State Department reaction to all suggested changes relevant to the passport controversy. Were the United States to engage in retaliatory steps against czarist Russia, such measures would prove counterproductive in terms of American needs.[19] For these reasons, from now on, Wolf would be unable to oppose such State Department affirmations with any degree of credibility.

Thus it would appear that altering the passport matter, contingent as it was upon Russia's abandoning its doctrine of perpetual allegience, would be wellnigh impossible. Secretary Hay had already failed in his attempt at obtaining a naturalization treaty with Romania, itself only a Russian satellite.

During the opening years of the twentieth century, all avenues seeking a reduction in anti-Jewish pogroms in Russia, and securing recognition of the American passport for naturalized American Jews of Russian origin, were closed. In the summer of 1902, Wolf, urged on by several Democratic congressmen, managed to arrange a meeting with President Roosevelt on these issues. He chided Wolf for having come without first making adequate arrangements, and reminded him that it was difficult to speak openly in the presence of others. As for the problems at hand, there was little the United States could do. Would American Jews, queried Roosevelt, have wanted him to go to war against Russia and its neighbor Romania?[20]

For public consumption, Wolf put the best possible light on the passport problem and, by implication, the ultimate improvement in the state of Jewish affairs in the empire. It ought to be added that he was beguiled into this attitude by constant reassurances from the State Department, backed by Russian connivance, that changes in the terms of the treaty were being contemplated.[21] So, for example, 1904, an election year in America, coincided with vague Russian affirmations of fashioning a more liberal regime, including a commission that would look into the Jewish question. Wolf, thereupon, tempered his criticism of America's lack of concern for the accepted freedoms due every citizen with assurances that this government was doing all in its power to ameliorate the situation. He based his hopes on communications between Robert McCormick, the American minister at St. Petersburg, and the Russian foreign minister, Count Lamsdorff, who affirmed that the newly formed commission would shortly be revising passport regulations.[22]

This gesture was soon to prove as barren of results as those which were to follow. Although the period from 1904 to 1905 was once again marked by anti-Semitic pogroms, Wolf remained optimistic. Secretary of State Root had warned him that the United States could not undertake any action that would improve the lot of Russian Jewry at that juncture in time, yet Wolf took heart. He relied on the secretary's good word, for Root dredged up a promise of the czar that once the riots subsided, he would see to the creation of a new parliament free from religious prejudice. This enabled Wolf to boast that the czar's directive would lead to a "final victory for the recognition of the American passport." Wolf also claimed that his correspondence with Root (with its optimistic premises) became the basis for the State Department's replies to inquiries by angry citizens concerned over the Russian state of affairs. Unfortunately, by the summer of 1903, the first democratically elected Duma, or parliament, in Russian history was dissolved for having opposed Russian governmental policy. The American State Department now knew that emancipating Jews in the empire would take place only within the framework of granting equal rights to all nationalities in that land.[23]

Despite such bleak prospects, Root and Wolf continued their pious communications, with Root believing that "at least in practice," the Russians were becoming "less exacting" in processing American passports. In 1907, Root's confidence stemmed from the State Department's eagerness to conclude a naturalization convention with Russia. Ever alert to possible changes, Wolf now contacted Robert Bacon, an assistant secretary of state. Their letters sounded like a repetition of the Root Wolf exchanges. Yet nowhere in his note did Bacon indicate if the naturalization agreement would be negotiated, much less whether the passport item was to be included in its agenda. At last, however, Wolf had to recognize the indeterminateness of State Department pronouncements. He admitted in his *Report* that "the vexing passport question would be the revision of the Russo-American Commercial Treaty.[24] For in truth, the ax was about to fall. After many conversations, Alexander Izvolsky, the Russian minister of foreign affairs, informed Nicholas Riddle, the American chargé d'affaires at St. Petersburg, that Russia "could not possibly consider a naturalization treaty; it would bring up the whole Jewish question."

Although the Bacon letter promised Wolf nothing and his earlier correspondence with the State Department was equally vague, relying as it did on mendacious Russian reports, Wolf chose to trust the department's moral affirmations. Experienced politician though he was, he refused to confront his own doubts or to recognize the department's dilatory tactics. Accordingly, his Board of Delegates reports consistently read like happy auguries of better treatment for Russian Jews and for naturalized Americans in Russia. His earlier pique of righteous indignation, which led him to sign a petition seeking the elimination of the Russo-American Commercial Treaty, was momentary. It had melted into thin air.[25]

Why then did Wolf during all those years from 1894 on persist in such optimistic posturing? The answer is to be sought in terms of his patriotic fervor. He could not face the fact squarely that to conclude a commercial or naturalization agreement with Russia was at best amoral. Such a project had nothing whatsoever to do with political or humanitarian ideals. If, on the other hand, any new arrangement would further Russo-American trade, while yet reducing Jewish mass migration to this country, so much the better for all concerned. Or, if Russian intransigeance had to be accepted as a constant factor, then the shapers of American foreign policy would have to adjust their future relations with Russia accordingly.

To Wolf such behavior did not smack of duplicity. It was for him, at the very worst interpretation, merely a pragmatic approach to a difficult situation. Given his sense of overwhelming allegiance to this country, he would act accordingly.

This explains his ingratiating letters to those in command, which sometimes led him to shift part of the blame away from the Russian instigators of the massacres to their victims. It was but a small step from agreeing, for example, with Secretary Root in 1905,[26] that the time was historically inopportune for negotiating a new Russo-American commercial agreement to justifying the existence of certain anti-Semitic prejudices. To Count Sergei Witte, the Russian ambassador to the United States, Wolf wrote that the Jews' "financial wizardry," which led them to the control of the press and public opinion, especially in the United States, and to a lesser degree in the rest of the world, would also redound to Russia's credit, would it emancipate its Jews. Having humored Witte with stereotypical notions of Jewish wealth and power, Wolf then expanded on the same theme in a letter to Andrew White, former diplomat and then president of Cornell University. White had written about the dangers of ghettoization in the crowded urban centers of the world, and of the deleterious influences exerted by "Talmudic" rabbis. In this instance Wolf had invited White's reply when he asked the then current educator "what American citizens of the Jewish faith ought to do to bring about better results in Russia itself." And the answer, given White's views on Jews and Judaism, was to be expected. White repeated to Wolf what Wolf obviously wanted to hear: powerful financial Jewish interests outside Russia, "the great money power in the world," so "largely in the hands of Israelites," ought to withdraw support from Russia, and sustain Japan, who was fighting . . . indirectly for Jewish emancipation in Russia."[27] Like Wolf, White maintained a profound trust in the public pressure generated by the Kishineff Petition and asked Wolf to utilize that document toward altering Russia's policy toward its Jews.[28] But by the time White responded to Wolf's query, the Kishineff Petition, organized in America at Wolf's instance, had already failed in its initial purpose. Basically, the petition had been America's reaction to a widespread pogrom at Kishineff, where hundreds of victims were wounded, with more than twoscore killed, thousands impoverished overnight, their property damage mounting into millions of rubles. But the czar refused to acknowledge the contents of the petition, which expressed the public wish of the American people that such depredations cease. This message was sent as an official memorandum from the American executive and the State Department, but was so arrogantly dismissed by the Russian authorities that it never reached the czar.[29] At best, therefore, the White-Wolf correspondence was intended for public consumption in the United States.

The Kishineff Affair had begun like other blood-libel accounts. During the Easter season in 1903, a Christian child had been found murdered in the city. Later investigation revealed that he had been killed by a relative. The motive was financial. But the Russian clergy and the press, abetted by the government, immediately laid the charge of ritual murder against the Jews. Allegedly, they had done the child to death in order to use his blood for the Passover. There followed an orgy of bloodletting, rape, and plunder that lasted for three days, from April 19 on. It had taken the American ambassador to Russia, Robert McCormick, almost three weeks to ascertain the extent of the horror, but he finally learned the truth from dispatches in the *London Standard*. Meanwhile, the American press continued to decry the suffering of the Jews in Kishineff. Editorials on Russian barbarism multiplied.[30] Such agitation culminated in the Kishineff Petition.

Wolf was the moving force behind the document. Not only had he alerted Hay to the dangers at Kishineff, but after the American embassy at St.

Petersburg persisted in denying the existence of any pogrom, it was Wolf who urged the president of B'nai B'rith, Leo N. Levi, and its executive, to organize a public protest. Meanwhile, Wolf had obtained an interview with Secretary Hay and President Roosevelt. By then Levi and Wolf and their colleagues had already drawn up the petition, decrying the outrage. In response, Roosevelt noted that at his request, the governor of Kishineff had already been removed, and that between "three to four hundred perpetrators . . . had been arrested." Nevertheless, Roosevelt was eager to send the document off as soon as possible, while Wolf and Levi and Oscar Straus, who now joined them in the deliberations, were worried lest there be insufficient time to collect a representative sampling of signatures from all Americans, one that would truly reflect the weight of American public opinion. Aware too, that there had been semiofficial indications of the czar's refusal to receive the document, Levi, Straus, and Wolf also debated the need to precede the document's actual transmittal to Russia with a letter of inquiry as to its reception. Were its signatures only partially completed or its acceptance in Russia rebuffed, its value as a historic document might be lost. On the other hand, Wolf reasoned that inasmuch as its contents had been broadcast worldwide, it mattered little whether the Russian government would or would not accept it. Wolf also wondered whether the frank tenor of its message might play new havoc with the fate of Jews still resident in Russia. In the end, however, all such doubts were resolved in favor of sending the document. At Roosevelt's direction, the American chargé d'affaires at St. Petersburg, Nicholas Riddle, was instructed to ask for an audience with the Russian minister of foreign affairs, at which time a request would be made to have the czar receive the petition. Straus delivered these presidential instructions to Secretary Hay for transmission abroad, while Levi received the original draft as a historic memento. Though, as expected, the Russians remained indifferent, by now 13,000 signatures had been added to the document. These loose sheets were then "bound in polished levant, placed in a specially prepared ebony case, along with a separate volume containing a brief account of the Petition. . . ." Wolf delivered the case to Secretary Hay; their final destination was the National Archives.

For his efforts Wolf seemed gratified. Roosevelt thanked him for the admirable "good sense" he had shown in the entire affair, and sent him an autographed picture.[31]

In this public account of the preparation for Kishineff, Wolf seemed beset by reasonable doubts, as to both the effectiveness of the document and its reception in Russia. Privately, however, in helping to shape the petition he agonized over an entire series of possible mishaps. His mentor at B'nai B'rith, Levi, had warned him against allowing the Zionists to twist Kishineff to their own purposes and inveighed against forcing B'nai B'rith to bear the brunt of the massacre's financial costs. Words of protest were therefore in order, but no monies were to be sent. More immediately, Wolf wondered whether the suddenness of the government's decision to send the document posthaste were not due to Ambassador McCormick's temporary absence from his post. Wolf knew full well that all that was necessary in this instance was for an accredited American diplomat to present his government's demands to the Russian foreign ministry for transmission to the czar. If, however, the message were to go through such regular channels while McCormick was away, would it get lost in the Russian bureaucratic maze? Yet even to conjure up such perilous notions that might have cast aspersions on the purity of governmental motive seemed treacherous. So harried was Wolf by Secretary Hay's note asking for an immediate release of the Petition that he felt it would be "hazardous" to send anything in writing to Roosevelt, including a request to meet with him in person. Yet Wolf knew that the success of the petition, if it were realized, would boost Roosevelt's political aspirations. In this connection Roosevelt himself was eager to curb the effects of Democratic Congressman Henry Goldfogle's resolution of 1902, calling for an accounting of federal action on the passport matter. That, the president was convinced, would prove inimical to the country's interests and awkward for his administration.

Other fears gnawing at Wolf during this period included his sensitive reaction to the document's being called "The Jews' Petition." He imagined the very title bore anti-Semitic overtones that would diminish the universal appeal of its contents. And over the entire affair there hovered slights to his personal dignity and public image. He had to make certain that Cyrus Adler's book on Kishineff, then in the process of publication, would not impinge upon the publicity due the petition. From a more personal point of view Wolf was also highly incensed that a reporter for the Heart Press had "tricked him" into signing one of the many circulars being drawn up in connection with the Kishineff Affair. Since Hearst was presumably angling for the presidential nomination on the Democratic ticket, Wolf's name on a memorandum sponsored by his political rivals would prove to be a distinct embarrassment.[32]

The supreme irony inherent in all these conjectures and situations was simply that the petition, having been sent, was not received. Yet the document acquired historic significance, and Wolf's hopes were not dimmed. In fact, the personal victory he achieved in the way of public acknowledgment for his appeals on behalf of persecuted Russian Jewry was overwhelming. So moved was he by the outpouring of sympathy for his cause, that toward the end of the year he again informed his Board of Delegates that several legislators and the State Department were working to "right the wrong" in the matter of the Passport Controversy. In unvarnished terms, however, nothing fateful had been accomplished as a result of Kishineff. For Russia in no way had been moved to alter its policies; its autocracy remained totally indifferent to the rights of its own native Jews and to any demand for such rights that the sentiments of foreigners may have created.[33]

Furthermore, Kishineff, in its own sad way, could also be reckoned as a repetition of Wolf's first official encounter with Russian anti-Semitism. Back in 1869, he had received public acclaim in America for having protested a Russian edict decreeing the expulsion of Bessarabian Jews into the interior of the empire.[34] Then, too, as later at Kishineff (1903), no significant change occurred in Russian attitudes, but in each instance, Wolf's public image grew.

The American Jewish Committee, having been formed partially in response to the failure at Kishineff, to the ongoing anti-Semitic persecutions in Russia, and to that country's obstinacy on the passport issue, found the last factor a vehicle neatly trimmed to its specifications. The Committee latched on to an ineptly worded communiqué from Secretary Root, warning American Jews against traveling in the Russian empire. This message was to become the Committee's catalyst in its campaign to abrogate the Russo-American Commercial Treaty.[35] All its other plans were to be subordinated to this endeavor. Committee members were especially annoyed with Wolf for having engaged them in that ill-fated publicity concerning the supposed injustice meted out to a sailor in the Boston area, when they should have expended all their efforts on the passport controversy. This incident so infuriated Herbert Friedenwald, the Committee's secretary, that when he prepared an account of his organization's proceedings, he deliberately omitted Wolf's name. Wolf never forgave him, and declared that throughout he was the recipient of Friedenwald's "contemptible behavior." Yet once the campaign to eliminate the treaty moved into high gear, whenever the Committee needed Wolf as one of its Washington contacts, it did not hesitate to call upon him.[36]

The Committee began its formal attack with a memorandum, addressed to the president of the United State, which cited the legal and moral need to abrogate the Russo-American Commercial Treaty.[37] Meanwhile, in 1908, Wolf's son-in-law and law partner, Meyer Cohen, attended the Republican Convention in Chicago. He wanted to make certain that the party's plank would decry foreign discrimination against American citizens abroad. At the same time, Wolf besieged delegates to the Democratic National Convention, meeting in Denver, with appropriate letters.[38] Ever mindful of his political obligations, he made certain to inform President Roosevelt that congressmen like Henry Goldfogle, William Sulzer, and Burton Harrison were prepared to wield the passport issue as a political club. For after all, why should the Republican party have been saddled with a problem created during a Democratic administration, under Buchanan's leadership?[39] But unity carried the day, and Taft, the successful Republican candidate for the presidency, spoke up against the practice of submitting Americans to religious inquiries by a foreign power.[40] In truth, Taft had never agreed to an abrogation of the treaty, and followed the lead of the State Department in seeking, or better still, equivocating about its revision.[41] By 1909 the Senate ratified an earlier agreement with Russian regulating the position of commercial companies in both countries, but leaving the restrictions against American citizens intact.[42] Such action reinforces the impression that Secretary of State Root had misled Wolf with vague talk of renewed negotiations.[43] If, as did Schiff,[44] Wolf knew that Russia had rejected an American overture to revise the treaty, he did not let on. Instead, he kept silent when he presided over a Commission of the Council of the Union of American Hebrew Congregations dealing with the passport matter, and decided it was an American rather than a Jewish concern. The Commission had skirted the issue because it now contained the threat of ending the Commercial Treaty and not all the delegates to the Union were as intrepid as the members of the American Jewish Committee. To save face, the Commission issued an innocuous appeal to men of good will everywhere to cooperate so that the "integrity of the American passport may be fully and rightfully preserved." Such platitudes merely angered the members of the Committee who grew even more incensed when they insisted that unlike their American coreligionists, Jews from Western Europe were accorded special treatment as a result of a series of specific agreements between Russia and the Western Powers, including England, France, Germany, and Austria. The State Department denied this and claimed that in no way did Russia favor any group of English, French, or German Jews. The situation then reached a fever pitch once President Taft had extended the benefit of minimum tariff rates to the Russian empire, in accordance with the passage of the Payne-Aldrich Tariff Act. Taft announced this new program posthaste, without even considering a request from the Tariff Board that such a course be delayed until some changes occur in a Russian understanding of the passport problem.[45]

In the winter of 1911, President Taft asked to meet with prominent Jewish leaders on the passport controversy. To hear Wolf tell it, it was he who suggested the makeup of the conference: Schiff, Marshall, and Sulzberger from the American Jewish Committee; Adolph Kraus, Philip Stein, and Jacob Furth representing B'nai B'rith; and Bernhard Bettman, together with J. Walter Freiberg of the Union of American Hebrew Congregation. The president then invited Wolf to serve as the third representative from the Union.[46]

Taft's interpretation of the treaty shocked his guests. The chief executive could not see how, in the absence of treaty obligations, any nation could be prevented from excluding whomever it wished. Taft also recalled that several secretaries of state had seen no illegalities in the Russian position on the treaty. Since American had merely requested that its people be treated as "citizens of the United States" when they entered Russia, the president was at a loss to understand why it was necessary to request an end to commercial arrangements with Russia. In this connection, Taft was well aware that the Western European powers merely protested against Russian treatment of their Jewish nationals, but never went so far as to sever relations. The president then listed the seemingly dire consequences that would ensue if the treaty were terminated: sizable American economic investments in the empire would be jeopardized; an uncontrolled exodus of Russian Jews would be catapulted to this country, with consequences involving problems of transport over Germany; and a multiplication of tragic deportations for untold numbers. Taft reminded his hearers that he was the chief executive of the entire country and had to view the problem in its total perspective. He tried to lighten the chilling impact of his words with a reference to an optimistic belief that conditions for Jews in the empire were improving.

Even Wolf was overwhelmed by the totality of Taft's rejection, and he worried lest publicizing the president's conclusions would prove "highly injurious" to the Jews in Russia. But Schiff, who had grown livid with anger, wanted the president's attitude broadcast to the world. While the other members present tried to respond by emphasizing the sanctity of American citizenship, Taft delivered the final blow when he reminded his audience of Rockville's views on the subject. The former American minister to St. Petersburg thought that the Russians were justified in excluding Jewish nationals of foreign countries, lest the taste of such freedoms would allow native Russian Jews greater freedom in exploiting the peasant class. Schiff was mortified, and after lecturing the president, left without saying good-bye.[47]

Taft's perceptions were colored by the State Department's comprehensions of the issue. Secretary of State Philander C. Knox believed that alien travelers on Russian territory came wholly within the purview of Russian law. His aides buttressed this approach with legal arguments: they felt that matters of access and immigration or exclusion were aspects of a nation's sovereignty that might well be included in regulations detailing commercial arrangements.[48]

Meanwhile, Knox's minister to St. Petersburg, Curtis Guild, and his predecessor, William Woodville Rockhill, insisted that the treaty be retained to safeguard America's commercial, political, and moral interests.

Commercially, outlawing the treaty would play havoc with America's two-million-dollar investment in Russia, resulting in a ruinous tariff war. Politically, it would upset the balance of power in the Far East, forcing two enemies, Russia and Japan, into imperialist designs. It would estrange America from its West European allies, and force it into a relationship with Germany, whose Asiatic interests conflicted with those of the United States. Morally, it would subject America to the charge that it was willing to forego friendly relations on the basis of foreign discrimination against a miniscule portion of one of its minority groups. The United States would look foolish in the eyes of other nations since it still practiced discrimination against blacks, yet maintained friendly relations with Australia, which excluded some 19,000 Afro-Americans from its territory. Guild reinforced the dilemma in terms of principle by wondering why the United States in the past had not broken off relations with countries such as Morocco, Romania, and Turkey, who had also practiced anti-Semitism. The ministers were likewise convinced that terminating the treaty would set latent anti-Jewish forces in motion in the empire. American Jews would then lose all visiting and testamentary rights. Both diplomats bolstered their argument with insinuations that abrogationists were radicals in disguise, who placed this government in the indefensible position of protecting Jewish racial and religious solidarity against Russian nationalism.[49] Meanwhile, Taft and the State Department continued to feed Wolf false information.[50]

In publicizing their disaffection with the executive branch, members of the American Jewish Committee prevailed upon Congress to drive the abrogation measure to victory. The detailed story of how the Committee's maneuvers bore fruit by December 1911 has already been recorded. With the exception of Oscar Straus, the members of the Committee did not doubt the rightness of their decision to seek abrogation.[51] Wolf, however, was caught between two alternatives: to fight for "the cause" along with the Committee, or to persist as he had in the past, in interpreting the executive viewpoint to his coreligionists. Wolf's letter to Marshall, in March 1911, implied a choice of nightmares. There Wolf restated some State Department arguments. America's policy of Oriental exclusion would make her the laughing stock of other nations for her idealistic defense of the passport; restricting alien entry was a local police regulation reserved to Russia by the treaty's terms; the United States and Russia had just concluded a secret agreement in the event of war with Japan; and so on. Yet at the same time, Wolf agreed with the moral principles on which the abrogationists based their argument. Privately, Marshall suspected Wolf of engaging in deceptive talk with the administration, which was determined to do nothing about the passport controversy.

It is recalled that although Marshall refused to trust Wolf, he also had to rely on him for bits and pieces of information. In the spring of 1911 the State Department had it bruited about that Russia would adopt a more favorable approach on the passport matter. Wolf then imparted this news to Marshall, with President Taft's reassurance that the material was authentic.[52] On his own initiative, Wolf subsequently urged a prominent citizen from Texas, Felix Bath, to desist from agitating against the treaty's nullification, since he, Wolf, had it on good authority that a resolution urging abrogation would not pass during the current session of Congress. Wolf also repeated the promise he received from President Taft that negotiations would save the day.[53]

Wolf's hasty acceptance of Russian avowals taken at face value incurred the wrath of the American Jewish Committee. Hebert Friedenwald, its secretary, had it on personal authority from Ambassador Guild that no instructions of any sort were received from the State Department or the president. Friedenwald also informed Judge Mayer Sulzberger, the president of the Committee, that none of the correspondence between Bath and the State Department indicated that it was protesting the treaty. Friedenwald in turn cautioned Marshall that the Committee would have to rethink the extent of its cooperation with others, for Wolf had been playing "a double game." So paranoid had Friedenwald become on the entire matter that he suspected Adolph S. Ochs, publisher of the *New York Times*, had lost much of his enthusiasm for abrogation because of Wolf's change of attitude in the Bath episode. Meanwhile, Sulzberger was prepared to retaliate against any Committee member who had worked with Wolf directly, and wanted to know by what right Wolf dared to interfere with the Committee's plans to abrogate the treaty.[54]

No one came forward to execute Sulzberger's command, but the distrust between Wolf and the Committee persisted. Each one's prerogatives in obtaining public recognition on the passport matter were too great to be overlooked. Friedenwald, who managed the daily affairs of the Committee, accused Wolf, as chairman of the Board of Delegates, of deliberately withholding names of senators and representative favoring abrogation from the Committee. Wolf based his refusal to share such lists on the grounds that Friedenwald had questioned the efficiency of the Board of Delegates on the passport problem. Friedenwald, Wolf contended, had not only demeaned the work of the Board, but also regarded the Committee as the sole agency of any consequence in the field. Friedenwald then accused Wolf of "malicious misrepresentation," but Marshall cooled Friedenwald's rage and cautioned him that since all three organizations, the Committee, the Board, and B'nai B'rith, had decided to cooperate, it would be necessary to conciliate Wolf.[55]

In fulfilling his role as a dispenser of presidential attitudes, Wolf walked a tightrope. He had to persuade the Committee that to counter the pressures of a dilatory government, he had to expend his energies to the utmost. At the same time, he always looked for hopeful portents of change either in Washington or in St. Petersburg, and clutched at any notion designed to prevent a break in relations between the two countries. This Janus-faced approach revealed itself in a series of letters to Marshall who, it appears, was his go-between with the Committee. Sometimes, Wolf would inform Marshall of forceful conversations had with Taft, where the president would be taken to task for his lack of action on the passport, and warned of the influence of the Jewish vote. Then Wolf would vitiate his own efforts in the same breath, and wonder whether there was anything the president could have done rather than cancel the treaties. To such complaints Marshall would reply that he feared neither a termination of the treaty nor an upsurge of anti-Semitism in this country together with an increase in Jewish immigration to America.[56]

In a last ditch effort to stave off the treaty's demise, Taft, Guild, and former-president Roosevelt had opted for arbitration as a successful alternative to terminating the arrangement with Russia. Wolf conveyed this information to Marshall and added that he had seen the president "on Saturday by appointment," and had given him "silver tablets of the law," on the occasion of his twenty-fifth anniversary. It was then that the president conceded that he would ask for a new agreement with Russia only if an international arbitration tribunal would uphold the Russian interpretation of the treaty. With the exception of Oscar Straus, Marshall and the other members of the Committee regarded the administration's projected proposal as another delaying tactic designed to postpone what they thought should have been inevitable. Wolf, however, was not to be outdone. As late as August 1911, when the American Jewish Committee had already received senatorial confirmation of a December hearing on the treaty's termination, Wolf was still comforting Marshall with "positive assurances" received by the State Department from St. Petersburg that there would be a happy solution to the problem. What Marshall and his colleagues had to cultivate, Wolf suggested, was a "long, enduring patience."[57]

If, throughout his career, Wolf's patriotism made him desist from forthright criticisms of the State Department, now his ambivalent attitude toward the Russo-American Commercial Treaty may be explained by his lifelong friendship with Taft. When Taft rejected the reasoning of the abrogationists, Wolf was obliged to follow suit. Much in the same vein, Wolf tried to fend off any criticism directed against Taft by spokesmen for the Jewish community. By the time Taft realized he would be a presidential candidate, Wolf was able to advise him on both general and specifically Jewish issues. For example, Wolf suggested that George B. Cortelyou, former secretary of commerce, become chairman of the Republican National Committee. Cortelyou, Wolf reasoned, would have "prominent Wall Street connections" confirming Taft's success in the venture.[58] (As matters turned out, Frank Harris Hitchcock managed Taft's 1908 presidential campaign, but this does not deny Wolf's easy access to the candidate.) Insofar as special interests were concerned, Wolf instructed Taft on what to say before a Jewish audience. In typical "Wolfean" terms, Taft was to stress the Jews' contribution to civilization and the happy rapidity with which they assimilated to the American way of life, and to list those of their coreligionists whose ties to Ohio paralleled Taft's own ancestral origins. At the same time, Wolf was eager to erase any notions, prevalent among New York Jews, that Taft had shown any sympathy for Russia. Specifically, by 1908, Wolf told a friend that in 1904, when Taft was homebound from the Philippines via Siberia and St. Petersburg, Roosevelt directed him to speak to the czar about Russian anti-Semitism and the passport matter. However, the Russian ambassador to the United States lodged a protest with the State Department and urged that the meeting not take place. As usual, the excuse was that "pending treaty relations" made any such conference impractical. Taft complied with the request. Wolf imparted this information to Oscar S. Straus, secretary of commerce and labor, who told him that he would neither campaign nor use such an argument in the hustings—namely, that Roosevelt and Taft had been in accord with the Jewish point of view concerning the American passport. Wolf then decided that he would see

> the President if possible, and have a full and exhaustive conversation with him, for he more than any other living American, is a born politician and understands the importance of things as *trifling as this seemingly is*. [italics mine][59]

Aware of the prestige Wolf enjoyed during the Taft incumbency,[60] and of his prior ability to reach Roosevelt when necessary, Marshall made certain to channel his proabrogationist sentiments through Wolf to President Taft.[61] In fact, long after the American Jewish Committee had succeeded in terminating the treaty, Wolf's close affiliations with the former president warranted an explanation from John Hayes Hammond, entrepreneur, engineer, and Taft's personal friend. Hammond assured Wolf that a scheme to develop the cotton industry in Turkestan, at the height of the passport issue, in no way detracted from federal sympathy for American Jewry. Hammond insisted that both he and Taft had only the most genuine of feelings for the victims of Russian oppression. Yet Hammond's decision to embark on his business venture under Russian control was undertaken at the suggestion of a Russian agent, Gregory Wilenkin, at the very height of the empire's failure to recognize the American passport.[62]

In the light of the cordial relations that existed between Taft and Wolf, it grew doubly difficult for him to alter a pattern of polite parleying with federal officials. Throughout his life he had access to governmental sources of power and information. He was convinced that he could achieve his goals only by the calculated positioning that was characteristic of an earlier era. He found it well-nigh impossible to abandon his ways, since statements from the executive generally made his optimistic evaluations appear credible. Despite the fact that the Russians had constantly rebuffed American requests to discuss the Jewish aspect of the 1832 treaty, the State Department always maintained that talks with officials of the Russian foreign ministry were continuing. Until the last moment, when terminating the treaty had become inevitable, Ambassador Guild reassured Taft that negotiations with the Russians would produce results.[63] Much in the same spirit, Taft, in a message to Congress on the very eve of the treaty's planned demise, declared that conferences with the Russians looking toward an amicable settlement were proceeding apace.[64] How could Wolf not have believed such hopeful signs, when he so desperately wanted to believe them, and when his entire role as a good Jew, a loyal Republican, and a confidante of presidents would have been at stake?

Scarcely had the ink been dry on the terms of the treaty's termination than the State Department, in its haste to effect a new arrangement with the empire, moved surreptitiously to avoid congressional censure. What Knox wanted in essence was an exchange of notes leading to a modus vivendi to allow commercial relations between both countries, which would ease the difficulties for Russia and America. Rights of entry and residence by respective nationals would be reduced to brief periods for specific purposes. This way Russia would be granting a special favor in allowing American Jews to enter its territory, while the United States could impose limits on "an objectionable class of Russian immigrants."[65] The response of Knox's aides to these suggestions was varied, yet each proposal submitted was intended to court Russia even more eagerly than the scheme conceived of by the secretary himself.[66]

Saved at last by information from the Commerce Department that discriminating ties between countries may be relied on through an exchange of notes, Knox opted for this plan in place of the modus vivendi, which would have needed Senate confirmation. Conveniently, a State Department memorandum now contended that the stipulations of the Russo-American Commercial Treaty of 1832, involving immigration, length of residence, and the disposition of alien property, had in the course of history become local legislation, no longer operative; principles of international law would preserve the consular rights and functions accorded to diplomats in either country.[67]

Wolf, however, who would receive information about cabinet plans from his good friend Secretary Nagel, now realized that some sort of rapprochement was being considered by the State Department. Wolf communicated his concern to the president. Taft assured him that the government did not intend to fashion a modus vivendi or invoke any other arrangement to change the existing situation resulting from an absence of any treaties. All the government was doing, Taft insisted, was examining the state of current agreements with the Russian government.[68]

Learning of Taft's message to Wolf, Ambassador Guild was perplexed on two counts. Who was this Wolf that he should have merited Taft's attention? And did Taft's letter signal a rupture between Russia and America? On the first point, Guild was told that Wolf, representing Jewish organizations active in combating the passport question, deserved a reply from the White House. And as for the alleged break between the two countries, the very absence of an official treaty would allow both Russia and America to adjust their commercial relations on a de facto basis. What must have appeared to Wolf as official confirmation of a rupture in Russo-American relations was rather an explicit admission by the chief executive, verified by the State Department, that regardless of treaty severance, the commercial rights of Russian aliens in this country would not be abridged. For its part, Russia gave no such assurances concerning American Jewish commercial travelers in the empire. But in return for American favors extended to its citizens in this land, Russia agreed to maintain a minimum tariff schedule for American imported goods.[69]

More than idealism had prompted Wolf's inquiry to the president. The Executive Council of B'nai B'rith wanted to award Taft a medal on behalf of his concerns for American Jews. Yet Kraus, its president, was disturbed by talk of a new commercial treaty. If this were so, then the entire abrogation story would be regarded as a cheap political trick, with Taft eyeing the forthcoming presidential election. In addition, Wolf had grown doubly anxious. He and B'nai B'rith planned a dinner in Secretary Nagel's honor. It would be inappropriate for the president to be overlooked, while his cabinet member was being feted. But with Taft's supposedly reassuring answer, the question solved itself, and the social events proceeded as planned. B'nai B'rith executives, with their wives, attended a luncheon at the White House in the president's honor in January 1913. There, they awarded a medal to Taft for his efforts at promoting peace, harmony, and humanitarian ideals among the peoples of the world. During the same period Secretary Nagel was honored at a dinner for his work on behalf of the immigrants.[70]

During the Wilson years the passport matter died with a whimper. When there was an indication of an attempt to revive negotiations for a new treaty, Wolf again inquired if such were the case, only to be told that no new plans were contemplated.[71] In truth, however, Taft's explanation that informal arrangements between the two countries, where all those questions associated with abrogating the treaty would be "left unprejudiced,"[72] now prevailed. This meant that the program that regulated Russo-American trade was set by minimum tariff schedules established by the 1909 Tariff Act. At the same time, the rights of citizens in either country were to be regulated by international law. Therefore, czarist Russia, despite its denunciations of Jewish control over the American media and offices of government, did not engage in economic reprisals against America.[73] It is true that a well-orchestrated publicity campaign and an aroused American public opinion, outraged by Russian insensitivity to bigotry, assured the American Jewish Committee success in abolishing the Russo-American Commercial Treaty. And under the new arrangements, the volume of trade between the two countries did diminish. But this was only temporary. By 1916, with Russia at war, American exports to that country had increased from $27,000,000 to $500,000,000 per annum.[74] The czarist regime had not altered its attitudes toward the rights of foreign Jews, but with the abrogation of the treaty, the question of American naturalized Jews seeking entry to Russia was moot.[75] When Secretary of State Robert Lansing rebuffed the request of the American ambassador to Russia, David R. Francis, that another commercial treaty be negotiated, the rejection was devoid of any practical consequences, Lansing was able to assert that no new treaty could be contemplated until Russia removed its restrictions against American Jews. At the same time, however, the Russian government decided to postpone the matter until the following year.[76] But by then the czarist government had collapsed and the passport issue had expired. Wolf, old though he was, sought other areas in which to do battle.

11
Wolf: Classical Anti-Zionist

There can be no doubt that Wolf dearly loved his people, the Jews he so frequently represented. Yet he had always fought violently against one of his clients' most persistent aspirations: the fulfillment of the Zionist dream. Ever since the loss of Palestine and their dispersion at Roman hands, Jews everywhere had continued to pray for the restoration of their homeland. For centuries they, together with Christian millenarians, had based their Zionist formula upon religious requisites. By the beginning of the World War I, however, political Zionism, steeped in all the aspects of nationalistic ideals, burgeoned forth as an issue over which nations contended.

Although he respected the spiritual aspects of Zionism, Wolf's own identification with the unalloyed features of Reform Judaism made it inevitable that he would emerge as a classical anti-Zionist. His opposition to political Zionism knew no bounds. Ultimately, it would lead him publicly to denounce the Balfour Declaration of 1917, that document which validated the hopes of those people who understood Zionism to be the only viable foundation for a Jewish state. More immediately, Wolf had all along affirmed that Judaism incorporated individualistic orientations to life and that it partook in no way of that specificity of custom, habit, and tradition unique to an ethnic community. For Wolf had inherited the fear of the German liberals—whatever smacked of Jewish particularism, ritual, or nationalism would have invoked the ire of the anti-Semites, as it had earlier incited Prussian officials to paranoid visions of Jewish supernationals conspiring against the individual state and the world as a whole. In fact, in its own fashion, Wolf's explosive reaction to the Zionist idea carried its own anti-Semitic echo. Though his motives were not to be impugned, immediately after the formation of the Basle Program, in 1897, looking to the establishment of a state, Wolf raised the specter of dual allegiance. In his report to the Board of Delegates the following year, Wolf wondered how Jews could be loyal citizens of the United

States while they proclaimed their allegiance to another sovereignty, a Jewish commonwealth in what was Palestine.

He therefore cherished what the leading proponents of Reform Judaism had said as far back as 1855—that Judaism comprised a rational religion, whose revelations assumed the progressive nature of man's unfolding maturity. Such a system was not to be bound by legalistic formulas defining the tribal customs of a Hebraic group in bygone times, but was supposed always to accommodate itself to those prophetic utterances of the Hebrew Scriptures whose messages remained forever true, despite the flux of time and circumstance.[1] Yet like the movement of which he was a part, Wolf was beset by the paradox to be found in Reform Judaism's idealization of the Jews' mission to the world. Judaism had been intended as a humanizing faith, striving for universal ideals, while the Jew, though deprived of his ethnicity, had nevertheless to persist in the chosen task of teaching God's word to mankind. Put more bluntly, the Jew within Wolf's purview had to remain distinctive, while he had yet to be denuded of any identifiable characteristics. Try as he might, Wolf was unable to dissolve that mystic bond which tied his coreligionists, as he was wont to call them, together. It has been seen how he argued, poetically if lamely, that despite their baptisms, both Heinrich Heine and Benjamin Disraeli were still Jews. Yet his essays and speeches are replete with references to the universality of Jewish values and the commonality of human attributes Jews share with the rest of mankind.

At the beginning of World War I, American Zionists, whose ranks were filled later by thousands of immigrants from Eastern Europe, were beset by no such ironies. They neither felt obligated to teach Judaism's message of pure monotheism to the world, nor did they have to square an understandable pride in the heritage of the Jew (witness Wolf's constant harping on Jewish contributions to the civilization of the world) with avowed declarations by Reform Jewish theologians that Jews were merely akin to other enlightened religionists, likeminded Christians who were also laboring for the arrival of the messianic era. Instead, the Zionists whose adherents by now included Reform rabbis who had strayed from the mainstream of their native theology, worried about implementing the Basle Program, and about the conditions Jews in Central and Eastern Europe would face once an armistice were signed.[2]

With such goals in mind, the newly strengthened and refurbished Federation of American Zionists, led by Justice Louis Dembitz Brandeis, invited members of the American Jewish Committee to consider activating a joint relief program for the Jewish victims of the war in Palestine and Europe, and to create a democratically elected assembly to speak for the Jews to the governments of the world. But the Committee fudged and hedged, and suggested its own alternate autocratic methods of electing delegates to any future conference. Except for acceding to the creation of a comprehensive

relief agency, which it managed at last to control, the Committee reacted to
Brandeis's invitation by repeated attempts to redirect the thrusts of Zionist
intentions.[3] It was not about to relinquish its preferred method of achieving
diplomatic results through private contacts with noteworthy individuals for
raucous democratic conventions where the masses of American Jews would
voice their nationalistic concerns, approaches that were anathema to Louis
Marshall and his peers. Members of the American Jewish Committee feared
that Jews would bring ridicule upon themselves were they to elect delegates
to any "Jewish" congress. Schiff, too, was convinced such a gathering would
stir up the anti-Semites.[4] For Marshall, Schiff, Adler, Straus, and others who
directed the affairs of the Committee knew full well that once hostilities had
ceased, the Zionists would be prepared to ask the Allied Powers to recognize
nationality rights for the Jews. Such a state of affairs would wreak havoc with
the principle the Committee stood for: Jews were members of a faith community, owing political allegiance to the countries wherein they were
domiciled. This view fitted neatly into the prevailing American scheme that
here in the United States faith and citizenship were separate entities. Within
this sort of comprehension, Judaism then was the third major creed in an
open democratic society. Any assault upon it, either in agnostic terms by
secular Zionists and some of their brethren in arms, Yiddishists, Socialists,
and members of the working class, or by other misguided Jews intent upon
asserting the peoplehood of Israel, would weaken the security of American
Jewry as a whole. More particularly, it would unhinge the entrenched
position the earlier German Jewish arrivals had already obtained in this
country. It is well to recall that Schiff, Marshall, Wolf, and others like them
were the products of three or more decades of adaptation and acculturation
for immigrants. Most of these German Jews were members of the Republican party. Under Roosevelt's tutelage they had learned to dislike the
hyphenated American. They were not prepared to grant to the newer immigrants the richness of ethnic diversity. They feared that such pluralism would
endanger the new way of life in America, a life replete with freedoms
unknown on the continent.

To such biases were added the implications flowing from President
Wilson's dislike of Germany, and the czar's alliance with England and France
in 1914. American Jews had always mistrusted Russia: its anti-Semitic persecutions had caused them endless pain and trouble.[5] Viewed in retrospect,
however, these people never equated Germany's hatred for the Jew with
Russia's barbaric treatment of him. Thus, German-American Jewish immigrants, triple hyphenates, were petrified lest other Jews from diverse European backgrounds might, in voicing Zionist ideals, unlock the whole
Pandora's box of a questionable allegiance by Jews to this country.

It was precisely his determination to avoid such problems, and to reinforce
his entrenched belief in the efficacy of private negotiations on delicate

matters with federal officials, that Wolf brought with him in his old age. Then he stood on the sidelines and cheered the Committee in its contentions with the Zionists and their allies who were clamoring for a Jewish congress. Though the Committee had long ago, at the instigation of Herbert Frieden-wald, derogated Wolf's claims to leadership, now he was prepared to forget old slights. In letters to Marshall, written in the summer of 1915, after the American Jewish Committee had been forced to set the stage for still another meeting with the Zionists and their colleagues demanding a democratically convened congress, Wolf continued to fulminate against Zionist statements.[6] He took sharp exception to Brandeis's classic pronouncement that linked American ideals to the Zionist cause. The jurist had declared that "loyalty to America demands that . . . each American Jew become a Zionist."[7] Wolf was furious. Though he was almost "tempted to answer Brandeis's ridiculous statement that unless we are Zionists we are not Jews," Wolf feared that such a procedure would result in "more publicity" and more "glory" for the Zionists. He relied instead, on a future conference planned for October 1915, where the Committee would set American Jewry straight on the Zionist issue. In an additional note, Wolf recalled his correspondence with Rabbi Jacob Voorsanger of San Francisco, Wolf's own protégé, who said, " 'It is the weakness of the Zionists to cast aspersions on the loyalty of their opponents.' "[8] Wolf agreed completely. But he need not have put so much trust in that forthcoming October session. It simply was not to be, for the Committee had second thoughts about accepting the demands of one of its constituent members, the *Kehillah*, or federated New York Jewish com-munity. The Committee now decided that the term "conference" was pre-ferable to "congress." Though participating organizations would still be able to determine the means by which delegates were to be chosen, the topic would be limited to matters affecting Jews "in belligerent lands." In this way, the Committee was prepared to resort to autocratic methods, designed to prohibit any open-ended discussions of political events. Louis Marshall and his peers feared that frank assessments by the Zionist masses of Jewish nationalistic aspirations would spell disaster for their coreligionists caught between opposing forces in war-torn lands. For their own part, the Zionists were appalled at the Committee's attempts to stifle public opinion. Brandeis and his followers responded with mass demonstrations and the reorganiza-tion of the Congress Organization Committee.[9] The truth was that mutual distrust between the members of the American Jewish Committee and the Zionists made any meeting of minds an impossibility. But before still another attempt at discussion between the two groups was to fail, B'nai B'rith tried to mediate the dispute. Its president, Adolph Kraus, Wolf's close friend, chaired the parley, whose delegates promptly retreated from the quarrel. Their ambiguous statements, that Jewish demands for equal rights were justified and ought to be presented to the "proper authorities," at a propitious moment, in no way addressed the dispute. The choice of holding a congress as the Zionists demanded, or convoking a conference in accordance with the wishes of the Committee, was left unresolved.[10]

Had Wolf attended that B'nai B'rith session he would have had no doubts on how to vote. For him, any publicly acknowledged meeting with the Zionists was out of the question. His immigrant's sense of an overwhelming allegiance to the United States, his deep distrust of Jewish nationalists, and his life-long association with leaders of classical Reform Judaism made his support of anti-Zionism inevitable. He rejected any accomplishments of the Jewish settlement, the *Yishuv*, in Palestine, including those which were apolitical in nature. Earlier, in 1914, he scorned the furor over the intended language of instruction at the Haifa Technical Institute, or Technicum, as it was then called. He was less concerned with whether courses were to be conducted in Hebrew or in German than with the seemingly astounding notion that Jewish Nationalists ought to establish a scientific school in the first instance. He had boasted that of the entire B'nai B'rith executive, he alone was "unalterably opposed" to the "whole scheme."[11] He charged the Zionists with being paradoxical. Presumably, they persisted in their obstinate adherence to Orthodox Judaism, while they drew on the financial resources of the Reform Movement to sustain them in their "Zionist craze." His hatred for Zionism was so intense that he managed to regard both religious Jews and secular ones as misguided half-wits. For this reason, in his estimation, Palestine would always be plagued by temporary plans, lacking in solid achievements. No good would come of all those insubstantial changes hatched by the "Russian-Zionistic-Anarchistic and Socialist elements." He was convinced that living in New York, close to "that hotbed of Zionist activity," was what had impaired Schiff's judgment. Wolf simply could never comprehend how or why Schiff was so generous in sustaining Jewish institutions and enterprises in Palestine. Wolf had nightmares lest a "compact" body of Jews in Palestine advocate any cause whatsoever that would in turn lead to a "calamity for Jews everywhere."[12]

Neither Wolf's derision, nor B'nai B'rith's indecision stopped the fated swell of sympathy for the Zionist cause. Having successfully rallied Jews of all sorts of opinions under Brandeis's leadership, the Zionists literally forced the members of the American Jewish Committee to meet with them in executive session. Both Zionist and non-Zionist at last agreed that any convocation ought to seek full freedom for the persecuted. But Marshall, Straus, and their friends were determined to limit the talk to removing civil disabilities where applicable and to postponing the official opening of an American Jewish Congress until after the war had ended. Though personal animosities still delayed the final decision, all parties soon realized that compromise was essential. No one institution would be able to withstand defeat—the Committee because it lacked popular support, and the Congress Organization

Committee because it lacked funds. Thus the terms for a future congress included more democratic methods of representation, which irritated the Committee members, and limitations on discussing theories, or philosophies, which irked the Zionists. At the same time, however, a temporary congress was to be convened before hostilities would cease. Where the issues were pertinent, Jews were prepared to discuss group rights. Later, Marshall amended this term to "people's rights" to calm the sensitivities of German Jews who were frightened by any implications that they may have constituted a separate body politic. [13]

In this connection it is well to recall that Kohler and Wolf's work, *Jewish Disabilities in the Balkan States*, was published in 1916 under the auspices of the American Jewish Historical Society. This was a scholarly group, which included Wolf among its founding members. The society's roster bore the names of some of the leading intellectuals of the day, men such as Cyrus and Mayer Sulzberger, Oscar Straus, Kohler, Louis Marshall, Cyrus Adler, and others, all of them staunch advocates of the American Jewish Committee. *Jewish Disabilities in the Balkan States* had not only their blessing, but also that of the Board of Delegates on Civil and Religious Rights of the Union. At least officially, its chairman, Wolf, had coauthored the book. Though he modestly declined to admit even a minimal share in the effort, by his signature he reestablished the primacy German Jews had already achieved in trying to safeguard civil, political, economic, and religious rights for Jews in Europe's southern and eastern tiers. Long ago, Wolf had been involved with his good friend Peixotto in trying to mitigate the suffering to which Romanian Jews, as a group, had been subjected. The record of their past achievements in *Jewish Disabilities* could well have refuted the criticisms of the Congress people and the Zionists that German Jews cared little for the collective nature of others who shared their faith, and sometimes even their fate. [14]

Although Wolf was an avowed anti-Zionist, his position in the Jewish community assured him delegate status at any future congress. On that score Kraus had gone to great lengths to avoid offending Wolf, so that Marshall was obligated to invite the old man. Yet Wolf remained strangely silent about the whole incident. Instead, he informed Kohler that at the proper time B'nai B'rith would appoint its own commission to deal with "securing equal rights for Jews at the peace table." [15]

By the summer of 1917, Wolf imagined that this state had already been achieved, and he was therefore determined to disassociate himself from the Congress movement. Wolf argued that the Russian Revolution had already attained its happy goal for a newly democratized Russia, and that Romanian promises of equal freedom for its Jewish minority would invalidate any new attempts at liberation. It would strain the reader's credulity to think that Wolf, clever and perceptive as he seemed to have been, would place his trust in Romania. Only a year before, he had accepted the premise of his *Jewish*

Disabilities with its unrelenting record of Romanian anti-Semitism clearly documented through 1913. He could perhaps have been forgiven his optimism over the Russian turn of events. With countless other Jews, he too rejoiced in the hope that the Kerensky government in Russia would introduce parliamentary reforms. But his faith in Romania at best served as a pro forma excuse for refusing to attend a congress session. A more valid reason was Wolf's other contention—that since America was now a belligerent, talks of Jewish equality before a settlement could be reached were premature. Earlier, the American Jewish Committee had arrived at a similar conclusion, based, however, on dissimilar circumstances. Its argument had been that this country's neutrality, and Wilson's antiannexation policy, outlawed the need for considering the Jewish position in Europe and the Near East. History now enabled it to refurbish its earlier image of noninvolvement. Before the end of the war, it would appear imprudent to convoke any large, official gathering in the name of resolving the "Jewish problem." Indeed, America's entry into World War I freed many anti-Zionists, such as Wolf, and some non-Zionists from having to face up to Jewish demands accepting Zionist premises. Wolf, Marshall, and the others would not now have to agree to scheduling a congress where their nationalistically inclined brethren would embarrass them with questions casting doubt on Jewish loyalty to the government of the United States. For how could patriotic citizens even dream of being involved in peace negotiations when their country was still at war? Wolf's second argument for postponing a meeting of the American Jewish Congress was that "the government sent a Commission to Palestine."[16]

Wolf was unaware of its secret nature.[17] It had been devised by Henry Morgenthau, former Ambassador to Turkey, who imagined that by speaking privately to certain Turkish diplomats, he could neutralize Turkish fears of Germany, whose two warships had trained their guns on Constantinople. Morgenthau was intrigued with the possibilities of his own diplomatic clout. Were he able to persuade the Turks into signing a separate peace treaty with the Allies, then the German naval vessels would be removed, and the allied naval forces would be able to retaliate against German submarines. The convoluted nature of such a maneuver demanded that it be kept secret. Its cover would be that a commission had been delegated to investigate the conditions of the Jews in Palestine. Earlier, there had been reports of Turkish massacres of Jews in the Holy Lands, which the Germans vigorously denied. Publicly, then, the Morgenthau Mission called for considering the Jewish situation on humanitarian grounds. All that was necessary now to corroborate Wolf's view was that here was an American commission, dedicated to the safety of the Jews in Palestine. What need was there then for a Congress? Of course, Wolf was unaware of the dark diplomacy in which Morgenthau was about to engage. Privately, he was to meet with representatives of the Allied Powers to decide on a future course in their relations with Turkey. He had already prepared for this conference in earlier conversations with Turkey's prime minister, Talaat. At that time Morgenthau presented some harebrained scheme in which Palestine would be bought for the Zionists. Since any planned parley would have to include them, Morgenthau wanted Felix Frankfurter, a member of the Advisory Board of the Provisional Zionist Executive Committee, to accompany him to Gibraltar, the proposed setting for the session. Secretary of State Lansing accepted Morgenthau's suggestion that Frankfurter be present. The secretary also agreed to Morgenthau's second stipulation. To prevent the Zionists from passing resolutions condemning the Turkish atrocities, postponing the Congress had become a necessity. But under no circumstances was Brandeis to know that delaying the assembly was Morgenthau's original idea.[18]

In his ignorance, Wolf thought happily that such a change was the result of his overweening influence. On 11 June 1917 he sent a letter to President Wilson, asking his opinion about the wisdom "of holding a Congress at the present juncture." He went on to tell the president that any such assembly "would embarrass the government." Delegates there would make statements that "might seriously affect the situation," or "would damage the interests of the Jews in the United States."[19] Three days later the president's secretary, Joseph P. Tumulty, telephoned Wolf to tell him that the president "concurred . . . in the opinion as to the advisability of postponing the Congress." Though he was not eager to "rush into print," Wolf transmitted the presidential information to Kraus, Schiff, Marshall, and Judge Julian W. Mack. Prodded by his good friend and avid Zionist, Rabbi Stephen S. Wise, Kraus called Wolf again to make certain that there were no misunderstandings regarding Wilson's statement. Wolf, in turn, was reassured by Tumulty that the president had indeed thought it prudent to postpone the American Jewish Congress. Wise was livid and rushed to the White House. There, on 29 June 1917, Wilson reassured him that while the congress effectively served both Jewish and American interests, the "urgency of public business [would necessitate its] postponement." The president had used Wolf's message for administration purposes. Never was there any mention of Morgenthau's mission. But Wilson made certain to tell Wise that if Wolf's judgment were correct—holding a Congress would be detrimental to American interests—then the meeting had better not take place.[20]

The incident alerted Wise to the dangers posed by "poor, dear, old Simon Wolf." His "measure [having] been taken" . . . "neither more nor less harmlessly benevolent he, nor his rather more malevolent allies will have any opportunity to be heard hereafter on any Jewish question without their statements being . . . checked . . . by men whom the White House trusts." For the moment this sounded like scant consolation indeed.

Having relayed this account of the matter to Harry Cutler of Providence, R.I., a prominent legislator, Wise also thanked Kraus "for averting the evil that would have come to pass had it gone unchallenged."[21]

Meanwhile, the Morgenthau mission, which occasioned the president's telephone message (he had cautioned Tumulty against writing it down) and indirectly buoyed Wolf's hopes, came to resemble an opéra bouffe. Lansing received a hurried statement from the British Foreign Office on 14 June 1917, saying that the purpose of the mission was now public knowledge, and that both Armenians and Zionists objected to it. They feared that the plan would endanger the separate aspirations of their respective peoples to carve out independent states on the lands of the former Ottoman empire. Then, the British Foreign Office, eager to protect its sphere of influence in the Near East, sent Chaim Weizmann down to talk Ambassador Morgenthau out of doing anything precipitate. Weizmann succeeded, and the mission reduced itself to passing the time of day in trivialized social amenities.[22]

Wilson's views on Jews and Zionism have occasioned much comment. But his response concerning the Congress, his delay in endorsing the Balfour Declaration as the British Foreign Office desired, and the fact that Wilson's alter ego, Colonel House, maintained ambiguous attitudes to Jews and Zionism, are indications that Wilson was first and foremost the president of the United States. Whoever reached him with a plausible plan to protect American interests gained his sympathy: Wolf, with the notion that Americans at the American Jewish Congress might make some statements that were injurious to the war effort; Morgenthau via Lansing that political comments on Turkish atrocities in Palestine would undermine a contemplated peace with the Ottoman empire; and Colonel House, who sometimes worried about the "many dangers lurking in the Zionist movement." Most researchers of the period, moreover, agree that such positive attitudes as Wilson developed toward Zionism grew not only from his own religious background, but were carefully nurtured by Justice Brandeis.[23]

Wilson did in fact greet the Zionist movement with a warm acknowledgment of the "birth of new ideals, of new ethical values, of new conceptions of social justice." Yet nagging doubts remain as to the extent of his devotion to the cause. That speech was delivered after a ten-month delay in his administration's approval of the Balfour Declaration. It permitted Rabbi Stephen S. Wise and other Zionist leaders to hope that their goals were at last about to be realized, but Wilson spoke after he had been informed that the German government was intent on securing Zionist support. An overwhelming bit of evidence, which would indeed confirm an ambivalent presidential approach to the entire Zionist issue, was Wilson's response to an inquiry by Ambassador Walter Hines Page, the American minister to London. Page wanted to know how American Jewry reacted to the Balfour Declaration. Wilson responded by showing him a torn leaf from the *Reader's Digest* summarizing pro- and anti-Zionist attitudes.[24]

It bears remembering that when Wilson issued his pro-Zionist declaration, on 31 August 1918, the British campaign in Palestine was succeeding, and for all practical purposes America was not at war with Turkey. Therefore, a sympathetic public hailed Wilson as the harbinger of a new peace,[25] while for the president's benefit, anti-Zionists, Wolf included, excoriated Zionist policy.

Instead of a national home for Jews in Palestine, Wolf's cause célèbre had been, like that of other anti-Zionists, the dream of equal rights for all men everywhere, including Jews. Oscar Straus, as one of the moving spirits in the Jewish Publication Society, had sponsored Max Kohler's "Jewish Rights at the Congress of Vienna," an essay that was to serve as a clarion call affirming Jewish rights to legal equalities on an international basis. Though Wolf, as seen, denied any meaningful share in the preparation of another work by Kohler, *Jewish Disabilities in the Balkan States*, he remained staunchly loyal to the premises inherent in both treatises. The law demanded equality for Jews in the Balkan States, and by implication, recognition for all Jews everywhere to the prerogatives of citizenship, without any formal acknowledgment of the effects of nationalism upon the Jews in the lands of Eastern Europe. Ultimately, certain members of the American Jewish Committee had to accept the concept of group rights insofar as the Jewish delegations at the Paris Peace Conference were concerned. This became the burden of Marshall's efforts at the convocation.[26] Wolf, however, insisted on distinguishing between an individual's rights to freedom and the justifications of a collective body to the equal privileges of citizenship. He turned a deaf ear to Marshall's pleas for unity among Jews. Nothing that Marshall said could assuage the octogenarian. Even if such cooperation among disparate individuals within the American Jewish community meant keeping silent on Zionist efforts to establish Palestine as a "centre (not the centre) for Jewish learning and culture," Wolf would not refrain from disparaging comments. In vain did Marshall explain that he too "refused to recognize the possibility of dual allegiance," but that the term "national rights" might be the only method by which Jews, along with the other nationalities of Eastern Europe, could be helped to "attain their civil, religious, and political rights." But Wolf had earlier dismissed such claims with his own obiter dictum that "never before . . . (in world history) have Jews as citizens . . . (of their respective countries) been more influential or have played a greater role in shaping the destinies of mankind than at this present moment without losing their identity as Jews, or without forfeiting their loyalty to the heritage which has been transmitted to them." As evidence of their supposedly exalted influence he cited its effects in "England, France, Germany, Austria, and Italy," and threw in "free Russia," which had effectively rid itself of czarist shackles.[27]

It was almost as though Wolf wrote these words for posterity, so that his peroration included the usual argument that young Jews "must enlist not as Jews, but as the great bodyguard of perfecting and maintaining republican institutions." He would allow those who wished to "migrate to Jerusalem or any other place in the world, to do so individually, or as a colony." But to foster or "advocate the creating of a state which would become the buffer of other states and be the constant target for attack" he felt was detrimental to everything Jews and Judaism represented. Together with Dr. David Philipson, Rabbi Henry Berkowitz, Max Senior, and Professor Marcus Jastrow, all leaders in Reform Judaism, Wolf honestly believed that anti-Semitism would intensify both in Palestine and in the emerging states of postwar Europe were Jews to be regarded as a national entity. Taking a leaf from Zebulon Vance's address "The Scattered Nation," Wolf asked that the Jews be the "gulf-stream for all nations, purifying, ennobling, and exalting the people" it comes into contact with.[28] Here was the same old cry of Reform Judaism's mission to improve the world being used as a weapon against any reinterpretation of Jewish nationalism. Reconstituting the Jews as an identifiable collectivity had to be demolished at all costs. For Wolf and his colleagues, the Zionist determination to turn Palestine into a Jewish state became the ultimate treachery. Its consequences would cast into doubt the patriotic loyalty of all other Jews in their respective lands in the Diaspora, and jeopardize the legitimate Arab claims to ethnic identity in the Holy Land.

Such notions formed the burden of an anti-Zionist petition hand-delivered to President Wilson in March 1919, when the chief executive had returned from Paris for a brief stay in this country. Though he was now eighty-two years old, Wolf had lent his name to this last-ditch effort to invalidate the Zionist purpose. As early as January 1918 he and Philipson had discussed the possibility of convening an anti-Zionist assembly whose deliberations would produce an appropriate resolution condeming the Jewish nationalists, a statement to be presented at a future peace conference. Philipson then contacted J. Walter Freiberg, president of the Union of American Hebrew Congregations, who had already written to Wolf on the issue. But Wolf's own hopes for fashioning a dramatic "non-Zionistic" statement were dashed once Philipson informed him that others were already at work on such a critique. A conference would therefore prove unnecessary. To assuage Wolf, Philipson assured him that his name would be suggested as one of the signers of that historic message. Berkowitz, Senior, and Jastrow, who was to draft the anti-Zionist manifesto, Philipson continued, had already consulted him for his expertise on the subject, so that Wolf would not have to take any further action. Philipson, Berkowitz, and their colleagues then enlisted the aid of a congressman from California, Julius Kahn of San Francisco, who had reneged on his earlier belief in the Zionist cause, to present the petition to President Wilson. The statement itself appeared in the *New York Times* on 5 March 1919, and was then deposited by Kahn, Ambassador Henry Morgenthau, and Rabbi Isaac Landman with the American Peace Commissioners at Paris.[29] But Wolf had to be content with having his signature appended to the document.

This must have been a bitter pill for him to swallow, the more so since a

later communication from Berkowitz asked Wolf to append a list of prominent anti-Zionists who might be invited to a convention. To bolster his need
for calling an assembly, Berkowitz enclosed a tirade against Zionism from his
British ally, Claude G. Montefiore, who fulminated against the "insane folly
of Wise and Company . . ." and worried about an "enormous increase in
Anti-Semitism." Montefiore could not understand how Berkowitz and the
others permitted such a state of affairs to continue, without some "grand
protest." Yet Philipson's advice against holding a meeting made it impossible
for Wolf to act. Why Berkowitz should have asked for a "powerful and
impressive demonstration to commend attention," when he himself was part
of that original group that thought an assembly unnecessary, is inexplicable,
unless, of course, he and Philipson had decided to call a later meeting.[30]

Such consolation then as Wolf could derive in his declining years was that
the diehards of the anti-Zionist movement had still to acknowledge his
presence. Sometimes his antinationlist paranoia made itself felt in other
quarters too. As late as October 1919, ex-President Taft, apparently impressed with Wolf's approach to Zionism, wrote:

> I do not hear encouraging account of the proposal to colonize Palestine
> with Jews. It is reported to me that the present occupants, the Syrians
> and the Arabs are in a state of rebellion against it. What do you hear?[31]

Taft's references echoed the general tenor of anti-Zionist reports, which
had begun to grow in intensity in 1918 and 1919. Such views were the
considered judgments of Christian missionaries. In addition, State Department personnel drew comfort from the internecine squabbles over Zionist
philosophies between American and European Jews. Such disparate approaches to the Zionist program heartened the Arab propagandists. The
latter, together with other anti-Jewish proponents, acquired the chance to
plead their cause once Wilson refused to be bound by secret agreements
between England and France for partitioning Turkey. The president believed
that the only course to pursue was "scientific settlement" based on justice for
the native populations. They alone were to determine their future political
configurations. Since the Allied Powers wrangled among themselves as to
who should constitute a commission of inquiry to determine the needs of the
indigenous populations, Wilson decided to dispatch an investigative group
under American auspices to Syria and Palestine. His instructions were given
to members of the American delegation, technically known as the American
Section of the Interallied Commission on Mandates in Turkey, more popu-
larly called the King-Crane Commission. Its appointees included men for
whom the Balfour Declaration was an alien document. Their technical
adviser was William Yale, who thought he detected separatist and negative
tendencies in Zionism. He saw only bitterness and factionalism among Jews,

Christians, and Moslems, if a Jewish National Home were to be implemented. The results of the King-Crane Commission were not publicized until much later, but the opinions of these leaders made their case against the Zionist presence in the land a foregone conclusion.[32]

The opposition that Zionists faced in many quarters were matched by the difficulties that non-Zionists, led by Louis Marshall as the spokesman for the Jewish delegations, encountered in their meetings with the American peace commissioners at Paris. In the final wording of the draft proposals, representatives of the Wilson administration at Paris did recognize certain aspects of the Jewish point of view. Clauses in the new Minority Treaties now regarded Jews in the emerging states of Eastern Europe as an ethnic group, assured of directing autonomous cultural, social, and religious institutions. Yet after many confrontations, when representatives of the new states signed their various agreements, they did so protesting alleged intrusions upon their sovereignty. These, they felt, were implicit in those clauses giving Jews certain unique privileges. On paper, then, while these "Minorities Treaties assured citizens who differed from the majority of the population in the new and enlarged states, group rights in religious, civic, and political spheres," in reality, Wilson's principles of freedom and justice for all regardless of race, religion, or origin were to become matters for international appeal. Only member nations of the League Council would be able to call the organization's attention to infractions of intranational rights. Moreover, only a majority of the Council of the League of Nations would be empowered to make any changes in the Minorities Treaties. Differences between the League and the signatories to the Treaties would have to be "submitted to the Court of International Justice." Max Kohler realized the impending failures in such a system, but blamed the Jews of Eastern Europe for this state of affairs because of the insistent demands of Jewish nationalists for rights to identifiable ethnic privileges.[33]

Certainly, Wolf was as perceptive as Kohler, and as skilled a negotiator with the power brokers in Washington. It could only then have been the ingrained habits of a lifetime that made him overlook the obstacles deliberately placed by the new emerging states of Poland and Romania against fulfilling the religious liberty clauses of the Minority Treaties, guaranteeing freedom to Jews in the expanded territories. It could simply not have been that Wolf was unaware of the future perils Jews faced in Eastern Europe, were the provisos securing their social, cultural, economic, and religious existence to fail. And fail they did. Ultimately, the League of Nations itself foundered, not only because the United States Senate refused to ratify the League's Covenant, but also because the League's jurisdiction was unenforceable. For how could a group logically protest the deprivation of its rights against its own government before an international tribunal? And what state would be a party pledged to listen to its own accusers?[34] Before signing the Minority Treaties both Poland and Romania held out as long as they could against securing any substantial rights for the Jews. Even after these two nations accepted the terms of the Treaties, Poland continued as late as 1922 to engage in an officially sanctioned economic boycott, begun in 1912, against the Jews. For its part, Romania persisted in denying them the option of citizenship by every possible means, including chicanery. But Wolf maintained that Wilsonian principles of international honor and individual freedoms were being implemented. In the fall of 1921 he announced that Poland, in adopting the minority rights clauses, was "beginning to accord to her Jews . . . under desirable conditions . . . full legal rights, though the economic boycott is still in force." He thought that Romania presented "a remarkable picture," one in which Jews, "enjoy all civil, religious, and political rights," a country where Jews were now appointed to teaching and governmental posts. Such trouble as there was, Wolf attributed to that minority among Jews who refused to opt for Romanian citizenship, "claiming Jewish nationality instead."[35]

Facts dictated otherwise. In the year that Wolf penned his report, Jews who had settled in Bukowina, Transylvania, and the Banat were expelled from their homes. Ukrainian Jewish refugees in Romania were being either systematically impoverished or shot by border guards; an anti-Semitic pamphlet was officially circulated in Bucharest; regulations for Jews entering non-Romanian colleges were being hedged about by new restrictions; Romania was willing to have its own Jews emigrate, provided they promised never to return. The lists of such deprivations appeared endless. Perhaps Wolf's sanguine account rested in part on the fact that Romania in 1920 had witnessed no large-scale pogroms, but rather smaller acts of anti-Jewish violence. Furthermore, for 1921, the American Jewish Committee did report that conditions for Jews in Romania had improved somewhat, though four years later Marshall indicated that "hateful discriminations" still abounded in that benighted land.[36]

In trying to account for such negativism, Wolf was one with the anti-Zionists, who viewed prejudice as the result of an unhappy confrontation between the bona fide residents of a country and Jews who insisted upon flaunting their nationalism. For Wolf, Zionists then were defined as members of distrustful groups who refused to participate in the growth of their respective countries. In Wolf's lexicon, whatever failures there were in the execution of the provisions guaranteeing minority rights were to be found in "Zionistic will-o'the-wisps." By the time Marshall recorded his view of "hateful discriminations" plaguing Romania, Wolf had already been dead for two years. During his lifetime Wolf did not comprehend that any postwar amelioration for the Jews in that country was at best temporary, the result of immediate pressures exerted by the Minority Treaties. Furthermore, Wolf was completely in the wrong concerning Poland, where anti-Semitic excesses highlighted the pitiful civil, economic, and political plight of the Jews in that nation. Yet like Ambassador Henry Morgenthau, sent by this country to investigate conditions in Poland, Wolf believed that Polish Jews had only themselves to blame for their nationalism, which led the citizenry of that country to ostracize them. Louis Marshall knew better, however, and detailed the gross persecutions to which Polish Jews were sometimes subjected. Instead, for Wolf, Zionism had become an excrescence in the lands of Eastern Europe, and its practitioners equally abnormal or excessive in their alienation from their Christian neighbors. Wolf's mind set was such that he honestly believed that a ghettoized, insular life-style among nationalistic Jews was at the base of all the troubles in their relationships with non-Jews.[37] So paranoid had he become over the Zionist cause that he accused its followers of "pigeon-holing" the report of the King-Crane Commission, that investigative assessment of conditions in Palestine, because it was so detrimental to the aspirations of Jewish nationalists. In this instance, however, that other arch foe of Zionism, Rabbi Isaac Landman, reassured him that the report was not made public because the result would have wrecked the secret agreements made by England and France with the Arab nationalists, and the Zionists, giving Great Britain control over Palestine and Transjordan, and France a free hand in Syria.[38]

Landman's reply provided scant comfort. Events had taken an irrevocable turn. The year 1922 was the year of San Remo, when Britain had been granted the mandate over Palestine with its "national home for the Jewish people." And Wolf was now too old to fight. He would shortly enter upon the last year of his life.

12
The Search for Lasting Recognition

Such a public career, full of measurable achievements, secured Wolf's fame during his lifetime. In his dealings with government officials in Washington he had scored some noteworthy successes, not the least of which was saving more than 100,000 immigrants from deportation.

The very nature of the society he encountered in America made those victories feasible. Here were fluid class lines, where jockeying for position, or for an attainable goal, meant polite, social maneuvering in an open democratic milieu. In such a setting federal representatives from the lowliest subordinate to the president himself were readily available for consultation at all times.

Carl Sandburg relates that streams of visitors continually flowed in and out of Lincoln's office. The president never knew how many callers he might have in one day. Whoever could be accommodated took his or her turn, waiting on the stairwell leading to the presidential suite.[1] When Wolf, for example, wanted to see Lincoln in the matter of the soldier who was to be shot the following morning, the president was there, in his office, at 2:00 A.M., talking with Wolf and Senator Thomas Corwin from Ohio. If Wolf wanted to question a Union general's motives, he had only, having been granted a presidential pass, to ride out to headquarters. If on another occasion, Wolf was perturbed by Secretary of State John Hay's inability to negotiate a naturalization treaty with Romania, there was at least the honor of reading the news on the diplomatic cable before it was publicized.[2]

Such access to the sources of political power was based primarily on a system of careful bargaining, where despite the rewards and failures of the political game, the petitioner had something to offer. Thus, Wolf's visit to Secretary Hay's office was ultimately the result of B'nai B'rith's cooperation in attempts to limit Romanian Jewish immigration to this country.[3] Similarly, back in the early days, Wolf's stumping Ohio and Indiana for the Republican national candidate had brought no assurances that Hayes would abandon his protemperance attitudes, or that he would issue a statement favoring the German ethnic vote. Wolf deemed such measures essential for a meaningful Republican victory;[4] their omissions, however, did not change Wolf's relationship with Hayes. For this reason, even after the loss of his recorder-of-deeds post, Wolf moved on to other sinecures. Schurz had managed to obtain a judgeship for him in the District of Columbia, and thereafter succeeded in having Garfield appoint him consul-general to Egypt.[5] In this instance, Wolf's loyalty to the Republican party had been his contribution in all those quid pro quo arrangements.

Such a system of canceling obligations by bestowing favors was scarcely unique to Wolf. During his brief sojourn in Egypt, his correspondence had been full of requests for social or political commitments of one sort or another. Even General Sherman, of marching-through-Georgia fame, whose record concerning Jews was blemished, sought a personal request from Wolf. Would the consul-general see to the comfort and safety of certain American travelers, friends of Sherman, who wanted to marvel at the wonders of the Nile?[6]

When Wolf returned to the United States from Egypt, the pattern was still the same. Formally, he again became the skilled legal practitioner in the District of Columbia, while he continued to serve on the boards of various local institutions; informally, however, his very presence in the capital, his charm, savoir-faire, and political clout with the German and Jewish communities and with the Republican party brought results. In 1884, Senator Zebulon B. Vance of North Carolina asked Wolf's help in freeing an imprisoned young clerk, who allegedly stole merchandise from his Jewish employers in Sherman, Tex. Vance wanted Wolf to persuade the owners of the emporium to "release the boy guilty or innocent," with the "assurance" that the purloined goods would be restored. Vance recalled that as governor of North Carolina he once pardoned a Jewish prisoner because of the "good character of his race."[7] In his request, the senator had basically repeated what was Wolf's method for incurring and discharging social and political obligations.

Inasmuch as such modes of relying on personal contact to achieve desired ends was common practice, Wolf's success as a minor governmental functionary in appointing others to office should occasion no wonder.

More significant was his ability to wield effective personal influence when he was no longer part of any federal bureaucracy. Commissioner Sargent's comment, "I know Mr. Wolf and esteem him highly," became the watchword for the success of Wolf's persuasive powers. In that instance, Sargent was referring to Wolf's uncanny ability to reverse deportation proceedings for three Romanian families, all of whom had *legally* been candidates for repatriation.[8]

Wolf's faculty for achieving almost impossible goals reached new heights, we may remember, when he interceded directly with the State Department, to obtain the release of an American naturalized Jew from a Russian jail, and to rescind the deportation of three American businessmen, then resident in Memel and Berlin, to Russia.[9]

Equally indicative of the weighty influence Wolf wielded was his participation in revoking a military decision. In 1911 a commanding officer, Col. Gerard, at Fort Meyer Va., reasoned there were "few communities where Jews [would be] received as desirable associates." There was no point then for a Jewish soldier, Frank Bloom, to take the entrance examination to West Point. Wolf brought the case to the attention of President Taft, who ordered an investigation. Secretary of War J. M. Dickinson indicated that the candidate's poor grades on an earlier test should normally have disqualified him, but because of the religious slurs impugning his character, he would be permitted a second examination. Dickinson was prepared to discipline the superior officer involved.[10]

Such official confirmation of Wolf's claims to justice reinforced his conviction that he knew best how to approach those in command. Sometimes, however, there were issues that were too complex for any one individual to contend with. Even Wolf's role as an accredited representative for the Board of Delegates of the Union and B'nai B'rith did not always assure him unqualified success. He had protested bravely against attempts by the National Reform Association to create a christological basis for the Constitution,[11] and countered state legislative procedures to introduce the reading of the Bible into the school curriculum. However, the fact that all sorts of sectarian efforts were constantly being introduced into state and national legislatures[12] was beyond Wolf's control. On one occasion, a colleague of his on the Board of Delegates reported that a measure in the Maryland State Assembly calling for Bible readings in the schools had been defeated, and the chief justice of the North Carolina State Supreme Court, Walter C. Clark, commended Wolf for handily eliminating similar amendments.[13] Yet such initiatives did not change the basic patterns. There were constant attempts to blur the separateness of church and state. When he could reverse such trends, Wolf then took due credit. But these were isolated moments, barely sufficient to gain him lasting fame as a dedicated secularist.

Beyond these problems which were too complex for any one person to confront, Wolf's own intense loyalty to this country made it difficult for him to remain the Jews' impartial advocate. He had always to prove how good the Jew was for America. During the Gilded Age, for example, when anti-Semitism burgeoned forth,[14] he was determined to present the Jews' impeccable behavior as citizens, soldiers, and patriots. Reference has already been made to his book whose title paraphrases this expression. He was convinced that were he to demonstrate numerous instances of bravery by Jews on the battlefield, in Latin American settlements, in the armies of Europe, and during the life of this republic, the specter of hatred for his coreligionists would somehow disappear. He must have imagined that his eagerness to detail the considerable contributions of the Jews to world civilization was contagious. His readers too would become sympathetic to the plight of the Jew through the centuries, and marvel at his intellectual prowess. Yet to expect the disinterested and disaffected to experience a change of heart after perusing *The American Jew as Citizen, Soldier and Patriot* would be asking too much. Praise from the critics for Wolf's *American Jew* notwithstanding,[15] lengthy prose essays, no matter how well-intentioned, do not transform bigots. It is all the more remarkable that so experienced a lawyer, a born politician, could not have recognized such a basic observation. Perhaps he did, and simply refused to acknowledge reality.

Such ease at compartmentalizing his own disparate attitudes can be seen, for example, in several other attempts at half-heartedly defending those who were opposed to changing Russo-American relations. One recalls his ambig-uous letters to Marshall in the matter of abrogating the Russo-American Commercial Treaty. As eary as 1903, he told his good friend, Rabbi Bernhard B. Felsenthal, that the Committee [of congressmen invited to the White House at Wolf's request] "could not accomplish much with the President and Secretary of State" in amending the Russo-American passport controversy. Wolf did, however, hope for a successful outcome,[16] a result constantly anticipated in his annual reports to the Board of Delegates of the Union.[17]

If, on the one hand, Wolf waffled in his attempts to sway the unconvinced, on the other, in his defense of the Jew, both as American citizen and as immigrant, he ascribed the positive actions of the group to the outstanding behavior of its more notable leaders. It is also true that in his ardor to lash out against the anti-Semites,[18] he made certain to isolate the few wayward Jews from the law-abiding members of his faith. But his belief in the suitability of the Jew for this country was so great that the motivations for his criminal behavior were to be laid at the feet of the Christian majority.

> What other condition can you expect among a certain number of . . .
> victims of your hate and antagonisms [than that] there will be found a
> lower strata of humanity . . . [because] Christian churches permit the
> persecution of the Jew as they did the enslavement of the Negro.[19]

It would be difficult to see how so general a condemnation of the religious forces in this country could lend credibility to his conviction that America needed the Jew as a civilizing force for mankind.

The obverse of that principle, which he likewise held dear, that the Jew needed America, worked ultimately to his disadvantage. He sincerely felt that citizens could serve only one civil and political master. He feared that the nationalist sentiments inherent in Zionism would sully the patriotism of

American Jews. Though his apprehensions were not fulfilled, his own entrenched anti-Zionism alienated him from a large segment of the American Jewish community. By the time American Zionism was about to emerge as an international phenomenon, Wolf busied himself with obfuscating its dream. His delaying actions merely angered the idealists and distanced him even from those Reform Jews who preferred to call themselves non-Zionists. His biased defense of those he wished to protect, his inability to do battle with issues that were beyond the purview of any one person, and his hatred of Zionism were but signposts along the way that his name would not long endure. More poignantly, what he had really lent his heart and soul to in his halcyon days died.

Tied inextricably to his vision of America as the ideal land was the righteousness of its trust in the potential of the individual. He had spent the most significant portion of his public life secure in the knowledge that America's freedom was inexorably bound to its welcome for the alien. Yet no sooner had he become the immigrants' champion than his view of this country as the haven for the oppressed began to erode. In the end, he failed because the doors here swung shut. Furthermore, despite his protests against Russian mistreatment of naturalized American Jews, rooting out the consequences of such bigotry was not his victory. That belonged to the American Jewish Committee.

With its formation in 1906, Wolf was no longer able to claim a nationwide constituency. Though the Committee made a great show of principle in lecturing legislators and executives on its prime objectives in the passport controversy, it too, like Wolf, relied on personal contact to achieve its goals. It succeeded because of its emphasis on decisions arrived at collectively.[20] Wolf, however, despite the brilliant legal contributions of his younger colleague Kohler, operated as an individual. This does not deny Wolf's consultations with his peers on matters that were of common interest to the American Jewish community. Yet except for Kohler's work, there were no noteworthy attempts to mold the Board of Delegates to changing times. So effectively had Wolf structured the organization of his Board, that his death would shortly signal its demise.[21]

Having, in short, outlived his usefulness, Wolf would not in the long sweep of American history be forever remembered as one of the outstanding leaders in Jewry. This was unfortunate. For in his lifetime he had labored strenuously and accomplished much on behalf of other human beings. In an attempt to cheer him on in old age, Marshall, who once dubbed Wolf "Lupus Washingtoniensis," now wrote:

> You, of all people should be happy in the respect and honor which you are held, and in looking back at the years of your activity you have only cause for rejoicing that it has been given to you to help your fellowmen.[22]

Throughout the last decade of his life, Wolf may indeed have had the satisfaction of knowing that his was a force to be reckoned with in the corridors of American power. Yet thereafter, as the years of the twentieth century sped by, the number of his admirers who thought of him as the "Nestor of American Jewry"[23] declined. Today, few would know who he was, or what he had accomplished. *Sic transit.*

Notes

Abbreviations Used in Notes

Cyrus Adler Papers, Archives of the American Jewish Committee, New York City	CAP, AAJC
Alliance Israelite Universelle	AIU
American Jewish Archives, Hebrew Union College–Jewish Institute of Religion, Cincinnati, Ohio	AJA
American Jewish Historical Society, Library, Waltham, Mass.	AJHS
American Jewish Historical Society, Publications	PAJHS
American Jewish Historical Society, Quarterly	QAJHS
American Jewish Yearbook	AJYB
Annual Reports of the Board of Delegates on Civil and Religious Rights of the Union of American Hebrew Congregations	*Annual Reports . . .* (date)
Board of Delegates of American Israelites	BDAI Files
Philip Cowen Papers, American Jewish Historical Society, Library, Waltham, Mass.	PCP
Hamilton Fish Papers, Library of Congress, MS Division General Records of the Department of State National Archives Record Group	HFP NARG HFP
General Records of the Department of State, National Archives Record Group	NARG
Rutherford B. Hayes Papers, Library, Freemont, Ohio	RBH
Hebrew Immigrant Aid Society	HIAS
Jewish Scientific Institute, New York City	YIVO
Jewish Social Studies	JSS
Max J. Kohler Papers, at either AJHS or AJA as indicated	MJKP
Adolph Kraus Papers, AJA	AKP

Louis Marshall Papers, at either AAJC or AJA as indicated   LMP

Benj. F. Peixotto Papers are mostly at the AJHS; if not, either
NARG or RBH will be indicated   BFPP

Proceedings of the Council of the Union   *Proceedings*

Theo. Roosevelt Papers, Library of Congress, MS Division   TRP

Jacob H. Schiff Papers, Schiff Collection, AJA   JHSP

Carl Schurz Papers, Library of Congress, MS Division   CSP

State Department Files, Washington, D.C.   SDF

Cyrus Sulzberger Papers   CSP AAJC

Mayer Sulzberger Papers   MSP AAJC

Wm. Howard Taft Papers, Library of Congress, MS Division   WHTP

Wm. Williams Papers, New York Public Library, MS Division   WW Papers, New York

Woodrow Wilson Papers, Library of Congress, MS Division   WWP

Simon Wolf Papers
   at American Jewish Historical Society   SWP AJHS

   at American Jewish Archives   SWP AJA

Introduction

1. Max Kohler, "Simon Wolf," *AJYB* 5685 (1924–25), pp. 404–19; D. H. & E. L. Panitz, "Simon Wolf as United States Consul to Egypt," *PAJHS* 47 (1957): 76–100; idem, "Simon Wolf: Liberty under Law" (Washington, D.C.: Jewish Tercentenary Comm., 1955), pp. 1–17; E. L. Panitz, "In Defense of the Jewish Immigrant, 1897–1924," in *Jewish Experience in America*, ed. A. J. Karp (New York: Ktav, 1969), 4:31–62; idem, "The Polarity of Jewish Attitudes towards Immigration, 1891–1924," *Experience*, 5:23–61; idem., "Simon Wolf," in *Encyclopedia Judaica* (1974), 16:408; Albert Vorspan, *Giants of Justice* (New York: Thos. Y. Crowell, 1960), pp. 3–21; D. H. Panitz to Leonard Hall, 2 Mar. 1956; Floyd McCaffree to Panitz, 9 Feb. 1956, in author's personal possession.

2. Wolf to R. B. Hayes, 22 June and 14 Sept. 1876, Abe L. Nebel Collection, RBH; Wolf to Roosevelt, 12 Oct. 1904; Wolf to Taft, 23 June 1908, SWP, AJA.

3. Wolf, *The American Jew as Patriot, Soldier and Citizen* (Philadelphia: Levytype Co., 1895), pp. 1–576; idem, *The Presidents I Have Known from 1860 to 1918* (Washington, D.C., 1918), pp. 1–459; idem, *Some of the Personal Reminiscences at Home and Abroad* (Washington, D.C., 1914), pp. 1–38; *Selected Addresses and Papers of Simon Wolf* (Cinn: Union of American Hebrew Congregations, 1926), pp. 30–306.

4. *Washington Star*, 28 Oct. 1921, SWP; Panitz, "Liberty under Law," pp. 12–13.

5. Kohler, "Wolf," p. 411; *Baltimore Jewish Times*, 15 June 1923; *Jewish Review and Observer*, 15 June 1923; *London Jewish Chronicle*, 15 June 1923; *Washington Star*, 5 and 9 June 1923, SWP, AJHS; Panitz, *Encyclopedia*, sup.; idem, "Liberty under Law," pp. 12–13, SWP.

6. Frank J. Coppa and Thos. J. Curran, "From the Rhine to the Mississippi: The German Immigration to the United States," in *The Immigration Experience in America*, ed. Coppa and Curran (Boston: Twayne, 1976), p. 59. By 1900 the German-American Alliance was the largest ethnic organization in this country; see also R. Baker Harris to D. H. Panitz, 9 July 1956. The Wolf Collection in the Washington, D.C. Library of the Supreme Council 330 of the Free-

masons contains 800 volumes of Hebraica, 450 of which are in German. Wolf donated these
books in 1909; they include the *Jewish Encyclopedia* (1904), the Babylonian Talmud, Gratz's
History of The Jews, The Menorah Monthly, and *The Occident.*

7. Marshall to J. H. Schiff, 9 Feb. 1911, Chas. Reznikoff, *Louis Marshall, Champion of
Liberty* (Philadelphia: Jewish Publication Society, 1957), 1:77; Marshall to Herbert Friedenwald, 2 Dec. 1912, LMP, AAJC.

8. Marshall to Friedenwald, sup.

9. See chap. 10, n. 52–55.

10. Vorspan, sup.

Chapter 1. The Urban and Urbane Politico

1. Messages to Harry Fischel, Chrmn., Simon Wolf Banquet, Nov. 1916, *HIAS* Papers,
YIVO Archives.

2. *Jewish Immigration Bulletin* 6 (1916): 2–13.

3. Panitz, "Liberty under Law," pp. 1, 5–9, 11–12.

4. Elbert Aidline, "Simon Wolf at Eighty," *American Hebrew,* 20 Oct. 1916, p. 839.

5. *American Hebrew,* 27 October 1916, p. 886.

6. Ibid., 20 Oct. 1916, p. 839.

7. T. V. Powderly, "To Simon Wolf at Eighty," *American Hebrew,* 27 October 1916, p. 875;
Jewish Immigration Bulletin 6 (1916): 2.

8. *American Hebrew,* pp. 874–75, 893.

9. Panitz, "Liberty under Law," pp. 10–12.

10. Wolf, "Fifty Years at Home and Abroad," *The Temple* 2 (1898): 8, SWP.

11. See below, chap. 8, nn. 22–25; chap. 12, nn. 14–16. Wolf was particularly concerned
with Haym Salomon's patriotism having gone unrewarded. In "Are Republics Ungrateful?" (Feb.
1893), SWP, he urged federal payment of the debts then due Salomon's heirs. See Wolf,
American Jew, pp. 24–26.

12. Panitz, "Liberty under Law," p. 1.

13. Wolf, *Reminiscences,* p. 10; Panitz, "Wolf as Consul," p. 83; see also, Introduction, n. 5.

14. Wolf, "Fifty Years," p. 7.

15. "Youthful Reminiscences," n.d., SWP.

16. Rachel Mann Wertheimer, *The Review* 6 (1910): 14.

17. "Description of Cleveland in 1848," Speech, 3 May 1912; Peixotto et al., Testimonial to
Wolf, 7 Aug. 1861, Cleveland, Young Men's Hebrew Literary Society, SWP.

18. "'Auld Lang Syne,' Reminiscences of Chicago," 1923, SWP.

19. *Jewish Exponent,* 31 July 1891, p. 1.

20. Ibid., pp. 1–2; Wolf, *Presidents,* p. 3; "Reminiscences of Cleveland," n.d., SWP. At the
Democratic convention, in 1860, President Buchanan personally greeted each one of the
delegates, including Wolf, who was serving as an alternate. Cf. Isaac Markens, *The Hebrews in
America* (New York, 1888), p. 235. Wolf may well have met Stephen Douglas because of
Peixotto, who, as editor of the *Cleveland Plain Dealer,* was on "close terms" with Douglas until
the latter's death in 1861.

21. Wolf, "Fifty Years," p. 7.

22. Ibid., p. 8.

23. *Jewish Exponent,* p. 2.

24. Ibid., p. 2; see also *Jewish Independent,* 8 June 1923, SWP. Caroline Hahn was the
sister of Herman Hahn, who later became president of the Michael Reese Hospital in Chicago.

25. Kohler, p. 405; *American Hebrew* 24 (1916): 840. Before starting his legal career Wolf
had entered into a business partnership with Marks S. Mayer, his future brother-in-law, and
with Adam Baum.

26. "Reminiscences of 1861," SWP.

27. Ibid.; *Jewish Exponent*, p. 2.

28. *Jewish Messenger*, 11 Dec. 1863, p. 200.

29. Wolf, "Reminiscences of 1861," SWP.

30. *Jewish Messenger*, 24 Jan. 1862.

31. Carl Sandburg, *Abraham Lincoln: The War Years* (New York: Scribner's 1945), 3:163–68.

32. *A Partial Outline of Jews and Jewish Institutions*, n.d., Archives, Washington Hebrew Congregation, Washington, D.C.

33. *Jewish Messenger*, 24 Jan. 1862.

34. Cyrus Adler and A. M. Margalith. *With Firmness in the Right: American Diplomatic Action Affecting Jews, 1840–1945* (New York: American Jewish Committee, 1946), pp. 299–322.

35. "Reminiscences of 1861"; *Presidents*, pp. 9–11.

36. *Occident* 20 (1863): 496–97; *Presidents*, pp. 35–43.

37. *Occident* 26 (1868): 225–36; Markens, pp. 233–44.

38. *Jewish Times*, 12 Nov. 1869, p. 9.

39. Address, Washington Literary and Dramatic Association, pp. 4–5, SWP.

40. "Reminiscences of 1861."

41. "Lincoln, An Appreciation by Simon Wolf," Republican National League House, Washington, D.C., Feb., 1888; *National Jewish Monthly*, Feb. 1956, p. 8. See also Gen. Benj. F. Butler to Myer S. Isaacs, 9 April 1864, BDAI Files, AJHS. These refer to Nathan Grossmayer's having secured a pardon for Morris Waldauer, who had gone AWOL to visit his dying mother. Lincoln did pardon many deserters. The universality of this practice must have lent a legendary air to more than one such incident of brave, heartsick boys and their terminally ill parents.

42. Penciled note on white-lined paper, 24 Aug. 1862, SWP. See also Wm. S. McFeely, *Grant: A Biography* (New York: W. W. Norton, 1981), pp. 183–84.

43. "Reminiscences of 1861"; *Presidents*, pp. 9–11. Wolf indicates that his arrest took place at the "height of the war." Soon after he reached Washington, he began to represent Jews who were accused of being blockade runners. By December of that year, the Jews as a class were indicted for engaging in illegal trade across Union and Confederate lines. See n. 23; see also Bertram W. Korn, *American Jewry and the Civil War* (Philadelphia: Jewish Publication Society, 1951), pp. 169–71, for the view that Baker harbored anti-Semitic prejudices.

44. Panitz, "Liberty under Law," p. 3; Korn, pp. 121–24; Sandburg, 3:15.

45. Rob't Scott et al., *Wars of the Rebellion: Official Records of the Union and Confederate Armies* (Washington, D.C.: GPO, 1890–91), 1:17, pt. 2, p. 424; Panitz, "Liberty under Law," p. 7.

46. Korn, p. 137. Korn believes that Wolf must have seen "the delegation from Paducah." Yet given Wolf's gregariousness and his need to be visible in all matters pertaining to the Jewish community, he would certainly have mentioned the Kaskel group in his papers. Since, currently, there seems to be no reference to these leaders, either he did not meet with them or perhaps, more simply, was never consulted. Years later, however, in his *Presidents*, he did recall his protests in the matter of Order no. 11. (See below, nn. 47, 48.)

47. *Occident* 20 (1863): 496–97.

48. Korn, p. 164; Sandburg, 1:279; *Jewish Messenger*, 26 Feb. 1864, p. 60.

49. *Presidents*, pp. 35–43; Korn, pp. 158–74; Panitz, "Liberty under Law," p. 4.

50. Wm. S. Hesseltine, *Ulysses S. Grant, Politician* (New York: Frederick Ungar, 1935), chap. 5; McFeely, pp. 266–73; Wm. Starr Myers, *The Republican Party: A History* (New York: 1928), pp. 160–79.

51. Myers, pp. 180–97; Hesseltine, pp. 116–30; See David H. Donald, *The Republican Party, 1864–76, History of U.S. Political Parties*, ed. A. M. Schlesinger, Jr. (New York: Chelsea House, 1973), pp. 126ff., for Republican attempts to unite the party nationally.

52. *Presidents*, p. 64.

53. Wolf, *Selected Addresses and Papers*, pp. 102, 104.

54. *Presidents*, pp. 51–53, 60–62; *Reminiscences*, pp. 7–9.

55. *Presidents*, pp. 64–70.

56. Joseph Lebowich, "General Ulysses S. Grant and the Jews," *PAJHS* 17 (1909): 74–76; Korn, pp. 138–44. Like Lebowich, Korn contends that Grant himself was responsible for Order No. 11.

57. *Presidents*, p. 69.

58. Donald, p. 1283.

59. Korn, pp. 134–35, 277; *Hebrew Leader*, 4 Sept. 1868, p. 4.

60. *Presidents*, p. 85.

61. Floyd McCaffree, researcher, Republican party, to D. H. Panitz, 9 Mar. 1957, in author's personal possession.

62. Naomi W. Cohen, *Encounter with Emancipation: The German Jews in the United States, 1830–1914* (Philadelphia: Jewish Publication Society), pp. 150–52; Korn, p. 134.

63. Hesseltine, pp. 159–60.

64. *Presidents*, p. 73; Riddle to Hamlin, 11 Dec. 1868, SWP AJHS.

65. *Jewish Times*, 6 Mar. 1869, p. 9; Hesseltine, pp. 139–42, 153–55; McFeely, pp. 290–303.

66. *Jewish Times*, 19 Mar. 1869, p. 6.

67. *Presidents*, p. 72; Essay, "Early Relations with President Grant," n.d., SWP.

68. Riddle to Hamlin, 19 Apr. 1869, SWP AJHS.

69. *Senate Executive Journal* 17:201, 241; *Washington Post*, 20 Nov. 1927; *Congressional Record*, Appendix, Apr. 24, 1959, p. 6536, courtesy Recorder of Deeds Office; G. M. Thornell, Sec'y, Board of Commissioner's Office, to D. H. Panitz, 13 Mar. 1957.

70. *Jewish Times*, 30 Apr. 1869, p. 9.

Chapter 2. Recorder of Deeds

1. *Presidents*, p. 73.

2. Ibid., p. 71.

3. Ibid., p. 74.

4. Ibid., p. 97; *Encyclopedia Judaica* 16: 408.

5. *Presidents*, pp. 73–74; *Encyclopedia Judaica* 16: 357.

6. *Presidents*, pp. 88, 90–92; "A Glimpse of Washington," 1904, SWP.

7. *American Hebrew*, 20 Oct. 1916, p. 841. For information on the nature of the recorder-of-deeds post, see chap. 1, n. 69.

8. *Presidents*, pp. 91–92.

9. Wolf to Hayes, 22 June and 24 Sept., RBH; *Presidents*, pp. 84–85; see also chap. 1, n. 61.

10. *American Hebrew*, 20 Oct. 1916, p. 841.

11. Leonard D. White, *The Republican Era, 1869–1901* (New York: Macmillan, 1958), pp. 23–25.

12. See below, nn. 93 and 94.

13. *Jewish Times*, 15 Oct. 1869, p. 5.

14. Ibid., 29 Oct. 1869, p. 6.

15. Panitz, "Attitudes-Immigration," p. 37; Letter to *New York Herald*, 9 Dec. 1869, SWP AJHS; *Jewish Times*, 10 Dec. 1869, pp. 10–11 and 24 Dec. 1869, p. 7. See also ibid., 11 June, p. 9, 20 Aug., p. 7, and 24 Sept. 1869, pp. 4–5, for references to famine and cholera to which these Russian Jews were subjected. Quite aside from the decree banishing them to the interior, these factors made their lives tenuous at best.

16. *Jewish Times*, 24 Dec. 1869, p. 7.

17. Wolf to Editor, *Jewish Times*, 3 Dec. 1869, p. 3. The text of the petition is in M. S. Isaacs to Fish, NARG 59 Miscellaneous Correspondence 2 (1869): 284. See also Evelyn L. Greenberg, "An 1868 Petition on Behalf of Russian Jewry," *Jewish Experience in Africa* 3 (1969): 355–56, for a reprint of the document.

18. *New York Herald*, sup.; *Jewish Times*, 10 Dec. 1869, p. 6. Wolf saw the president's affirmative reply as further evidence of his lack of prejudice.

19. *New York Herald*, sup.; *American Israelite*, 10 Dec. 1869, pp. 10–11.

20. Panitz, "Attitudes-Immigration," pp. 37–38, n. 33.

21. *Jewish Times*, 24 Dec. 1869, p. 3.

22. Andrew G. Curtin to Hamilton Fish, "Memorandum of the Jews in Russia and Especially on Their Removal from Besserabia," *Jewish Times*, 4 Feb. 1870, pp. 6, 8–9; Adler and Margolith, pp. 173–74; Kohler, *The Board of Delegates of American Israelites*, PAJHS, 19 (1925): 51.

23. *Jewish Times*, 4 Feb. 1870.

24. Central Committee of the Alliance Israelite Universelle to Wolf, 7 Jan. 1870; enclosure, courtesy M. Weill, Sec'y, to D. H. Panitz, 28 July 1959. For the original text of the letter, see Panitz, "Attitudes-Immigration," n. 33.

25. Panitz, "Attitudes-Immigration," pp. 31–39; Zosa Szjakowski, "Emigration to Europe or Reconstruction in America," *PAJHS* 47 (1952): 165–67; idem, "The Alliance Israelite Universelle and East European Jewry," *JSS* 4 (1942): 137–55; E. Lifschutz, "An Unsuccessful Effort for a Mass Migration to America," [Yiddish] *Yohrbuch fun Amopteil fun YIVO* (1938), p. 48.

26. Weill to Panitz. When the Nazis captured the Paris office of the Alliance, they destroyed its files. At that time the bulk of the correspondence between Crémieux and Wolf disappeared.

27. *American Israelite*, 10 Dec. 1869, pp. 10–11; Alliance to Wolf, 7 Jan. 1870, enclosure in Weill to Panitz; *Hebrew Leader*, "The Approaching Arrival of Russian Jews in America," 15 Apr. 1870.

28. Cf. Alliance to Wolf, 2 Mar. 1870, enclosure in Weill to Panitz.

29. *Jewish Times*, 1 April 1870, p. 70.

30. Alliance to Wolf, 2 Mar. 1870; see below, chap. 5, nn. 23, 24.

31. *Jewish Times*, 15 Oct. 1869, p. 5.

32. Ibid., 15 Apr. 1870, p. 8.

33. *The Hebrew Leader*, sup., is a prime example.

34. Panitz, "Attitudes-Immigration," p. 39.

35. *Jewish Times*, 15 April 1870, p. 8.

36. *Jewish Messenger*, 6 May 1870.

37. *Jewish Times*, 22 Apr. 1870, p. 20; *Jewish Messenger*, 29 Apr. 1870.

38. *Jewish Times*, 29 Apr. 1870, p. 136; *Jewish Messenger*, 1, 27 Apr. and 6 May 1870.

39. *Presidents*, pp. 72–73; *Jewish Times*, 4 Feb., p. 8, and 11 Feb. 1870, p. 9.

40. *Jewish Times*, 1 Apr. 1870, pp. 225–30.

41. Adler and Margolith, pp. 99–100; Lloyd P. Gartner, "Consul Peixotto in Bucharest," *AJHSQ* 18 (1968): 30–32.

42. NARG 84, Letters Received, vol. 75, HFP.

43. Peixotto to Wolf, 22 Nov. and 26 Dec. 1869, and 9 Mar. 1870, SWP AJHS.

44. Peixotto to Wolf, 22 Nov. 1869, SWP AJHS.

45. Peixotto to Isaacs, 28 June 1870, BDAI Files, AJHS.

46. Gartner, p. 44; Peixotto to Isaacs, 7 June 1870, BDAI Files, AJHS.

47. Peixotto to Wolf, 28 June 1870, SWP AJHS.

48. Peixotto to Isaacs, 7 June 1870, BDAI Files, AJHS.

49. NARG 84 Letters Received, sup., Wolf to Fish, 2 June 1870, asking that Buchner be appointed consul at Bucharest; see also Gartner, pp. 44, 46, 49–50, for the Seligman effort on Peixotto's behalf.

50. Peixotto-Wolf Correspondence, 22 Nov. 1869–28 June 1870, BFP. Peixotto berates Wolf for his seeming lack of interest, first with reference to Peixotto's wish to study law in San Francisco, and second, his desire to secure the Bucharest consulate; see also Markens, pp. 235–36, for Peixotto's associations in Cleveland. See also chap. 1, n. 17, for Peixotto's friendship with Douglas. Note, too, Peixotto et al., *Testimonial Resolution to S. Wolf, Esq. by the Y[oung] M[en's] H[ebrew] L[iterary] S[ociety] of Cleveland,* 7 Aug. 1861 (5621), wishing Wolf success in his new legal venture at New Philadelphia, Ohio. SWP.

51. Wolf to Peixotto, 14 June 1870, enclosure in Wolf to Fish, 21 Dec. 1870, vol. 74, HFP.

52. Peixotto to Wolf, 7 Sept. 1870, SWP.

53. Peixotto to Joseph Seligman, 17 June 1871, Letter Files, vol. 75, HFP.

54. Copy in SWP.

55. Fish to Wolf, 14 Jan. 1871, SWP.

56. Peixotto to Jos. Seligman, 4 Jan. 1871, Letter Files, vol. 75, HFP.

57. Wolf to Fish, 21 Dec. 1870, with enclosure, Wolf to Peixotto, 14 June 1870, vol. 74, HFP.

58. Fish to Wolf, 14 Jan. 1871, Letterbook, HFP.

59. Wolf to Kohler, 1 Feb. 1915 and 4 Nov. 1916, MJKK.

60. Adler and Margalith, pp. 104–6; Wolf to Isaacs, 16 April and 17 Sept. 1872, BDAI Files; #922 Fish to Wolf, with enclosure, 12 April 1872, HFP; Isaacs to Wolf, 29 Mar. 1872, HFP, copy in SWP; *Jewish Messenger,* 19 July, p. 3, 26 July, p. 3, 12 Aug. 1872, p. 2; Wolf and Kohler, *Jewish Disabilities in the Balkan States, PAJHS* 24 (1916): 24.

61. Wolf to Fish, 26 Mar. 1872, SWP.

62. NARG 59 Consular Dispatches, Bucharest vol. 2 (Jan. 10, 1870–Mar. 30, 1881) disp. #15 Peixotto to Grant, Nov. 6 1871 and Peixotto to Wm. C. Clement, Nov. 10, 1871; Peixotto to Wolf, Dec. 20, 1871, with enclosures, Peixotto to W. Hunter, Oct. 14, 1871 and Hunter to Peixotto, June 6, 1871, SWP AJHS.

63. Panitz, "Attitudes-Immigration," pp. 39–40; see also Peixotto to Isaacs, 3 Dec. 1872, BDAI Files, AJHS.

64. *Jewish Messenger,* 19 July, p. 2; 26 July, p. 3, and 2 Aug. 1872. In 1872, Wolf raised $2,000 for the Romanian mission.

65. Peixotto to Wolf, 17 Mar. 1873, SWP.

66. Wolf to Isaacs, 12 May 1873, BDAI Files, AJHS.

67. *Jewish Messenger,* 4 Feb. 1873.

68. Ibid., 11 Apr. 1873.

69. Gartner, pp. 108–14.

70. Peixotto to Wolf, 15 May 1876, SWP; *Memphis Appeal,* 27 Dec. 1876, p. 2; *Cincinnati Enquirer,* 25 Sept. 1876, p. 2; *Ohio State Journal,* 23 Oct. 1877, MJKP.

71. NARG 59 Applications and Recommendations for Office (Benj. F. Peixotto). Peixotto to Gov. Hayes, 8 Oct. 1876; unsigned memorandum [Mar. 1877] that "Mr. Peixotto's appointment has been personally asked by letter and in person by Senators Matthews, [Jon H.] Mitchell, [Aaron A.] Sargent, [Newton] Booth, [Chas. W.] Jones," by numerous congressmen from California, Ohio, was endorsed by Ohio's two former Governors, [Edward F.] Noyes, and Thomas Young, and strongly seconded by prominent citizens from San Francisco, Cincinnati, Cleveland, and New York; Wolf to Kohler, 4 Feb. 1915, MJKP.

72. Cf. NARG 59, L. Austin to [R. B.] Hayes, 17 Nov. 1877, worrying whether Peixotto's "sympathy for the Turks" would constitute an objection to his nomination to St. Petersburg; Peixotto to Hayes, 8 Dec. 1877, RBHP.

73. Peixotto to Hayes, 17 Dec. 1877, asking for an appointment to the consulship at Lyons, France. RBHP.

74. Wolf to Kohler, 4 Feb. 1915.

75. NARG 84, Cons. Disps. Lyons 5–9 (1878–86).

76. Peixotto to Wolf, 8 May 1874, SWP.

77. *Jewish Times*, 4 Apr. 1874, p. 578.

78. Peixotto to Wolf, 13 Mar. and 15 Apr. 1874, SWP.

79. Peixotto to Wolf, 10 Mar. 1873, 8 May 1874, SWP; Wolf to Fish, 21 Dec. 1878, copy, SWP; Wolf to Kohler, 4 Feb. 1915, MJKP.

80. Peixotto to Wolf, 10 Jan. 1872, 20 Dec. 1873, SWP; Peixotto to Wolf, 11 Aug. 1874, SWP.

81. Peixotto to Wolf, 25 Dec. 1881, SWP.

82. *The Story of the Roumanian Mission, Menorah Monthly*, vols. 1–4 (1886–88).

83. See below, n. 87.

84. NARG 59, Peixotto to Blaine, 13 Mar. 1889, BFPP.

85. NARG 59, A. R. Whitney to Benj. Harrison, 11 Mar. 1889, BFPP.

86. NARG 59, Peixotto to Blaine, 11 Mar. 1889.

87. Hannah Strauss Peixotto to Wolf, 5 Oct. 1890. See also Wolf to Philip Cowen, 10 Dec. 1902, PCP. Here Wolf repeats the main areas of his involvement in the Peixotto mission from its very inception until shortly after Peixotto's death.

88. *19th Annual Report* . . . (1892), p. 2883; *Washington Star*, 5 June 1923. Wolf's second wife was Amy Lichtenstein, the niece of Julius Bien, a well-known cartographer and former president of B'nai B'rith. SWP AJHS.

89. *Jewish Times*, 24 Dec. 1869, p. 6.

90. Ibid., 15 Nov. 1869, p. 9.

91. "Reminiscences of 1861," SWP AJHS; see also Kohler, "The German-Jewish Migration to America," *PAJHS* 9 (1901): 102–3.

92. Wolf, "Essay on Relations with President Grant," n.d., SWP.

93. NARG 84, E. E. Vausant to Fish, Letters Received, 18 Sept. 1871; Korn, p. 137, claims Gov. John Geary of Pennsylvania was responsible for the Eckstein appointment.

94. Wolf, "Fifty Years," "The Temple," II (April 1898), pp. 3–6.

95. Ibid., p. 3.

96. Samuel E. Morison and H. S. Commager, *The Growth of the American Republic*, 4th ed. (New York: Oxford University Press, 1955), pp. 72–75. Directors of the Union Pacific Railroad organized a construction company, the Credit Mobilier of America, to which they "diverted enormous profits to their own use." In St. Louis "the 'Whiskey Ring' systematically defrauded the Government of millions of dollars in taxes on distilled whiskey."

97. Ibid., pp. 73–74.

98. Wm. E. Woodward, *Meet General Grant* (New York: Premier, 1957), pp. 243–45; idem, *A New American History* (New York: Garden City Publishing, 1948), p. 623.

99. U.S. Congress, House, 44th Cong., 1st sess., *Congressional Record* 4 (1876), 1361, 2197.

100. *American Israelite*, 28 Apr. 1876, p. 6; *Jewish Times*, 28 Apr. 1876, p. 134; see also 44th Cong., 1st sess., *The Proceedings of the Senate Sitting for the Trial of William W. Belknap* (Washington, D.C.: 1876).

101. Wolf to Editor, *Daily Journal*, 19 Apr. 1876 [copy in rough draft], SWP.

102. Wolf to Hayes, 22 June 1876, Nebel Collection, RBHP.

103. Wolf to Hayes, 14 Sept. 1876, sup.

104. Frederic Bancroft and Wm. Dunning, "A Sketch of Carl Schurz's Political Career, 1869–1906," in *The Reminiscences of Carl Schurz* (New York: Doubleday, 1916), pp. 338–53, 363–64, 368–70; Richard B. Morris, ed., *Encyclopedia of American History* (New York: Harper's 1953), pp. 252–53.

105. Bancroft and Dunning, pp. 377–80.

106. Ibid., pp. 376ff.

107. *Presidents*, pp. 102, 104; Wolf to Hayes, 28 Dec. 1876, RBHP.

108. "Fifty Years," p. 4; *Presidents*, p. 104; Wolf to Schurz, 17, 22 Apr. 1878, CSP; *Washington Star*, 5 June 1923, SWP.

109. *Jewish Exponent*, 31 July 1891, p. 2; *Presidents*, p. 104; *Senate Executive Journal* 21 (1877): 311.

110. *Jewish Times*, 13 Feb. 1874, pp. 777, 788, 790, 808; Wolf, "The B'nai B'rith of 1874 and the Statue of Religious Liberty," *B'nai Brith News*, May 1921, SWP.

111. *American Israelite*, 21 June 1878, p. 6.

112. Ibid., 5 July 1878, p. 6.

Chapter 3. Building a Constituency

1. *Jewish Messenger*, 27 May 1870. Wolf was added to the executive of the Board of Delegates in his capacity as representative of the Washington Hebrew Congregation and as spokesman for the District Grand Lodge of B'nai B'rith. See also Allan Tarshish, "The Board of Delegates of American Israelites" (Master's thesis, Hebrew Union College, 1932). Eager for a more representative standing, the Board enlarged its enrollment to include both congregations and agencies.

2. Chap. 2, nn. 9–12.

3. *Jewish Times*, 27 May 1870, p. 199.

4. Lilienthal to Wolf, 3 June 1870, SWP.

5. For a review of this period, see W. Gunther Plaut, *The Growth of Reform Judaism* (New York: World Union for Progressive Judaism, 1965), pp. 21–24; Moshe Davis, *The Emergence of Conservative Judaism* (Philadelphia: Jewish Publication Society, 1951), pp. 125–34; Wolf, *Selected Addresses and Papers*, pp. 97–107.

6. *Jewish Times*, 26 Nov. 1869, p. 6.

7. Ibid., 15 Oct. 1869, p. 5.

8. *American Israelite*, 8 May 1870, p. 8; *Minutebook*, Washington Hebrew Congregation, 8 May 1870.

9. Plaut, intro., pp. 10–12; Davis, pp. 123–34, 156.

10. See below, n. 15.

11. *Jewish Times*, 16 June 1871, pp. 248–49; 4 June 1875, p. 232; 2 July 1875, p. 280; 23 July 1875, pp. 328–29.

12. Ibid., 4 June 1875.

13. See below, nn. 25–28; *Jewish Times*, 4 June 1875.

14. *Jewish Times*, 18 June 1875, p. 246.

15. See chap. 2, nn. 9, 10, 12–13, 31, 33, 40.

16. Tarshish, p. 44.

17. *Jewish Times*, 8 July 1870, p. 297.

18. Tarshish, p. 67.

19. *Jewish Times*, 4 June 1875, p. 215.

20. Ibid., 16 June 1871, p. 245; 26 May 1876, p. 197; 2 June 1876, p. 212.

21. Ibid., 2 June 1876; *Proceedings*, 1:274; Kohler, "Board of Delegates," p. 113. Wolf served the Board in two different roles, as chairman of its Popularization Committee in 1874, and as its vice-president from 1871, until its dissolution in 1878.

22. *American Israelite*, 21 July 1876, p. 5.

23. Ibid., 20 Aug. 1876, p. 408.

24. *Proceedings*, 1:536.

25. Ibid., p. 345.

26. *Jewish Times*, 22 June 1877, p. 5.

27. *Proceedings*, 1:365.

28. Ibid., pp. 246–47.
29. Ibid., p. 380.
30. *Jewish Times,* 22 June 1877, p. 5.
31. *Proceedings,* 1:536.
32. Ibid., p. 426.
33. *Jewish Times,* 13 May 1877, p. 4.
34. Panitz, "In Defense-Immigrant," p. 60.

Chapter 4. Egyptian Interlude

1. *Presidents,* p. 104.
2. Ibid., p. 211.
3. Panitz, "Wolf-Consul," pp. 77–80.
4. *American Israelite,* 24 June 1881, p. 402; 8 July 1881, p. 13.
5. *Reminiscences,* p. 10.
6. Panitz, "Wolf-Consul," p. 82.
7. NARG 59, Instructions to Consuls Egypt 4, 5 Nov, 1875–1 June 1886, pp. 228–29.
8. *Reminiscences,* p. 10; Panitz, "Wolf-Consul," p. 83.
9. See below, n. 12.
10. Panitz, "Wolf-Consul," pp. 88–89.
11. *Reminiscences,* p. 13.
12. Panitz, "Wolf-Consul, pp. 87–88, 94–95; "Egypt," Encyclopedia Britannica, (1910) 8:92; *Reminiscences,* p. 31.
13. Panitz, "Wolf-Consul," pp. 89–91; see also Bernard Lewis, *The Arabs in History* (London: Anchor Press, 1950), p. 54; Philip K. Hitti, *History of the Arabs* (London: Macmillan, 1946), p. 166. The destruction of the Alexandria Library was attributed to General Omar Ibn El-Ass, who was loyal to the second Caliph, Omar Ibn Al-Khittab.
14. Panitz, "Wolf-Consul," pp. 91–92.
15. Ibid., p. 86.
16. Ibid., pp. 90–91, 97.
17. NARG 59, Consular Dispatches, Egypt 18, 23 June 1881–30 May 1882; disp. #16, Wolf to Blaine, 8 Nov. 1881; #36, Wolf to Blaine, 22 Nov. 1881; #62, Wolf to Freylinghuysen, 21 Mar. 1882; NARG 84, Misc. Letters Received, Cairo, Millikan to Wolf, 26 Sept. 1881.
18. *Reminiscences,* pp. 11–12; Panitz, "Wolf-Consul," pp. 84–85.
19. *Reminiscences,* pp. 16, 19.
20. Ibid., p. 27; Father Sylvester Malone to Wolf, 23 Mar. 1882, SWP. Malone, on advice from Peixotto, dissuaded Wolf from traveling to Palestine, a place considered dangerous to one's health. Malone argued that the food was bad, the roads hazardous there, and that one would have had to be a good horseman and of strong constitution to endure the rigors of the trip. However, Peixotto and Malone, then visiting Wolf at Cairo, did go off to Palestine and Syria, and left Wolf behind in Egypt.
21. *Reminiscences,* pp. 15–16, 21; NARG 84, Miscellaneous Letters Sent, Cairo 1878–83, Nicolas Comanos to president of the Council for Administering the Railways, 6 Feb. 1882, pp. 417–18.
22. *Reminiscences,* pp. 20, 23, 26. Others in Wolf's party included Peixotto, who had left Lyons to vacation in Egypt, and of whom Wolf wrote that "Peixotto had no enemy except himself," and Father Sylvester Malone, a Catholic priest from Brooklyn, N.Y., whose tastes and values Wolf described as "truly Catholic." In Malone, Wolf detected a kindred spirit. "Were there more Catholics in the world like Malone, and more Wolfs to appreciate them, peace and harmony would reign supreme." So Wolf mused.

23. Ibid., p. 13.

24. Ibid., p. 25.

25. Ibid., p. 19.

26. Ibid., p. 14.

27. *Reminiscences,* p. 16; Panitz, "Wolf-Consul," p. 97.

28. Jacob M. Landau, *Jews in Nineteenth Century Egypt* (New York: New York University Press, 1969), pp. 215–17.

29. NARG 59, Instructions to Consuls, Egypt 16, 5 Nov. 1875–1 June 1886), disp. #31, 24 Jan. 1882, Freylinghuysen to Wolf; Consular Dispatches, sup., 24 Jan. 1882. Wolf admitted that were he forced to ask for an additional 60 days leave, he would resign.

30. NARG 59, Wolf to President Arthur, 1 June 1882; cf. Panitz, "Wolf-Consul," pp. 94–95, 99, and nn. 83–86; Instructions to Consuls, sup., Freylinghusen to Wolf, disp. #31, 24 Mar. 1882.

Chapter 5. Champion of the Immigrant

1. Simon Dubnow, *History of the Jews in Russia and Poland* (Philadelphia: Jewish Publication Society, 1918), 2:363–69; Paul Masserman and M. Baker, *The Jews Come to America* (New York: Bloch, 1932), pp. 224–27.

2. *New York World,* 5 June 1881, in Panitz, "Attitudes-Immigration," p. 50.

3. See below, nn. 4, 8, 9.

4. Panitz, "Attitudes-Immigration," pp. 49–51.

5. Ibid., p. 51.

6. *8th Annual Report . . .* (1881), p. 1069. Meeting privately with Secretary Freylinghuysen, Wolf requested that the American minister to Russia cooperate with representatives of other European powers in seeking relief from persecution for Russian Jews. He also wanted the U.S. to renegotiate its Russo-American Commercial Treaty, a most-favored-nation arrangement, whose original terms, drawn up in 1832, allowed for discrimination against Americans of the Jewish faith, who may have been traveling in the empire, or doing business there. See also 46th Cong., 2nd sess., *Congressional Record,* p. 3131; *AJYB* 5670 (1910–11): 22–23. In 1882, Congressman Cox introduced resolutions requesting copies of diplomatic Russo-American correspondence dating from 1872, and dealing with anti-Jewish persecution in the empire, or with the maltreatment of American citizens there.

7. Adler and Margolith, pp. 211–13; *10th Annual Report . . .* (1883), p. 1418; *11th Annual Report . . .* (1884), p. 1562.

8. Panitz, "Attitudes-Immigration," pp. 49–51.

9. *Proceedings,* 3:2314.

10. Ibid., p. 2122, 1:526.

11. Ibid., 2:894–900.

12. Ibid., 3:1870.

13. *11th Annual Report . . .* (1884), p. 2641.

14. Panitz, "Attitudes-Immigration," pp. 51–54.

15. Adler and Margolith, pp. 217–21.

16. *18th Annual Report . . .* (1891), pp. 2815–17. Wolf and his colleagues on the Board of Delegates, in the Union of American Hebrew Congregations, and in B'nai B'rith were now convinced that Russia would not be deterred from pursuing its refurbished anti-Semitic measures.

17. John Weber and Walter Kempster, "Letter from the Secretary of the Treasury Transmitting a Report of the Commissioners of Immigration upon the Causes Which Incite Immigra-

tion," House Exec. Doc. #235, vol. 37 (1892): 1–12, 15–17, 21–27, 31–39, 148–71, 303–4. These proscriptive edicts included religious restrictions, forced conversions, occupational and residential limitations, burdens of military service, and the denial of first-class citizenship rights. Russia deemed all emigration from its lands illegal. Therefore, the majority of Jews so affected would remain overseas. However, of those bound for America, at least 52% had tickets prepaid by relatives in the United States. The attached *Minority Report* in the *Weber and Kempster Report* claimed that although Jews were only ¹⁄₂₀ of the total Russian population, they controlled ⅓ of the wealth of the country; their poorer brethren were obviously the undesirable ones who should never have been admitted here in the first place. Weber and Kempster also investigated immigrant conditions in Austria-Hungary, while other members of the team toured Western Europe, Italy, and England.

18. John Higham, *Strangers in the Land* (New Brunswick: Rutgers, 1955), pp. 143–44, 146–48.

19. Panitz, "Attitudes-Immigration," p. 57; Panitz, "In Defense-Immigrant," pp. 25–26.

20. Panitz, "Attitudes-Immigration," p. 52.

21. Samuel Joseph, *History of the Baron de Hirsh Fund* (1912; reprint, Fairfield, N.J.: A. M. Kelly, 1971), p. 272.

22. *Presidents*, pp. 160–62; Panitz, "Attitudes-Immigration," pp. 59–61; Panitz, "In Defense-Immigrant," pp. 33–35.

23. Panitz, "In Defense-Immigrant," pp. 38–39, 55.

24. Ibid., pp. 27–28.

25. Samuel Joseph, *Jewish Immigration to the United States from 1881 to 1910* (1914; reprint, New York: Arno Press, 1969), p. 40.

26. See below, n. 29.

27. Panitz, "In Defense-Immigrant," pp. 25–26.

28. Higham, pp. 177–86.

29. *Selected Addresses and Papers*, pp. 207, 209–10.

30. United States Industrial Commission, *Report of Immigration* (Washington, D.C., 1901), pp. [intro.: 11, 47, 62], 85, 95, 201, 240–54.

31. Ibid., pp. [intro.: 80], 30–31, 33, 43–44.

32. Ibid., pp. [intro.: 66, 75, 83], 248–54.

33. Ibid., pp. [intro. 23–27].

34. Ibid., pp. [intro.: 47, 50, 76, 83]. Wolf encountered a redoubtable opponent in Julius Rosendale, an immigrant inspector who thought Jewish immigrants immoral and unclean in personal habits, and insisted that they displaced native labor in special factories set up to assist them.

35. Joseph H. Kissman, "The Immigration of Rumanian Jews up to 1940," *YIVO Annual of Jewish Social Science* 2–3 (1938): 161–69, 174.

36. Levi to Wolf, 20 Oct. 1902, SWP; *26th Annual Report . . .* (1901), pp. 447–60. Wolf blamed the steamship companies for creating such unhealthy conditions among the immigrants that they contracted "loathsome diseases," and were then subject to deportation. He complained to Immigration Commissioner Terence V. Powderly. See also Wolf to Cowen, 17 July 1909, where Wolf observed that the steamship lines "scour Europe" for impoverished aliens who would never be able legally to enter the United States in the first place. (However, since the lines made a double profit, both in sending and deporting these people, the practice continued.)

37. Levi to Wolf, 27 Oct. 1902, SWP.

38. Ibid. See also *29th Annual Report . . .* (1902), p. 4662. So charged was the air with restrictionist sentiment concerning the admission of Romanian Jews that Wolf's successful intervention with Commissioner Sargent to reverse deportation proceedings against three Romanian families who had entered the United States illegally through Seattle acquired special

significance. See also Wolf to Cowen, 15 Mar. 1904, relaying Sargent's complaint that it was preposterous for people to come here by way of Siberia, Japan, and then Seattle, in the hope that they would evade American customs officials.

39. *29th Annual Report* . . . (1902), pp. 4658–59; Adler and Margalith, pp. 120–28, provide the text of the Roumanian Note.

40. *29th Annual Report* . . . (1902), p. 4658; *Presidents,* pp. 185–86; Roosevelt to Wolf, 22 July 1904, TRP.

41. Roosevelt to Wm. Williams, 23 Jan. 1903, in Elting E. Morison, ed., *The Letters of Theodore Roosevelt* (Cambridge: Harvard University Press, 1951–54), 3:411–12.

42. Williams to Roosevelt, 29 Jan. 1903, WW Papers, New York.

43. *Menorah Monthly* 34 (1903): 122.

44. Ibid., p. 127. Levi warned that B'nai B'rith would not join the general chorus of criticism directed against Commissioner Williams and his administration at Ellis Island. See also p. 123 for a negative evaluation of Williams's procedures by Lee K. Frankel, director of the United Hebrew Charities.

45. Ibid., pp. 157–58. However, see also Wolf to Cowen, 14 June 1904, in which Wolf details the evidence taken in Boston that large numbers of assisted immigrants were arriving in that city, PCP; see also Wolf to Jacob H. Schiff, 10 June 1904, that the "riff-raff of Europe, a large percentage of whom were Jews," were helped by the London Board of Jewish Guardians (to whose fund Lady Rothschild had contributed) to come to this country. Wolf explained that Commissioner Sargent then dispatched Robert Watchorn to investigate the matter. JHSP, Schiff Collection, AJA.

46. Industrial Commission, *Report,* pp. [intro.: 75–76, 82], 248–49.

47. *Report of the Commission Appointed by the President, Sept. 16, 1903, To Investigate the Conditions of the Immigration Station at Ellis Island* [hereafter cited as Ellis Island Commission, *Report*] (Washington, D.C., 1904), pp. 35–38; *Menorah Monthly* 35 (1903): 254. The members of the Commission were Ralph Trautman, chairman, Arthur Van Briesen of the Legal Aid Society, Eugene Philbin, a former district attorney, T. W. Hynes, commissioner of corrections, and Lee K. Frankel. See also Morison, 3:659–60. Writing to Trautman, Roosevelt thought that the commission had not supported Williams's policies aggressively enough.

48. *30th Annual Report* . . . (1903), pp. 5039–40.

49. M. J. Kohler and A. Elkus, "Brief in the Matter of Hersh Skuratowski" (New York, 1909), United States Immigration Commission, *Reports* [hereafter cited as *USCIR*] 41, p. 166.

50. Panitz, "In Defense-Immigrant," pp. 31–32, 62–63.

Chapter 6. Challenges to Power

1. *Presidents,* pp. 187–216; Cyrus Adler, *The Voice of America on Kishineff* (Philadelphia: Jewish Publication Society, 1904), pp. 479–80.

2. *29th Annual Report* . . . (1902), pp. 4676–77; Adler and Margalith, pp. 119–32.

3. *AJYB* 5664 (1903–4), pp. 127–28.

4. Zosa Szakowski, "The Alliance Israelite Universelle in the United States," *PAJHS* 39 (1950): 419, n. 60, 420–30.

5. Ibid., pp. 419–21.

6. *28th Annual Report* . . . (1901), pp. 4475–76; *29th Annual Report* . . . (1902), pp. 4660–61; *32nd Annual Report* . . . (1905), Appendix C; *33rd Annual Report* . . . (1906), Appendix D; *35th Annual Report* . . . (1909), p. 6070; Wolf to Roosevelt, 12 Oct. 1908, SWP.

7. *Proceedings,* (1909), pp. 6256–61; Reznikoff, 1:24–25.

8. Reznikoff, p. 19; Memorandum on the Formation of the American Jewish Committee, p. 2, Blaustein Library, AAJC.

9. Nathan Schachner, *What Price Liberty?* (New York: American Jewish Committee, 1948), pp. 13–14.

10. Minutebook, Executive, American Jewish Committee, p. 6, AAJC; Schachner, pp. 12–16. As it finally emerged, the American Jewish Committee was to consist of neither delegates from national organizations nor representatives of religious congregations. Instead, the new Committee was to comprise a core of 15 members, to be enlarged to 50. This body would then cooperate with various agencies in this country and abroad on matters of national and international moment to the Jewish people.

11. Minutes, American Jewish Committee, 19 May 1906, pp. 30–31, AAJC.

12. Schachner, pp. 19–22.

13. Schachner, p. 22.

14. Wolf to American Jewish Committee, 9 May 1907; cf. Herbert Friedenwald, 13 May 1907, Correspondence, File, AJC executive, AAJC.

15. "Memorandum of a Conversation Had with Simon Wolf," 5 Mar. 1908, CAP.

16. See File, Boston Sailor Case [hereafter cited as BSC] (1908), AAJC.

17. Clipping, "Barring of Marine Arouses Hebrews," *Boston Journal*, 29 Sept. 1908, BSC.

18. Wolf to V. H. Metcalf, 30 Sept., 1 Oct. 1908, BSC.

19. M. Sulzberger to Wolf, 13 Oct. 1908, BSC.

20. Clipping, *Jewish Tribune*, 27 Nov. 1908; Sulzberger to Wolf, 26 Oct. 1908; Williams to Metcalf, affidavit, 8 Oct. 1908; Friedman to Friedenwald, with ushers' affidavits, 9 Oct. 1908; Nathan Pinanski to Friedman, 8 Oct. 1908; Friedenwald to Adler, 12 Oct. 1908, all BSC.

21. Sulzberger to Wolf, 8 Jan. 1909, BSC.

22. See below, chap. 7, nn. 14, 15; chap. 8, nn. 18, 33; chap. 10, nn. 56, 57.

23. Marshall to Wolf, 28 Oct. 1921, Pers. Corresp. vol. 16, LMP, AJA.

24. See below, chap. 7, nn. 19–23.

Chapter 7. Justice for the Stranger

1. *AJYB* 5667 (1906–7), p. 898; *33rd Annual Report* . . . (1906), Appendix C. p. 5654.

2. *33rd Annual Report* . . . (1906), pp. 5646–48.

3. Ibid., pp. 5649–50; see also Watchorn to Wolf, 6, 7, 10, 12 Sept. 1900, SWP; "Mr. Watchorn's Report on Rumania," *American Hebrew*, 19, 26 Oct. 1900, pp. 647–48, 679, 682.

4. *33rd Annual Report* . . . (1906), pp. 5650–52.

5. Ibid., 5640–46; Dubnow, vol. 3, chaps, 35, 37; *AJYB* 5665 (1904–5), p. 24.

6. *33rd Annual Report* . . . (1906), p. 5652.

7. See below, chap. 9, n. 23.

8. *Protest vs. Pending Immigration Bill* Pamphlet (New York: Liberal Immigration League, 1906), pp. 5–6, 9–10; *34th Annual Report* . . . (1907), p. 5984; Schachner, pp. 12–16. The League furnished Wolf with reports on immigration matters in Congress.

9. See below, n. 16.

10. 59th Cong., 1st sess., *Congressional Record* (1907), 9152, 9159, 9194–95; 62nd Cong., 3rd sess., *Congressional Record* (1907), 862; Blair Bolles, *Tyrant from Illinois: Uncle Joe Cannon's Experiment with Personal Power* (New York: Norton, 1951), pp. 73–74; Henry Fairchild, "The Making of the Literacy Test," *Quarterly Journal of Economics* 31 (1917): 455.

11. Panitz, "In Defense-Immigrant," p. 44.

12. Adler to Friedenwald, 23 Jan. 1907. Cannon promised Wolf there would be no wavering in committee on the matter of the Immigration Bill including its health provisos. CAP AAJC.

13. *33rd Annual Report* . . . (1906), p. 5645; Adler to Friedenwald, 12 Feb. 1907, CAP.

14. Adler to Friedenwald, 23 Jan. 1907, CAP.

15. Adler to Friedenwald, 28 Jan. 1907, CAP.

16. Roosevelt to Cannon, 27 May, 5 Aug. 1906, in Morison, 5:285–86, 360–61; Panitz, "In Defense-Immigrant," p. 44.

17. Friedenwald to Sulzberger, 13 Feb. 1907, MSP AAJC.

18. *Recommendations Respecting Revisions of the Immigration Laws Made by the American Jewish Committee, the Board of Delegates on Civil and Religious Rights of the Union of American Hebrew Congregations, the International Order B'nai B'rith to the United States Immigration Commission* (New York, 1910), in *USCIR*, 12:183.

19. M. Kohler, Chas. Nagel and J. H. Schiff. *The Immigration Question* (New York: UAHC, 1911), p. 42.

20. *28th Annual Report* . . . (1901), pp. 4478–83; *29th Annual Report* . . . (1902), p. 4661; *31st Annual Report* . . . (1904), p. 5268; *32nd Annual Report* . . . (1905), p. 5511; *35th Annual Report* . . . (1908), p. 6069; *37th Annual Report* . . . (1909), p. 6392.

21. Wolf to Kohler, 9 Jan. 1911, SWP.

22. See for example, *28th Annual Report* . . . (1901), pp. 4478–83; *29th Annual Report* . . . (1902), p. 4662; *31st Annual Report* . . . (1904), p. 5269; *33rd Annual Report* . . . (1907), p. 5985.

23. Cf. *AJYB* 5672 (1911–12), pp. 316–28.

24. See below, nn. 26, 31, 33; see chap. 8, nn. 14, 15, 37, 40–42, 52; chap. 9, nn. 3–6.

25. "Skuratowski Brief," pp. 169–80.

26. Kohler, "Protecting Immigrant Rights," *American Hebrew*, 2 July 1909, pp. 296–97.

27. David M. Bressler, *The Removal Work, Including Galveston.* Speech, St. Louis, Nat'l Conf. on Jewish Charities, 1910, pp. 16–18; Wolf to Kohler, Feb. 1910, SWP. Officially, the agency was known as the Jewish Immigrants' Information Bureau.

28. See chap. 5, n. 22.

29. Panitz, "In Defense-Immigrant," pp. 34–35.

30. "The Galveston Case," *Correspondence between Simon Wolf and Secretary Benjamin W. Cable. Legal Aspect by M. J. Kohler, Jewish Exponent*, 5 Aug. 1910, pp. 1, 8.

31. 62nd Cong., 1st Sess., *Hearings on HR#166 To Investigate Office of the Immigration Commissioner of The Port of New York* (Washington, D.C., 1911), pp. 110–11.

32. Panitz, "In Defense-Immigrant," p. 35.

33. Kohler, *Immigration Question*, pp. 33–34, 39–42.

34. See above, n. 18.

35. 2 May 1912, SWP.

36. Higham, pp. 189, 191; Alpheus T. Mason, *Brandeis: A Free Man's Life* (New York: Viking, 1946), p. 42.

37. Kohler, *Immigration Question*, p. 42.

38. Wolf to Nagel, 19 Oct. 1911; Nagel to Wolf, 18 Oct. 1911; Wolf to Nagel, 15 July 1912. Taft's rather vulgar expression indicates the free relationship he and Wolf might have had. This may well account for the many favors Taft extended to Wolf. Not only did Taft promote a candidate to West Point at Wolf's suggestion (see chap. 12, n. 10), but he also reinstated Col. Chas. H. Laucheimer to his position as adjutant and inspector of the Marine Corps. Laucheimer had been relegated to a minor post in the Philippines, where he was a subordinate to several junior officers. But Wolf took up the matter and referred Taft to a House investigation by the Committee on Naval Affairs. As a result, Laucheimer was transferred to San Francisco (Items #952, 953, Wolf to Chas. D. Hilles, 14 May 1912). In the political arena, Wolf advised Taft on his 1908 campaign (chap. 10, n. 60), and against the president's wishes, urged him to seek renomination, to combat Wilson's popularity (Wolf to Taft, 15 June 1914; Taft to Wolf, 19 June 1914, WHTP AJA). Later, Wolf would be in touch with the ex-president on Zionist matters [chap. 12, n. 31], and on securing equal rights for European Jews (Wolf to Taft, 8, 11, 18, 23 Sept., with enclosures, Kraus to Taft, 1 Oct., Taft to Kraus, 4 Oct., and Kraus to Taft, 8 Oct. 1913; Wolf to Taft, 20, 29 Dec. 1915, 19 Jan. and 29 May 1916. WHTP AJA). These are but a few

of the examples attesting to the close ties between Taft and Wolf, expressed in correspondence that lasted from 1904 until Wolf's death in 1923.

Chapter 8. In the Shadow of Restrictionism

1. Higham, pp. 101–5, 149–56, 169–72; Panitz, "In Defense-Immigrant," pp. 40–42; E. Tcherikower, *The Early Jewish Labor Movement in the United States*, trans. A. Antonowsky (New York: YIVO, 1961), pp. 100–113, 131–47.

2. *Annual Reports* . . . (1903, 1909, 1910), pp. 4477, 4505, 4507, 4661, 5042–43, 6400, 6532.

3. *29th Annual Report* . . . (1902), pp. 4121–22. Wolf to Cowen, 9 Aug. 1899, PCP. McSweeny, having heard that some Jews consider themselves a nation, saw no harm in calling them "Hebrews."

4. Industrial Commission, *Report*, pp. [intro.: 80], 30–31, 33, 43–44.

5. *29th Annual Report* . . . (1902).

6. See below, nn. 19–21.

7. *30th Annual Report* . . . (1903), p. 5040.

8. Fulton Brylawski to Adler, 1 Feb. 1920, CAP AAJC; Roy L. Garis, *Immigration Restriction* (New York: Macmillan, 1927), p. 107.

9. *29th Annual Report* . . . (1902), p. 4662.

10. *30th Annual Report* . . . (1903), pp. 5042–51; Panitz, "In Defense-Immigrant," Appendix, pp. 62–63.

11. *30th Annual Report* . . . (1903), p. 5051.

12. W. W. Husband to Kohler, 24 Mar. 1927; Husband to Wm. H. Wheeler, 15 Dec. 1908, enclosure in Husband to Kohler, 21 Mar. 1927.

13. Higham, p. 125.

14. Though Kohler worked with Wolf on behalf of the immigrants enumerated in the "Skuratowski Brief," the American Jewish Committee underwrote its cost. Secure in his office, Commissioner Williams pursued a self-formulated policy of requiring a $25.00 cash minimum from every immigrant as proof of his not becoming a public charge. In this instance, the catalyst that led to the writing of the "Brief" was the fact that 11 of the 15 Jewish aliens involved were shipped out of the country before bonds attesting to their solvency could have been posted. The "Brief" then became applicable to the remaining four clients. See Panitz, "In Defense-Immigrant," p. 30.

15. *Skuratowski Brief*, pp. 178–79; Wolf, "Statement," *USCIR*, p. 278.

16. Chap. 7, n. 26.

17. Brylawski to M. Sulzberger, 27 Nov. 1909; telegram, Brylawski to M. Sulzberger, 30 Nov. 1909; Brylawski to Adler, 30 Nov. 1909; M. Sulzberger to Friedenwald, with enclosures to be sent to Wolf and Kraus, 28 Nov. 1909; M. Sulzberger to Julian J. Mack, telegram, 29 Nov. 1909, CAP AAJC.

18. M. Sulzberger to Friedenwald, with enclosures, to Wolf and Kraus, sup.

19. *USCIR*, pp. 267, 271.

20. Ibid., p. 269.

21. Ibid., pp. 271–74; see also *39th Annual Report* . . . (1912), pp. 7164, 7169. As chairman of a committee dealing with immigration matters, Wolf noted that the legislation contemplated by the Immigration Commission incorporated a new statute, barring members of the brown and yellow races from entering this country.

22. *USCIR*, p. 267.

23. "The Influence of the Jews on the Progress of the World" (1887); "The Jew as a Factor in the Development of the United States" (1906); "The Jew in Public Life" (1901); "The Life and

Service of the Rev. Dr. Isaac Leeser" (1868); "Patriotism and Religion" (1897). See also Wolf to Editor, *Jewish Tribune*, 6 Jan. 1903, comparing the tribulations of the French captain Alfred Dreyfus with those of the American commodore Uriah P. Levy, both of whom exhibited the "magnificent staying powers of their race" (SWP). For Wolf's legal testimony before governmental officials where he asserted the moral superiority of the Jews as a group that never allowed any of its members to become public charges, see the following: Letter to Secretary of the Treasury, Foster, *Presidents*, pp. 160–62; Industrial Commission, *Report*, pp. 245–54; Ellis Island Commission, *Report*, sup.; *30th Annual Report* . . . (1903), pp. 5039–40; *Galveston Case*, p. 1.

24. *Selected Addresses and Papers*, pp. 195–98.

25. *Presidents*, pp. 35–43; Panitz, "Liberty under Law," p. 4.

26. *Selected Addresses and Papers*, p. 266.

27. Ibid., pp. 266–67; Industrial Commission, *Report*, pp. 245–54.

28. *American Jew* (1895) was written to combat the anti-Semitism of the period. It is a collection of articles citing the Jews' historic contributions to civilization, their participation in domestic and foreign battles for just causes, and their financial support for the fledgling American republic. These examples are submitted as evidence of the Jews' unswerving devotion to the United States.

29. *21st Annual Report* . . . (1894), pp. 3354–57; *23rd Annual Report* . . . (1896), pp. 3649–50; *32nd Annual Report* . . . (1905), pp. 5515–24; *40th Annual Report* . . . (1913), pp. 7349, 7354–59; *43rd Annual Report* . . . (1916), pp. 8106–17.

30. See above, n. 21.

31. *Jewish Exponent*, 5 Feb. 1910, p. 4; Friedenwald to Kohler, 15 Dec. 1909, CAP; *Minutebook*, American Jewish Committee executive, 20 Feb. 1910, p. 270. Within the councils of the Committee, Judah Magnes was livid that Mack and Wolf should have opposed classifying Hebrews as a race. Much of the larger Jewish community of New York and its press also condemned Mack and Wolf for their position.

32. Kohler, "The Honorable Simon Wolf Slighted," *American Hebrew*, 17 Dec. 1909, p. 172; Friedenwald to Kohler, 15 Dec. 1909, CAP AAJC; "Recommendations," *Minutes of the Conference of Immigration Called at the Instance of Abram Elkus, Esq.*, New York, 19 Dec. 1909, pp. 1–5, MJKP AJHS; Adler to Friedenwald, 28 Jan. 1910; Adler to M. Sulzberger, 9 Jan. 1910; Wolf to Adler, 1 Feb. 1910, CAP AAJC; Wolf to Kohler, 21 Dec. 1909, SWP. Wolf now invited Kohler to join the executive of the Board of Delegates.

33. Adler to M. Sulzberger, 30 Jan. 1910; Wolf to Adler, 1 Feb. 1910, CAP AAJC.

34. Wolf to Adler, with enclosures, and Wolf to Henry Goldfogle, 2 Feb. 1910; Adler to Wolf, 24 Feb. 1910; Adler to Goldfogle, 25 Feb. 1910; Adler to C. L. Sulzberger, 24 Feb. 1910; Wolf to Friedenwald, 17 Feb. 1910, CAP AAJC; Goldfogle to Marshall, 26 Feb 1910, LMP AAJC; Wolf to Kohler, 24 Feb. 1910, SWP: *AJYB* 5672 (1911–12), p. 315. Judge Leon Sanders was allowed the privilege of making a statement before the Commission. But the organization he represented, the National Jewish Immigration Council, was not included among the sponsoring institutions listed below the written recommendations. These followed the oral hearings that had been presented in Mar. 1910.

35. *AJYB* 5672 (1911–12), pp. 315–34.

36. *USCIR*, pp. 183–84.

37. Adler to M. Sulzberger, 30 Jan. 1910.

38. *AJYB* 5671 (1910–11), pp. 71–77, 79–82.

39. *AJYB* 5672, sup.

40. Dillingham to Wolf, with enclosure in Kohler to Marshall, 15 Oct. 1910, LMP AJHS.

41. Kohler to Wolf, with proposed draft, 27 Sept. 1910, LMP AAJC; Wolf to Adler, 29 Sept. 1910; Friedenwald to Adler, 27 Sept., 12 Oct. 1910; Adler to Friedenwald, 10 Oct. 1910, CAP AAJC.

42. *AJYB* 5672, pp. 233–34; *AJYB* 5671, pp. 70–86.

43. *AJYB* 5671, pp. 70–86.

44. *AJYB* 5672, pp. 316–364; *AJYB* 5671, pp. 121–47; see also *Minutebook*, AJC executive, 28 Dec. 1909, p. 261, AAJC; see also *36th Annual Report* . . . (1909), pp. 6398–99. In the interests of a just application of the law, Wolf had also corresponded with officials in the Department of Commerce and Labor concerning the charge leveled by Prentice Hall and James Patton of the Immigration Restriction League that Jews were trafficking in white slavery. See 61st Cong., 2nd sess., Sen. Doc. #196, *Importing Women for Immoral Purposes*, pp. 1–61. Wolf cautioned the Board of Delegates about the need to refute the charge. Later, at the Mar. 1910 hearings, C. L. Sulzberger proved that not only were there fewer Jews in correctional institutions than native Americans, but that a smaller number of Italians and Hebrews engaged in prostitution than did other immigrant groups.

45. *39th Annual Report* . . . (1912), pp. 7164–74.

46. Minutes, Conference on Immigration, 30 Dec. 1911; informal conference at Louis Marshall's residence, 47 E. 72nd St., New York City, to consider matters re hearing granted by House Committee on Immigration to AJC, 12 Jan. 1912, MJKP.

47. Marshall to Lodge re Dillingham Bill, s 3175, 26 Jan. 1912, LMP AAJC; Kohler to Schiff re Williams's disregard for legal principles, 14 Mar. 1912, MJKP; Wolf to Nagel re the need to publicize the secretary's decision to admit an imbecile child, in order to mute widespread criticism, 15 July 1912, SWP.

48. Friedenwald, to Adler, 5 May 1911, CAP; Marshall to Lodge, 26 Jan. 1912, LMP AJHS; Friedenwald to Adler, 19 Feb. 1912, CAP.

49. Wm. Rae Gwinn, "Uncle Joe Cannon: Archfoe of Insurgency" (Ph.D. dissertation, University of Michigan, 1955), pp. 181–246.

50. *30th Annual Report* . . . pp. 7164–74; Kohler, "Objections to the Immigration Bill," *Jewish Exponent*, 7 Feb. 1914, p. 6; *AJYB* 5674 (1913–14), p. 444.

51. Panitz, "In Defense-Immigrant," p. 49, note 149.

52. *43rd Annual Report* . . . (1916), p. 8006; *44th Annual Report* . . . (1917), pp. 8269–70; *45th Annual Report* . . . (1918), p. 8427.

53. *39th Annual Report* . . . (1912), p. 7073; *40th Annual Report* . . . (1913), p. 7345.

54. Marshall to Wolf, 11 Feb. 1913; Wolf to Kohler, 2 Jan. 1914; Wolf to Schiff, 5 Jan. 1914; Schiff to Wolf, 6 Jan. 1914; Wolf to Schiff, 25 Apr. 1914, all SWP.

Chapter 9. Toward Racism: "An Expense of Energy"

1. Wolf to Kohler, 2 Jan. 1914; Wolf to Schiff, 5 Jan. 1914, both JHSP, Schiff Collection, AJA. In his correspondence Wolf refers to a 17-year-old boy "separated from an elder brother," and therefore seemingly "abstracted in mind" because of his "terror and loneliness" who was to be subject to deportation.

2. Panitz, "In Defense-Immigrant," p. 49–50.

3. Kohler, *Objectionable Provisions of the Immigration Bill HR 6060*, n.d., MJKP; I. M. Hourwich to Rob't LaFollette, 15 Feb. 1913; Kohler to Marshall, 24 Dec. 1914, LMP AAJC.

4. 63rd Cong., 2nd sess., *Congressional Record* 49 (1916), 2596; M. F. Behar, *Our National Gates, Shut, Ajar, or Open?* Pamphlet #204 (New York: National Immigration League, 1916), pp. 7–9.

5. *39th Annual Report* . . . (1912), p. 7173.

6. Marshall to Goldfogle, 24 Jan. 1914; Marshall to Adolph Sabath, 24 Jan. 1914; Marshall to Chas. S. Thomas, 21 Dec. 1914; Marshall to James A. Reed, 12 Dec. 1914, all LMP AAJC.

7. Panitz, "In Defense-Immigrant," p. 50.

8. Ibid., pp. 52–54; cf. Harold U. Faulkner, *Politics, Reform and Expansion 1890–1950*

(New York: Harper Torchbooks, 1950), pp. 91, 114-15, 128–37, 185–211; Gustavus Meyers, *A History of Bigotry in the United States* (New York: Random House, 1943), pp. 192–94, 203–6.

9. Leonard Dinnerstein, *The Leo Frank Case* (New York: Columbia University Press, 1968), pp. 37–61, 74, 85–90, 96–101, 107–13, 121–29, 139–41; *New York Times* 8 March, p. A12; 23 Dec. 1983, p. A10; *N.Y. Times* 14 Mar. 1986, p. 16A. Alonzo Mann, a 14-year-old office boy at the National Factory, at the time admitted that he had witnessed Conley's dragging the girl's body down to the basement and that Frank was therefore innocent. In 1986 the Georgia Board of Pardons and Paroles granted Frank a posthumous pardon, but refused to declare him innocent. I am indebted to Dr. Raphael Panitz, of Washington, D.C., for continuing to supply me with current material on the Frank matter, and to Mr. Newtom Roemer, attorney, of Clifton, N.J., for clarifying the legal sources in the Frank case.

10. Wolf to Schiff, 25 Feb, 30 Nov. 1912. JHSP, Schiff Collection, AJA.

11. Marshall to Wolf, 27 Sept. 1913, Reznikoff, 2:276–77.

12. Dinnerstein, "Leo M. Frank and the American Jewish Community," *AJA* 20 (1968): 112–13.

13. Dinnerstein, *The Leo Frank Case*, pp. 91–95, 114–18, 121, 129–30.

14. Dinnerstein, "Frank-Community," p. 124, n. 46.

15. Wolf to Schiff. 30 Nov. 1914, Schiff Collection; see also 59 Law Ed. 969, pp. 343–46, 345–50, line 2 [349] (37 U.S. Reports). This is part of Justice Holmes's dissent; there is no statement by Justice Day.

16. Dinnerstein, "Frank-Community," p. 123; see also Marshall to Wolf, 8 Oct. 1921, Pers. Corresp. 16, AJA; *41st Annual Report* . . . (1914), p. 7653. Arnold Foster, of the Anti-Defamation League of B'nai B'rith, informs me that there was no connection between that institution's formation and the Frank case. Conversation had with Foster, 11 Oct. 1982, Yonkers, N.Y.

17. Higham, pp. 141–44; Walker to Wolf, 14 Nov. 1879. Walker wanted to know how many "defective and delinquent" classes there were among the Jews and how many charities were set up by the "'Hebrew Orders' to provide for these people"; see also Wolf to Kohler, 21 Dec. 1909, SWP. Wolf protests that Friedenwald of the American Jewish Committee, in publicizing studies of Jewish population statistics, omitted all references to him. Though the *Proceedings of the Council of the Union* (1876), 1:356, credits only Wm. B. Hackenburg for having undertaken the assignment, Wolf insisted he helped Hackenburg gather the necessary material. See also Henry Berkowitz, "Some Notes on the History of the Earliest German Jewish Congregations in America," *PAJHS* 9 (1901): 123, for the view that Wolf and Hackenburg together compiled a book entitled *Statistics of the Jews in the United States*, which was published under the auspices of the Union of American Hebrew Congregations, and the Board of Delegates [ca. 1878].

18. See above, chap. 8, n. 21.

19. Panitz, "In Defense-Immigrant," pp. 53–54. The Dillingham Bill in the Senate added new classes of excludable people, barring them from naturalization, while its counterpart in the House, the Burnett measure, dealt exclusively with the literacy proviso. President Taft vetoed the combined Dillingham-Burnett Bill because of its educational requirement. By limiting their admission to those who passed the literacy test, the new 1914 Burnett Bill tied that requirement to a percentage scheme based on ethnic origins for incoming aliens. Gone was the distinction between the right to enter this country and the privilege to acquire citizenship via naturalization, a process dependent on being literate. In this way even the literacy measure had acquired racial connotations. See Kohler, "Objections to the Immigration Bill," *Jewish Exponent* 7 Feb. 1913, p. 6; Marshall, *The Injustice of a Literacy Test*, 7 Jan. 1915, LMP, Box 1, AJA.

20. Higham, p. 156.

21. See chap. 1, nn. 1–8.

22. Panitz, "In Defense-Immigrant," pp. 54–55, nn. 177, 178, 182; Higham, pp. 300–10, 313–14.

23. Wolf to Wm. B. Wilson, 23 Oct. 1919, SWP.

24. *38th Annual Report* . . . (1911), pp. 6868–69; *41st Annual Report* . . . (1914), p. 7651; *42nd Annual Report* . . . (1915), p. 7935.

25. Panitz, "In Defense-Immigrant," p. 55, n. 153.

26. *New York Times*, 20 Feb. 1921, p. 1; 7 Apr. 1931, p. 2; *AJYB* 5683 (1922–23), p. 45; *AJYB* 5671 (1921–22), p. 117.

27. *AJYB* 5673, p. 345; *48th Annual Report* (1921), p. 9019, Appendix A. It was Kohler who detailed the harshness of the new immigration measure; *Selected Addresses and Papers,* pp. 291–96, 325–29.

28. Panitz, "In Defense-Immigrant," p. 60.

29. *48th Annual Report* . . . (1921), p. 9022.

30. Panitz, "In Defense-Immigrant," pp. 60–61, nn. pp. 218–220; Higham, pp. 318–24; Garis, *Immigration Restriction*, pp. 171–74.

31. See chap. 8, nn. 8, 9, 11, 12, 20, 21.

32. Chap. 7, n. 25; chap. 8, n. 38; cf. Marshall to Wolf, 4 Jan. 1913, LMP AAJC.

33. Davis to Wolf, 5 Mar. 1923, SWP.

34. See *50th Annual Report* . . . (1923), p. 9470, for which Kohler was responsible. From 1910 until his death, Wolf relied increasingly upon Kohler's legal acumen to compile the Board of Delegates *Reports*.

35. Davis to Wolf, sup.; Wolf to Davis, 29 Mar. 1923, SWP.

36. See Higham, pp. 318–19. Of Welsh stock, Davis believed in "Nordic superiority" among the races. See also *AJYB* 5684 (1923–24), p. 377; Kohler, *Immigration and Aliens in the United States* (New York: Bloch, 1936). Measures to register the alien were brought forth at a time when diminished immigration coincided with an upsurge in economic activity. Such an emphasis on methods for screening out the immigrant can only be explained in terms of the Americanization process. By 1923 this movement had developed a momentum of its own. It was still spurred on by xenophobic and patriotic motives, but bore no significant relationship to the number of aliens who were arriving here. See also Burton J. Hendrick, *The Jews in America* (Garden City: Doubleday, 1923); pseudoscientific works, like Hendrick's, lent credence to the view that altering the life habits and thoughts of incoming aliens from the Southern and Eastern tiers of the European continent was an almost impossible task. As evidence, Hendrick pictured the Jew as an unassimilable, ignorant creature, perpetuating a cross-breeding of the worst traits of some bygone nomadic Semites with the religious rituals of ancient Asiatic hordes. By excepting German Jews from the opprobrium heaped upon their coreligionists, Hendrick thought to impart a veneer of impartiality to his book. Momentarily taken by this play of favoritism, Wolf saw some positive aspects to *The Jews in America*. See Hendrick to Wolf, 29 Nov. 1922, SWP. Such toadying did not, however, change the restrictionists' basic premise: for American experts on eugenics, believers in racism, leaders in the American Federation of Labor, and southern and western populists, aliens coming from Eastern Europe, Italy, Greece, and surrounding countries would insure the ruin of America. Therefore this country's hope lay in combining a program of rigid restrictionism with forced assimilation for those who managed to reach U.S. shores. It mattered little that since 1903 ships' manifests continued to include all the vital information for every alien aboard. Now, two decades later, the Immigration Service, with its secretary in the lead, believed that registering all immigrants with a view to forced attendance at appropriate courses was an absolute necessity.

Chapter 10. In the Russian Maze

1. Adler and Margolith, pp. 171–85.

2. Ibid., p. 178; 47th Cong., 1st sess., 22 House Exec. Doc. #192, *Condition of the*

Israelites, disp. #2, Evarts to Foster, 14 Apr. 1880, p. 30; disp. #9, Foster to Evarts, 17 June 1880, pp. 31–32.

3. Adler and Margalith, p. 178.

4. *9th Annual Report* . . . (1882), p. 1256. Acting on Wolf's request, Cox sought information from President Arthur about the alleged expulsions, urged that the mistreatment of native and American naturalized Jews in Russia cease, and conveyed these demands as the unanimous wish of the American people to the chief executive. President Arthur thereupon informed Wm. Henry Hunt, the American minister at St. Petersburg, that the rights of American nationals abroad were not to be jeopardized because of their religious beliefs. Cf. *AJYB* 5670 (1909–10), p. 23. In 1884 and again in 1886, Cox renewed his pleas for information concerning official discriminations practiced against Russian Jews, and protested the expulsion of a Jewish merchant from St. Petersburg.

5. Adler and Margolith, pp. 211–13; *10th Annual Report* . . . (1883), p. 1418; *11th Annual Report* . . . (1884), p. 1562.

6. *AJYB* 5665 (1904–5), p. 294.

7. *16th Annual Report* . . . (1889), p. 2314; *17th Annual Report* . . . (1890), p. 2639.

8. Panitz, "Attitudes-Immigration," pp. 54–55; *19th Annual Report* . . . (1892), p. 2926; Blaine to Smith, 18 Feb. 1891, *Papers Relating to the Foreign Relations of the United States* [hereafter cited as PRFRUS] (Washington, D.C., 1892), pp. 737–39; Adler and Margalith, p. 219.

9. See chap. 5, n. 22.

10. Blaine to Smith, 18 Feb. 1891, sup.; *19th Annual Report* . . . (1892), p. 2826. Members of Congress had legally to confine themselves to Russian mistreatment of American citizens, a practice that was a natural extension of the Russian interpretation of the 1832 Commercial Treaty.

11. *19th Annual Report* . . . (1892), pp. 2826–27. Traditionally restricted from criticizing the internal directives of a foreign power, Congress was forced to link its request for information concerning Russian discriminatory practices, with any such measures taken against American Jews in the empire. See *Message of the President,* 9 Dec. 1891, *PRFRUS* (Washington, D.C., 1892), pp. 12–13, where President Harrison emphasized America's right to remonstrate once immigration to its shores threatened its economic and social well-being.

12. Adler and Margalith, pp. 241–45; *23rd Annual Report* . . . (1896), p. 3650.

13. Wolf and J. B. Klein to State Dept., 16 Sept. 1889, Miscellaneous Correspondence Received, Register C, vol. 174, p. 470, vol. 175, p. 116; State Dept to Wolf and Klein, 20 Sept., 26 Oct. 1889; State Dept. to Klein, 27 Jan. 1891, State Department Correspondence Sent, Register D, vol. 173, p. 116; *22nd Annual Report* . . . (1891), p. 2639.

14. *Presidents,* pp. 157–58.

15. Wolf to State Dept., 19 Nov. 1897, Miscellaneous Correspondence Received, Register C; State Dept to Wolf, 26 Nov. 1897, Miscellaneous Correspondence Sent, Register D.

16. Wolf to Sherman, 25 Feb. 1893, SWP, B'nai B'rith Archives; *21st Annual Report* . . . (1894), p. 3134; *22nd Annual Report* . . . (1895), p. 3357–58.

17. Adler and Margalith, pp. 256–58; *22nd Annual Report* . . . (1896), pp. 3358–59.

18. *24th Annual Report* . . . (1897), p. 3780.

19. *29th Annual Report* . . . (1902), pp. 4475–76.

20. Interview reconstructed from: *Presidents,* pp. 185–86; *29th Annual Report* . . . (1902), p. 4659; Roosevelt to Wolf, 22 July 1902, TRP.

21. *31st Annual Report* . . . (1904), p. 5269; *32nd Annual Report* . . . (1905), p. 5512–13; *AJYB* 5672 (1911–12), pp. 42–43; *AJYB* 5665 (1904–5), pp. 283, 301–4; McCormick to Lamsdorff, 7 Oct. 1904, and Lamsdorff to McCormick, 4 Oct. 1904, in *AJYB* 5670 (1910), pp. 35–36.

22. Adler and Margalith, p. 283; Dubnow, 3:98–99. Russian expansionist adventures had brought on a debacle whose effects the imperial government tried to mitigate by promises of a

more liberal regime. An imperial edict in 1904 was intended to relax restrictions on the rights of residence for Jews in certain areas.

23. *32nd Annual Report* . . . (1905), pp. 5513, 5531–32; Adler and Margalith, p. 273; *33rd Annual Report* . . . (1906), p. 5655; Dubnow, 3:135.

24. *33rd Annual Report* . . . (1906), pp. 5655–56; Adler and Margalith, pp. 274–75; Dubnow, 3:135–53; *34th Annual Report* . . . (1907), pp. 5987–88; Adler to M. Sulzberger, 15 Nov. 1907, CAP AAJA.

25. SDF 711.612/18, Knox to Taft, 14 Dec. 1910, enclosures, Part 2, Rockhill, disp. #118, Summary-State Dept. Corresp. [hereafter cited as Rockhill, Summary], 20 Apr. 1910, pp. 42–43; see above, n. 17; Herman Bernstein, "Russia Hoodwinking Us about Passports for Jews," New York Times, 2 July 1911, p. 5, p. 1.

26. *33rd Annual Report* . . . (1905), pp. 5531–32.

27. Ibid., pp. 5525–28; Adler, pp. 171–75, 177–78; *Presidents*, pp. 218, 232–33. Though he urged the abolition of all anti-Jewish proscriptive edicts in a letter to Witte's predecessor, Count Cassini, Wolf nevertheless made certain to call the Jews the "storm-petrels of the [coming] revolution in Russia." This was written precisely at the time the Russian imperial government had accused Jews of being anarchists and revolutionaries. Though Wolf had equally little use for traditional rabbis, he nevertheless took umbrage at White's description of "Talmudic rabbis" (Philip Cowen, *Memories of an American Jew* [New York: International Press, 1921], p. 125). See also Irving Levitas, "The Japanese and the Jews," *Yonkers Jewish Chronicle*, 27 Jan. 1984, p. 9, for the view that Japanese perceptions of Jewish wealth, unlike those of the West, were positive. White's references to Japan also tied into Schiff's support for that country in its hatred for Russia, and to American public revulsion at Russia's anti-Semitic practices. See also Adler, *Jacob H. Schiff: His Life and Letters* (New York: Doubleday, Doran, 1929), 1:212–28.

28. White to Wolf, 5 May 1905, SWP.

29. Adler, [intro.: 14–25], pt. 2, pp. 231–64.

30. Ibid., pp. 237–464, 475; Cowen, pp. 135–36. A brief interview between Wolf and Roosevelt concerns the possibility of a new pogrom erupting after Kishineff, in December 1903. At that time, Roosevelt hinted that despite his sympathy for Russian Jewry, he doubted that he could effect any changes in czarist attitudes. Nevertheless, Roosevelt suggested that Wolf prepare a cablegram to be sent to the American ambassador to Russia, who would then urge the emperor to prevent further outrages.

31. *Presidents*, pp. 201–15; Adler, *Kishineff*, pp. 469–81; see also Wolf to Levi, 24 June 1903, where Wolf recounts how Roosevelt thanked him for having arranged a private conference on the Kishineff matter. The session, initiated at Levi's suggestion, included Roosevelt, Hay, and Wolf and set the stage for the official American procedure on the Kishineff petition. See also Hay to Wolf, 24 June 1903, Levi to Wolf, 29 June 1903, and Wolf to Levi, 29 May 1903, SWP. A preliminary, undated copy of the petition is located in SWP. It asked the "Tsar" to stop the *illegal* persecution of the Jews, a unanimous wish of the American people. The petition emphasized that Russian pogroms resulted in an undesirable increase in Jewish emigration to this country and intensified the effects of American anti-Semitism. Given the Russian record, why the czar should have reacted to the petition, had he been allowed to see it, defies imagination.

32. Levi to Wolf, *29th Annual Report* . . . (1902), p. 4658; Levi to Wolf, 7 May 1903. Levi believed that the Russian government was prepared to "prevent similar outbreaks" elsewhere in the empire. Presumably, this was the spin-off from State Department comments alluding to the official punishment meted out to Russian police and other governmental factotums involved in Kishineff outrages. See Wolf to Levi, 29 May, 6 and 7 July 1903; Levi to Wolf, 23 Sept. 1903, SWP. So concerned were Wolf and Levi with Republican party loyalties that they were eager to "disassociate the Kishineff matter from the Manchurian Question," lest that connection with its "political associations" detract from Roosevelt's "humane intentions;" Peter Wiernik, *The His-*

tory of the Jews in America (New York: Jewish History Publishing Co., 1931), p. 355. Despite Levi's warning that B'nai B'rith not send any money overseas, other charities contributed a total of $100,000 from America. The Hearst Press led the drive and sent one of its reporters, Michael Davitt, to do an on-the-spot investigation; Adler, *Kishineff* [intro.: p. 15].

33. *Presidents*, p. 215; *30th Annual Report* . . . (1903), p. 5269.

34. Chap. 2, n. 14; *Presidents*, pp. 211, 214.

35. Root to Wolf, 27 Nov. 1906, SWP; *33rd Annual Report* . . . (1906), pp. 5654–55; *AJYB* 5669 (1908–9), pp. 248–54; *AJYB* 5672 (1911–12), pp. 23–33.

36. Wolf to Kohler, 23 Feb. 1916, MJKP: Adler to Friedenwald, 2 Dec. 1908 and 2 Jan. 1911. Adler advised that the Committee had better reserve its fire for abrogation and not dissipate its energies in battling any proposed extradition treaty with Russia. Wolf also thought that amending the current Russo-American Commercial Treaty (rather than abrogating it) was preferable to dealing with problems of naturalization involved in any extradition proceedings. See Wolf to Root, 9 Nov. 1907, SWP, and *34th Annual Report* . . . (1907), p. 5987.

37. Memorandum, AJC to Roosevelt, 8 May 1908, AJC Files.

38. *35th Annual Report* . . . (1908), p. 6070.

39. Wolf to Roosevelt, 12 Oct. 1908, SWP.

40. *AJYB* 5672 (1911–12), p. 40.

41. See below, nn. 57, 63, 64.

42. *AJYB* 5672, pp. 42–45.

43. *32nd Annual Report* . . . (1905), pp. 5512–13; *33rd Annual Report* . . . (1906), pp. 5655–56; *34th Annual Report* . . . (1907), p. 5987; *35th Annual Report* . . . (Jan. 1909), pp. 6070–71; *36th Annual Report* . . . (1910), p. 5404. By now, Wolf was no longer that optimistic over Russo-American cooperation on the passport.

44. *AJYB* 5672, pp. 40–41. Root himself informed Schiff that Russia refused to countenance any changes in the treaty.

45. Marshall to Goldfogle, 27 Jan. 1909. Marshall warned Goldfogle against introducing an abrogation resolution precipitately at the UAHC Convention in Philadelphia. This then provoked a quarrel and resulted in a "flatly emasculated resolution"; *Proceedings*, 1909, pp. 6142-74; *AJYB* (1909–10), pp. 37–42; *AJYB* 5672 (1911–12), pp. 46–50; Memorandum on Tariff Rates, n.d.; M. Sulzberger to Taft, 24 Feb. 1910; draft to Sulzberger, 10 Mar., with enclosure. Knox to Taft, 8 Mar. 1910, CAP; Friedenwald to M. Sulzberger, 25 June 1909, 11 and 31 Mar. 1910, MSP.

46. Marshall to Wolf, 18 Oct. 1916; Marshall to Kohler, 24 Aug. 1918, LMP AAJC; Kohler to Mortimer Schiff, 23 Aug. 1918, MJKP AJHS. The Committee's version of planning for the conference was somewhat different. At a Council of the Union meeting, held in January 1911, an address by Louis Marshall on the passport controversy and a resolution by Bernhard Bettman were presented. Both favored abrogation. This material was then transmitted to Taft, so that the reason for the presidential conference would be his reaction to the latest considerations. (However, see text and n. 45.) But telegrams from the White House to Freiberg of the Union of American Hebrew Congregations and to Kraus of B'nai B'rith indicate that these last two organizations were also represented. Taft to J. Walter Freiberg, to Adolph Kraus, 8 Feb. 1911, WHTP AJA; see also Marshall to Wolf, 28 Oct. 1916, SWP.

47. *Presidents*, pp. 311–13; *Minutebook*, American Jewish Committee, pp. 278–79; Wolf to Schiff, 23 May 1918, and Schiff to Wolf, 24 May 1918. Wolf apologized for including a reference to Schiff's hasty departure and promised to omit the episode in a later edition of *Presidents*. Yet Wolf gave Taft an exact rendition of Schiff's statement. See Wolf to Taft, 12 Dec. 1917, SWP AJA; see also Taft to Schiff, 23 Feb. 1911, and Taft to Nagel, 25 Feb. 1911, LMP AAJC; Schiff to Taft, 20 Feb. 1911, SWP.

48. SDF 711.612/18 Knox to Taft with enclosure, 14 Dec. 1910; 711.612/20 Rockhill to Knox, disp. #118, 20 Apr. 1910, p. 387; 711.612/59 J. V. McMurray to Miss Romey, "Some

Reasons Why We Should Not Favor the Abrogation of the Treaty of 1832 with Russia," 1 Feb. 1911; 711.612/55 E. E. Young, R. W. Flournoy, Memorandum on Abrogation, 11 Apr. 1911.

49. SDF 711.612/42 Guild to Knox, 2 June 1911; 861.111/54 Flournoy to Adee, 6 Oct. 1911; 711.612/2d disp. #118; 861.111/54 MacMurray to Adee, with enclosure, Schiff to Guild; 711.612/150 Guild to Knox, 15 Aug. 1911; 711.612/35 Memorandum on Abrogation, 11 Apr. 1911.

50. See below, n. 52, 54, 57, and cf. nn. 63, 64.

51. Naomi W. Cohen, "The Abrogation of the Russo-American Commercial Treaty of 1832," *JSS* 25 (1962): 3–41; Carl George Winter, "The Influence of the Russo-American Commercial Treaty on the Rights of American Jewish Citizens," *PAJHS 41 (1951): 163–94; see also* Cohen, *Not Free to Desist: A History of the American Jewish Committee* (Philadelphia: Jewish Publication Society, 1972), p. 74; idem, *A Dual Heritage: The Public Career of Oscar S. Straus* (Philadelphia: Jewish Publication Society, 1969), pp. 197–98.

52. Wolf to Marshall, 2 Mar. 1911, SWP; Marshall to Schiff, 9 Feb. 1911, Reznikoff, 1:77.

53. Wolf to Marshall, 10 May 1911, LMP AAJA; Brylawski to Adler, 24 May 1911, CAP.

54. Friedenwald to Adler, 16 and 26 May 1911; Friedenwald to Marshall, 18 May 1911; Friedenwald to M. Sulzberger, 24 May 1911; Sulzberger to Friedenwald, 29 May 1911, MSP; Brylawski to Friedenwald, 24 May 1911; Gus Karger to Julian Mack, 27 May 1911, CAP.

55. Friedenwald to Wolf, 1 May 1911; Marshall to Friedenwald, 6 May 1911; Friedenwald to Marshall, 8 May 1911; Brylawski to Friedenwald, 13 May 1911; Friedenwald to Marshall, 18 May 1911. AAJC Files.

56. Wolf to Marshall, 10 May and 14 July 1911; Marshall to Wolf, 20 July 1911 LMP AAJC; Friedenwald to M. Sulzberger, 24 July 1911, CAP.

57. Wolf to Marshall, 17 July and 10 Aug. 1911, LMP AAJC. As for the Tablets of the Law, Marshall had no use for "Jewish weaklings, rabbis included," who socialized with Taft, and thereby helped him relegate the abrogation issue to an "ignominious background." See also Marshll to Wolf, 20 July 1911, LMP AAJC; Theodore Roosevelt, "A Proper Case for Abritration," *The Outlook,* 4 Nov. 1911, pp. 592–93; SDF 711.612/82 Guild to Knox, 22 Dec. 1911; Marshall to O. Straus, 18 Oct. 1911, Reznikoff, 1:100. Straus himself originally suggested arbitration as a way of solving the passport problem.

58. Wolf to Taft, 6 and 23 Mar. 1908, SWP AJA; Taft to Schiff, 23 Feb. 1911, SWP.

59. Wolf to Cowen, 24 Sept. 1908, PCP.

60. Wolf to Taft, 23 June 1908. Wolf suggested that Geo. B. Cortelyou, with his "Wall Street connections," serve as the Republican National Committee chairman, thereby insuring New York State support for Taft in the forthcoming campaign. Cf. Meyers, pp. 377, 384; Wolf to Taft, 11 June 1908, SWP AJA.

61. Marshall to Wolf, 20 June 1911, LMP AAJC.

62. Hammond to Wolf, 13 Mar. 1918, SWP; Schiff to Wolf, 30 Nov. 1917, with enclosure; Wolf to Schiff, 28 Nov. 1917, Schiff Collection, AJA. Even Schiff admitted that Taft knew nothing about Hammond's being selected to head the Russian enterprise, until after Wilenkin had made the appointment. Schiff, however, did acknowledge that Taft and Wilenkin were on the best of terms.

63. SDF 711.612/129 Knox to W. E. Chilton, 31 Mar. 1911; Young and Flournoy, Memorandum, 11 Apr. 1911; 711.612/43A Knox to Shelby M. Cullom, 30 June 1911; 711.612/82 Guild to Knox, 22 Dec. 1911.

64. *PRFRUS*, p. [intro.: 21], 695.

65. SDF 711.612/121 Knox to Solicitor's Office, to the Division of Near Eastern Affairs, to the Division of Consular Services, to the Office of the Second Ass't. Sec'y of the Navy, 1 June 1912.

66. SDF 711.612/129 Memorandum, MacMurray to Knox, 5 June 1912; 711.612/124 MacMurray to Knox, to Wilson, 21 Dec. 1911; 711.612/126 MacMurray to Clark, 8 Mar. 1912; cf.

711.612/107 Osborne to MacMurray, 21 Mar. 1912; 711.612/109 Flournoy to MacMurray, 4 Apr. 1912; State Dept. to T. J. Scully, 14 Apr. 1912; 711.612/102 MacMurray to Osborne, 8 Mar. 1912; 711.612/124 Adee, Memorandum, 21 Dec. 1911.

67. SDF 711.612/45 Nagel to Knox, 31 July 1912; 711.612/154b Knox to Ambassador B. Bakhmetieff, 6 Aug. 1912; 711.612/182 Memorandum, 30 Nov. 1912.

68. SDF 711.612/65 Marshall to Taft, 15 Nov. 1912, in enclosure, Thompson to Knox; 711.612/188c Wolf to Taft, 22 Nov. 1912, and Taft to Wolf, 26 Nov. 1912, and Taft to Kraus, 26 Nov. 1912; Wolf to Kraus, 9 Nov. 1912, SWP. See also Wolf to Nagel, 15 Nov. 1912, SWP. In addition to seeking new information regarding cabinet plans for reviving a commercial treaty with Russia, Wolf also suggested that he and Marshall be named to any newly created passport commission, should such an agency be in the process of formation. See below, n. 70. Nagel replied that there was no thought of establishing a passport commission and reassured Wolf that the absence of a commercial treaty between Russia and America in no way affected the range of other existing agreements between the two countries. See Wolf to Kraus, 12 Nov. 1912. SWP.

69. SDF 711.612/204 Knox to Guild, disp. #187, 26 Feb. 1913; 711.612/180d Knox to Guild, 3 Dec. 1912. Dispatches to the State Department confirmed that Russia would neither engage in a tariff war with the United States—Guild's earlier warning notwithstanding—nor modify the policy of continuing to apply a lower duty on American imports. This permitted Russia to reap the benefits it had originally accrued under the 1832 Commercial Treaty without in any way altering its views of barring or restricting the entry of naturalized American Jews to the empire. See 711.612/184 Wilson to Guild and B. Bakhmetieff to Knox, 23 Dec. 1912; 711.612/99 Guild to Knox, 9 Mar 1913; 711.612/240A disp. #187 Knox to Guild, 26 Feb. 1913; 711.612/214 J. B. Moore to Francies A. Werner, 16 June 1913.

70. Wolf to Taft, 26 Nov. 1912; Kraus to Wolf, 21, 22 and 27 Nov. 1912; Wolf to Kraus, 29 Nov. 1912, SWP; *Presidents*, pp. 322–28. Although B'nai B'rith awarded the medal to Taft in 1912, it was not presented to him until a formal luncheon took place at the White House in 1913. At that time the Executive of B'nai B'rith posed with President Taft on the portico of the White House. Concerning the Wolf-Committee relationships, see also Marshall to Wolf, 22 Nov. and 12 Dec. 1912; Marshall to Friedenwald, 2 Dec. 1912, LMP AAJC. Fearing that the business community wanted to renegotiate a treaty to protect its exports, Marshall was furious with Wolf for having hastily broadcast Taft's disavowal of any such scheme to the wire services. Wolf explained that once the news left his office, he was no longer responsible for its dissemination. But Marshall worried lest "Lupus Washingtoniensis" was once more trying to extricate himself from a difficult position. As for State Department arrangements, see SDF 861.111/132 MacMurray to Wilson, Memorandum on Status of American Commercial Interests in Russia, 15 Mar. 1912; 711.612/273 Clark to MacMurray, Memorandum on Modus Vivendi, 28 May 1912; MacMurray, Memorandum, proposal for minimum tariff rates, 27 Nov. 1912..

71. SDF 711.612/223 Wolf to Bryan, 6 Dec. 1913; Moore to Wolf, 13 Dec. 1913. See also n. 69 above.

72. SDF 711.612/204 Knox to Guild, disp. #187, 26 Feb. 1913; disp. #187, 26 Feb. 1913; 711.612/180d Knox to Guild and Bakhmetieff to Knox, 23 Dec. 1912; 711.612/204A disp. #187, Knox to Guild, 26 Feb. 1913; Max B. Laserson, *The American Impact on Russia, 1784–1917* (New York: Collier, 1962), pp. 439–45.

73. SDF 711.612/214 Moore to Werner, 16 June 1813; 711.612/184 Wilson to Guild and Bakhmetieff to Knox, 13 Mar. 1913; 711.612/204A disp. #187, Knox to Guild, 26 Feb. 1913. See also n. 70 for its State Department references; Laserson, sup.

74. Cohen, "Abrogation," pp. 16, 22–33, 38; Thos. A. Bailey, *America Faces Russia* (Ithaca: Cornell, 1950), p. 230. Although American exports to Russia declined after the Treaty's termination, once Russia entered the war, they increased dramatically.

75. SDF 711.612/228 Wilson to Bryan, 25 Dec. 1913. Wilson thought that applying Russia's exclusionary policies to all of its varied nationalities was inexpedient.

76. SDF 711.612/248 Francis to Lansing, disp. #96 with enclosure, Straus to Francis, 26 May 1916; see also 711.612/248-½ Francis to Lansing, 16 June 1916.

Chapter 11. Wolf: Classical Anti-Zionist

1. David Rudavsky, *Reform in America, Modern Jewish Religious Movements: A History of Emancipation and Adjustment*, ed. Jacob R. Agus (New York: Behrman, 1967), pp. 298–30; Agus, *The Reform Movement: Understanding Judaism*, ed. J. B. Neusner (New York: Ktav, 1975), 2:16–19.

2. David Philipson, *The Reform Movement in Judaism* (New York: Macmillan, 1931), pp. 362–64; Wolf, *Selected Addresses and Papers*, pp. 30–76, 193–99, 242–42; Melvin I. Urofsky, *American Zionism, from Herzl to the Holocaust* (New York: Anchor Books, 1976), pp. 87–91.

3. "The American Jewish Congress, to the Jews of America: The Jewish Congress vs. the American Jewish Committee," pamphlet (New York: Jewish Congress Organization Committee, 1915), p. 6; *AJYB* 5676 (1915–16), pp. 359–65; Oscar Janowsky, *The Jews and Minority Rights, 1898–1918, Studies in History, Economics, and Public Law,* #384, ed. Faculty of Political Science (New York: Columbia University Press, 1933), pp. 165–67.

4. Marshall to Kraus, 12 Jan. 1915, Reznikoff, 2:50; Adler, *Schiff,* 2:296–97.

5. Plaut, pp. 34, 153–54; Urofsky, pp. 186–89. Despite their diverse origins, most American Jews remained strongly anti-Russian until the collapse of the czar's regime; Geo. S. Mowry, *The Era of Theodore Roosevelt and the Birth of Modern America, 1900–1912* (New York: Harper Torchbooks, 1958), pp. 92–93; Morison and Commager, p. 449.

6. *AJYB* 5677 (1916–17), pp. 311–17; Janowsky, pp. 184–85; "To the Jews of America," pp. 8–9; Wolf to Marshall, 6 and 7 July 1915, LMP AAJC.

7. "Zionism and Patriotism," cited in Mason, p. 446; cf., Brandeis, *The Jewish Problem, How to Solve It,* ed. O. Janowsky (reprint, New York: American Zionist Youth Commission, 1940), p. 14.

8. Wolf to Marshall, 6 July 1915, sup.; M. L. Raphael, "Rabbi Jacob Voorsanger of San Francisco on Jews and Judaism: The Implications of the Pittsburg Platform," *AJHSQ* 63 (1973): 200, n. 35.

9. "To the Jews of America," pp. 12–14; *AJYB* 5677 (1916–17), p. 312.

10. *AJYB* 5677 (1916–17), pp. 321–22; Bernard G. Richards, *American Jewish Congress, Jewish Communal Register* (New York: Kehillah, 1918), p. 1434.

11. Wolf to Schiff, 14 July 1914, Schiff Collection, AJA; cf. Israel Cohen, *The German Attack on the Hebrew Schools in Palestine,* pamphlet (London: *Jewish Chronicle,* 1918).

12. Wolf to Schiff, 22 May 1917 and 7 Jan. 1918, Schiff Collection, AJA; *AJYB* 5678 (1917–18), pp. 440–41, 447; "To the Jews of America," pp. 11–14.

13. Janowsky, pp. 178–88.

14. Nathan Straus to Kohler, 12 June 1917, MJKP.

15. Marshall to Wolf, 17 Nov. and 14 Dec. 1917, LMP, Pers. Corresp., vol. 7, AJA; Wolf to Kohler, 26 June 1916, SWP. See also Wolf to Wilson, requesting equal rights for Jews once the Armistice was signed. WWP LC and Wolf Collection, AJA.

16. Wolf to N. Straus, 5 July 1917, Schiff Collection, AJA; *AJYB* 5678, pp. 151, 254; *AJYB* 5680 (1918–19), pp. 656–67.

17. Wolf to Marshall, 16 June 1917, Schiff Collection, AJA. Wolf thought Brandeis ws involved in the Commission. See n. 18, below.

18. Frank Manuel, *Realities of American-Palestine Relations* (Washington, D.C.: Public Affairs Press, 1949), pp. 151–57; Leonard B. Stein, *Balfour Declaration* (New York: Simon & Schuster, 1961), p. 289, n. 16.

19. Wolf to Wilson, 11 June 1917, enclosure in Wolf to N. Straus, sup.; see also Wilson to

Tumulty, n.d., handwritten message on Wolf to Wilson letter (11 June 1917): "I don't like to answer this with a letter. Won't you get Mr. Wolf on the phone and tell him that I entirely agree with his judgment about this matter?" WWP LC; see also Marshall to Wolf, 15 June 1917, LMP, Pers. Corresp., vol. 8, AJA; Schiff to Wolf, 15 June 1917, Schiff Collection, AJA. Both Schiff and Marshall were opposed to holding a congress at the time.

20. Wolf to Straus, sup.; Tumulty, handwritten note on Wolf's letter to Wilson, sup., "phoned Mr. Wolf, 6/14/17," WWP LC; Carl Hermann Voss, *Stephen S. Wise: Servant of the People: Selected Letters* (Philadelphia: Jewish Publication Society, 1969), p. 81.

21. Voss, pp. 81–82; Janowsky, pp. 246–47.

22. Stein, pp. 352–57, 353 n. 11; Manuel, pp. 123–28, 155–58; *Felix Frankfurter Reminisces* (New York: Reynal, 1960), p. 151.

23. Selig Adler, "The Palestine Question in the Wilson Era," *JSS* 10 (1948): 304–10; Stein, pp. 599–600; Manuel, pp. 168–70; Richard Ned Lebow, "Woodrow Wilson and the Balfour Declaration," *Journal of Modern History* 40 (1968): 507–8; Mason, p. 451; Urofsky, pp. 197–98, 203–4, 228.

24. Adler, pp. 311 n. 43, 313–14, 317–18; Chas. I. Goldblatt, "The Impact of the Balfour Declaration on America," *PAJHSQ* 57 (1968): 460–64, 470–73, 477–78; Manuel, p. 171.

25. Ray Stannard Baker and Wm. Dodd, *War and Peace: The Public Papers of Woodrow Wilson* (New York: Harper, 1927), p. 243; Adler, pp. 313–14.

26. Straus to Kohler, 12 June 1907, MJKP; Wolf to Kohler, 26 May 1916, SWP; Janowsky, pp. 295–96, 311, 323–30, 338–39; Reznikoff, 2:563–64, 573–74, 595–96, 600–601.

27. Reznikoff, 2:724; Wolf to Marshall, 4 Mar. 1919, LMP Pers. Corresp., vol. 12, AJA; Wolf to Schiff, 22 May 1917, Schiff Collection, AJA.

28. Wolf to Schiff, 22 May 1917.

29. "Statement to the Peace Conference," Morris Jastrow, *Zionism and the Future of Palestine* (New York: Macmillan, 1919), pp. 151–59; Philipson to Wolf, 11 Jan. 1918, SWP; Morris Frommer, "The American Jewish Congress: A History, 1914–1950" (Ph.D. dissertation, Ohio State University, 1978), 1:132–33; A. Boxerman, "Julius Kahn," *California Historical Quarterly* 4 (1976): 340.

30. Berkowitz to Wolf, 31 Jan. 1918, SWP; Naomi W. Cohen, "The Reaction of Reform Judaism in America to Political Zionism, 1897–1922," *PAJHS* 40 (1951): 366–67; Reznikoff, 2:719–23.

31. Taft to Wolf, 23 Oct. 1919, SWP.

32. Manuel, pp. 221–26, 236–43, 248–52; S. E. Knee, "The King-Crane Commission of 1919: The Articulation of Political Zionism," *AJA* 29 (1977): 27–37.

33. *Selected Addresses and Papers*, pp. 312–14; Janowsky, p. 254–55, 326–27, 342, 353–57, 365, 385.

34. Herbert Hoover, *The Ordeal of Woodrow Wilson* (New York: McGraw Hill, 1961), pp. 279–99; Janowsky, pp. 239, 256, 351–53; Reznikoff, 2:599–633, 646–49.

35. *48th Annual Report . . .* (1921), p. 9020.

36. *AJYB* 5681 (1922–23), pp. 203–4, 345–51.

37. *48th Annual Report . . .*, sup.; Henry Morgenthau, *All in a Life-Time* (New York: Doubleday, Page, 1922), pp. 351, 383–84; Reznikoff, 2:629–31. Cf. Wolf to Kohler, 1 Nov. 1918, MJKP, where Wolf noted the extent of Jewish misery in Poland. At that time he thought it best for Jews to leave the country and emigrate even "to Palestine if necessary," but by 1920, his official anti-Zionist stance once more held sway.

38. Landman to Wolf, 30 Aug. 1922, SWP.

Chapter 12. The Search for Lasting Recognition

1. Sandburg, 3:163–68.
2. Chap. 1, nn. 30, 35.

3. Chap. 5, nn. 36–39.

4. Wolf to Hayes, 14 Sept. and 28 Dec. 1876; to Gov. Wm. Dennison, 10 Dec. 1880, Nebel Collection, RBH.

5. Chap. 2, n. 89; chap. 4, n. 5; Wolf, Essay-Grant, sup., SWP; later, after his election, Grant told Wolf it was General Sherman who was responsible for Order No. 11.

6. Panitz, "Wolf-Consul," pp. 95–97; Sherman to Wolf, 16 Aug. 1881, SWP.

7. Vance to Wolf, 22 Feb. 1884, SWP.

8. Chap. 5, n. 39; *29th Annual Report* . . . (1902), p. 4661.

9. Chap. 10, nn. 13–15.

10. *38th Annual Report* . . . (1911), pp. 6876–80. The soldier in question passed the examination, entered West Point, and then became an Army captain, stationed in the Philippines.

11. *21st Annual Report* . . . (1894), pp. 3549–50; *23rd Annual Report* . . . (1896), pp. 8016–17.

12. *American State Papers on Freedom of Religion*, 4th rev. ed. (Washington, D.C.: Religious Liberty Association, 1949), pp. 264–75, 281–308.

13. *43rd Annual Report* . . . (1916), pp. 3549–50; *23rd Annual Report* . . . (1896), pp. 8016–17.

14. Naomi W. Cohen, "Anti-Semitism in the Gilded Age," *JSS* 41 (1979): 190–95; "The American Jewish Historical Society," *Encyclopedia Judaica* (1972): 2.:286. Establishing the Society in New York in 1892 was an effort on an intellectual and scholarly level to prove how necessary Jews were to the moral and intellectual climate of America. An equally cogent motive was the attempt to defuse the growing anti-Jewish prejudice of the nineties. As a matter of fact, Wolf's speech "Are Republics Ungrateful?", urging Congress to indemnify the heirs of Haym Salomon, begins with the words, "in these days of anti-Semitism" (SWP); see also *Selected Addresses and Papers*, p. 25. Wolf was a charter member of the American Jewish Historical Society.

15. *Jew as Citizen*, pp. 1–11, 91–97, 99–105, 109–11, 145–48, 425–41, 485–525, 564–66. Written to disprove a statement by J. M. Rogers in the *North American Review*, that Jews did not take up arms for their country, the United States, the *Jew as Citizen* expands upon the Jews' alleged moral superiority as the motivation for the spiritual elevation and progressive improvement of mankind. See also Wolf to Gotthard Deutsch, Wolf's literary executor, 15 Sept. 1906. There Wolf declared that the *Jew as Citizen* "did more to disarm the prejudice and to call attention of the American people to the best characteristic of the Jew than any other publication in this country." As proof, he cited a five-column article in the *New York Sun* claiming the Wolf book was "undoubtedly the most exhaustive, and convincing [one] ever published on the subject." Wolf felt that "had (he) done nothing else [in his lifetime] . . . this (book) in itself would be sufficient compensation" (SWP AJA).

16. Wolf to Felsenthal, 11 June 1903, SWP AJA.

17. Chap. 10, nn. 23–25.

18. *Selected Addresses and Papers*, pp. 207–10.

19. U. S. Industrial Commission, *Report*, pp. 245–54.

20. A close reading of the correspondence of Adler, Marshall, Friedenwald, M. Sulzberger, Brylawski, and Schiff confirms this opinion.

21. *51st Annual Report of the Executive Board of the Union* (1924), p. 9621; *Proceedings*, p. 9799.

22. Marshall to Wolf, 20 Dec. 1921, LMP, Pers. Corresp., vol. 16, AJA; Wolf, "The Jew in Public Life," 6 July 1901, Chautauqua Lecture, SWP; *25th Annual Report* . . . (1898), p. 4002; *34th Annual Report* . . . (1907–8), pp. 5878–79; "The Beilis Affair," *AJYB* 5675 (1914–15), pp. 19–90. In his compassionate account of Wolf's concern for others, Marshall must have disregarded Wolf's apparent half-hearted concern to two events that stirred world Jewry. The first was the Dreyfus affair, popularized by Émile Zola, where a French captain was unjustly stripped

of his rank because of anti-Semitic prejudice prevailing in the French military establishment at the time, and the second, the Mendel Beilis ritual murder trial in czarist Russia. After his second court-martial, Dreyfus received a presidential pardon, and the Beilis matter ended in acquittal. But other than exclaim over the anti-Jewish atmosphere that made the Dreyfus matter possible, and compare the captain's suffering to that of Commodore Uriah P. Levy, or take note that justice had at last triumphed, Wolf lodged no official protest. This approach was far different from the efforts he put forth regarding the Kishineff pogroms. In both instances, as in the Beilis matter, Wolf was presented with the problem of aiding Jews overseas who were not American citizens. Why he chose to be immersed in Kishineff (other than to scoop Cyrus Adler and the Jewish Publication Society on that score), and distance himself from the Dreyfus or Beilis issues remains inexplicable. Wolf's lack of active involvement is all the more difficult to understand in view of a decision taken in 1908 that B'nai B'rith and the Board of Delegates of the Union would be concerned with both domestic and foreign affairs as they affected their coreligionists.

23. *The Jewish Voice*, 14 June 1923. See also *Jewish Times* (Baltimore), 8 June 1923. After having recovered the previous Wednesday from heart disease, Wolf then died of a recurrent attack on Monday night, 4 June 1923, at the Royal Palace Hotel in Atlantic City, where he and his second wife, Mrs. Amy Lichtenstein Wolf, were spending the summer (SWP).

Bibliography

Primary Sources

Manuscript Material

Cincinnati, Ohio. *American Jewish Archives*. Hebrew Union College–Jewish Institute of Religion. Jacob H. Schiff Collection.

Fremont, Ohio. Rutherford B. Hayes Library. Hayes Papers.

New York City. American Jewish Committee. Cyrus Adler Papers; Louis Marshall Papers [Photostats of the Marshall Papers are in the American Jewish Archives, Hebrew Union College–Jewish Institute of Religion, Cincinnati, Ohio]; Mayer Sulzberger Papers.

New York City. American Jewish Committee. Executive. Correspondence Files.

New York Public Library. MS Division. William Williams Papers.

Waltham, Mass. American Jewish Historical Society. Library.
Board of Delegates of American Israelites.
  Executive. Minutebook. Correspondence Files.
Philip Cowen Papers.
Max J. Kohler Papers.
Benjamin F. Peixotto Papers.
Simon Wolf Papers.
[Photostats in American Jewish Archives of the Cowen, Kohler, Peixotto, and Wolf papers. Other Wolf and Peixotto material may be found in General Records of the Department of State, National Archive Record Groups 59 and 84; Instructions to Consuls, Miscellaneous Correspondence; in the Hamilton Fish Papers, Library of Congress, MS Division; and at the Hayes Library, Fremont, Ohio. Additional Wolf papers are also to be found in the Roosevelt, Schurz, Taft, and Wilson papers at the Library of Congress, MS Division.]

Washington, D.C. General Records of the Department of State. National Archive Record Groups 59, 84. Miscellaneous Correspondence, 1870–1906; Instructions to Consuls. State Department Files 711.61, 861.111.

Washington, D.C. Library of Congress, MS Division.
Hamilton Fish Papers.
Theodore Roosevelt Papers.

Carl Schurz Papers.
William Howard Taft Papers.
Woodrow Wilson Papers.

Public Documents

Papers Relating to the Foreign Relations of the United States. Washington, D.C., 1892, 1894, 1897, 1904.

Report of the Commission Appointed by the President on September 16, 1903 to Investigate the Condition of the Immigration Station at Ellis Island. Doc. No. 10. Department of Commerce and Labor. Washington, D.C., 1892.

Senner, Joseph. *The Tide and Character of Immigration and Its Relation to Crime and Wages: Testimony before the Industrial Commission.* Publication No. 7. New York: Immigration Protective League, 1899.

U.S. Congress. House. United States Industrial Commission *Reports. Immigration and Education.* Vol. 15. 57th Cong., 1st sess., Doc. No. 184, 1901.

U.S. Congress. Senate. *Importing Women for Immoral Purposes.* Prepared by Wm. P. Dillingham. 61st Cong., 2nd sess., 1909.

U.S. Congress. House. *Hearings on H.R.#166 to Investigate Office of the Immigration Commissioner of the Port of New York.* 62nd Cong., 1st sess., 1911.

U.S. Congress. House. Committee on Immigration and Naturalization. *Hearings on H.R.#558. Statements.* Simon Wolf and Louis Marshall. 64th Cong., 1st sess., 1916.

U.S. Congress. House *Report* no. 3472, vol. 2. Senate Committee on Immigration and House Committee on Immigration and Naturalization. *Statement.* Simon Wolf. 51st Cong., 2nd sess., 1890, pp. 33–35.

U.S. Statutes at Large. Vol. 37. Washington, D.C., 1912.

Secondary Sources

Annuals, Press and Public Opinion, Reports

American Hebrew
American Israelite
American Jewish Yearbook
Annual Reports of the Board of Delegates of the Union of American Hebrew Congregations, Proceedings of the Union
Congressional Record
Hebrew Leader
Jewish Exponent
Jewish Immigration Bulletin
Jewish Messenger
Jewish Times
Menorah Monthly
New York Herald
New York Times

Washington Chronicle
Washington Star

Articles, Books, Pamphlets

Abbott, Edith. *Immigration: Select Documents and Case Records*. Chicago: University of Chicago Press, 1924.

Adler, Cyrus. *Jacob H. Shiff: His Life and Letters*. New York: Doubleday, Doran, 1929.

———. *The Voice of America on Kishineff*. Philadelphia: Jewish Publication Society, 1904.

Adler, C., and Margalith, A. M. *With Firmness in the Right: American Diplomatic Action Affecting Jews, 1840–1945*. New York: Americaan Jewish Committee, 1946.

Adler, Selig. "The Palestine Question in the Wilson Era," *Jewish Social Studies* 4 (1948): 303–34.

———. "Zebulon B. Vance and 'The Scattered Nation.'" *Journal of Southern History* 7 (1941): 357–77.

Agus, Jacob B. *The Reform Movement: Understanding Judaism*. Edited by Jacob Neusner. New York: Ktav, 1975.

The American Jewish Congress. "To the Jews of America: The Jewish Congress vs. the American Jewish Committee." Pamphlet. New York: Jewish Congress Organization Committee, 1915. Library, Zionist Archives.

Antonovsky, Aaron, trans. *The Early Jewish Labor Movement in the United States*. Rev. ed. Edited by E. Tcherikower. New York: YIVO, 1961.

Bailey, Thomas. *America Faces Russia: Russian American Relations from Early Times to Our Day*. Ithaca: Cornell University Press, 1950.

Baker, Ray Stannard. *Woodrow Wilson and World Settlement*. 3 vols. Garden City: Doubleday, Page, 1922.

Bancroft, Frederic B., and Dunning, Wm. A. "A Sketch of Carl Schurz's Career, 1869–1906." *The Reminiscences of Carl Schurz*. New York: Doubleday, Page, 1916.

Behar, Manoel F. "Our National Gates, Shut, Ajar or Open?" Pamphlet No. 204. New York: National Immigration League, 1916.

Brandeis, Louis. *The Jewish Problem: How to Solve It*. 1916. Reprint. Edited by Oscar Janowsky. New York: American Zionist Youth Commission, 1940.

Blau, Jos. L. *Religious Freedom in America*. Boston: Beacon, 1949.

Bolles, Blair. *Tyrant from Illinois: Uncle Joe Cannon's Experiment with Personal Power*. New York: W. W. Norton, 1951.

Boxerman, Alan. "Julius Kahn." *California Historical Quarterly* 40 (1976): 340–48.

Bressler, David. M. "The Removal Work, Including Galveston." Speech. St. Louis: National Conference on Jewish Charities, 1910.

Cohen, Israel. *The German Attack on the Hebrew Schools in Palestine*. Pamphlet No. 11. London: *Jewish Chronicle*, 1918. Library, Jewish Theologial Seminary.

Cohen, Naomi W. "The Abrogation of the Russo-American Commercial Treaty of 1832." *Jewish Social Studies* 1 (1963): 3–41.

―――. "Anti-Semitism in the Gilded Age." *Jewish Social Studies* 41 (1979): 187–210.

―――. *A Dual Heritage: The Public Career of Oscar S. Straus.* Philadelphia: Jewish Publication Society, 1969.

―――. *Encounter with Emancipation: The German Jews in the United States, 1830–1914.* Philadelphia: Jewish Publication Society, 1984.

―――. *Not Free to Desist: A History of the American Jewish Committee.* Philadelphia: Jewish Publication Society, 1972.

―――. "The Reaction of Reform Judaism in America to Political Zionism, 1894–1922." *Publication of the American Jewish Historical Society* 40 (1951): 361–94.

Dinnerstein, Leonard. "Leo M. Frank and the American Jewish Community." *American Jewish Archives* 20 (1968): 112–34.

―――. *The Leo Frank Case.* New York: Columbia University Press, 1968.

Dubnow, Simon. *History of the Jews in Russia and Poland.* 3 vols. Philadelphia: Jewish Publication Society, 1921.

Fairchild, Henry P. "The Literacy Test in Its Making." *Quarterly Journal of Economics* 31 (1917): 447–60.

Faulkner, Harold U. *Politics, Reform and Expansion, 1890–1900.* New York: Harper Torchbooks, 1959.

Faust, Albert B. *The German Element in the United States.* 2 vols. New York: Steuben Society, 1927.

Frankfurter, Felix. *Felix Frankfurter Reminisces.* New York: Reynal, 1960.

Franklin, Frank G. *The Legislative History of Naturalization in the United States.* Chicago: University of Chicago Press, 1906.

Frommer, Morris. "The American Jewish Congress: A History." 2 vols. Ph.D. dissertation, Ohio State University, 1978.

Garis, Roy L. *Immigration Restriction.* New York: Macmillan, 1927.

Gartner, Lloyd P. "Rumania, America, and World Jewry: Consul Peixotto in Bucharest, 1870–1876." *American Jewish Historical Society Quarterly* 58 (1968): 25–117.

Goldblatt, Charles I. "The Impact of the Balfour Declaration on America." *American Jewish Historical Society Quarterly* 58 (1968): 455–515.

Grusd, Edward. *B'nai B'rith: The Story of a Covenant.* New York: Appleton Century, 1966.

Gwinn, William Rae. "Uncle Joe Cannon, Archfoe of Insurgency: A History of the Rise and Fall of Cannonism." Ph.D. dissertation, University of Michigan, 1955.

Hesseltine, Wm. B. *Ulysses S. Grant, Politician.* New York: Frederick Ungar, 1935.

Higham, John. *Strangers in the Land.* New Brunswick, N.J.: Rutgers University Press, 1965.

Hoover, Herbert. *The Ordeal of Woodrow Wilson*. New York: McGraw Hill, 1961.

Janowsky, Oscar. *The Jews and Minority Rights, 1898–1918. Studies in History, Economics, and Public Law*. Edited by Faculty of Political Science. New York: Columbia University Press, 1933.

Jastrow, Morris. *Zionism and the Future of Palestine*. New York: Macmillan, 1919.

Joseph, Samuel. *History of the Baron de Hirsh Fund*. Fairfield, N.J.: A. M. Kelly Press, 1936.

————. *Jewish Immigration to the United States from 1881–1900*. 1914. New York: Arno Press, 1969.

Kissman, Joseph H. "Jewish Immigration to the United States of Rumanian Jews up to 1914." *YIVO Annual of Social Science* 2–3. New York: YIVO, 1948.

Knee, Stuart S. E. "The King-Crane Commission of 1919: The Articulation of Political Zionism." *American Jewish Archives* 29 (1977): 22–54.

Kohler, M. "The Board of Delegates of American Israelites 1858–1879." *Publication of the American Jewish Historical Society* (1925): 75–135.

————. *Immigration and Aliens in the United States*. New York: Bloch, 1936.

————. *The Injustice of a Literacy Test for Immigrants*. New York, 1912.

————. *Simon Wolf. American Jewish Yearbook* 5685 (1924–25), pp. 404–19.

Kohler, M.; Nagel, Chas.; and Schiff, Jacob H. *The Immigration Question*. New York, 1911.

Kohler, M., and Wolf, Simon. *Jewish Disabilities in the Balkan States. Publications of the American Jewish Historical Society* 24 (1916).

Korn, Bertram W. *American Jewry and the Civil War*. Philadelphia: Jewish Publication Society, 1951.

Landau, Jacob M. *Jews in Nineteenth Century Egypt*. New York: New York University Press, 1969.

Laserson, Max M. *The American Impact on Russia, 1784–1917*. New York: Collier, 1962.

Lebow, Richard Ned. "Woodrow Wilson and the Balfour Declaration." *Journal of Modern History* 40 (1958): 501–23.

Lewis, Bernard. *The Arabs in History*. London: Anchor Books, 1950.

Lifschutz, E. "An Unsuccessful Effort for a Mass Migration to America." [Yiddish] *Yohrbuch Fun Amopteil Fun YIVO* 1 (1938): 35–39.

Mackenzie, Ralph. "The Real Causes of the Failure to Recognize the American Passport." *Menorah Monthly* 34 (1903): 181–88.

Manuel, Frank. *The Realities of American-Palestine Relations*. Washington, D.C.: Public Affairs Press, 1949.

Markens, Isaac. *The Hebrews in America: A Series of Historical and Biographical Sketches*. New York, 1888.

Mason, Alpheus T. *Brandeis: A Free Man's Life*. New York: Viking, 1946.

McFeely, Wm. S. *Grant: A Biography*. New York: W. W. Norton, 1981.

Meyers, Gustavus. *History of Bigotry in the United States*. New York: Random House, 1943.

Morgenthau, Henry. *All in a Life-Time*. Garden City: Doubleday, Page, 1922.

Morison, Elting E., ed. *The Letters of Theodore Roosevelt*. 8 vols. Cambridge: Harvard University Press, 1951–54.

Mowry, George S. *The Era of Theodore Roosevelt and the Birth of Modern America, 1900–1912*. New York: Harper Torchbooks, 1958.

Myers, Wm. Starr. *The Republican Party: A History*. New York: Century, 1928.

Panitz, David H. and Esther L. "Liberty under Law: The Life and Contributions of Simon Wolf." Washington, D.C.: Jewish Tercentenary Committee, 1955.

———. "Simon Wolf as United States Consul to Egypt." *Publications of the American Jewish Historical Society* 47 (1957): 76–100.

Panitz, E. L. "In Defense of the Jewish Immigrant, 1891–1924." In *The Jewish Experience in America*, edited by A. J. Karp. Vol. 5. New York: Ktav, 1969.

———. "The Polarity of Jewish Attitudes to Immigration, 1870–1891." *The Jewish Experience in America*. Vol. 4.

———. "Simon Wolf." In *Encyclopedia Judaica*, 16: 408.

Philipson, David. *The Reform Movement in Judaism*. New York: Macmillan, 1931.

Plaut, W. Gunther. *The Growth of Reform Judaism: American and European Sources to 1948*. New York: World Union for Progressive Judaism, 1965.

Raphael, Marc L. "Jacob Voorsanger of San Francisco on Jews and Judaism: The Implications of the Pittsburg Platform." *American Jewish Historical Society Quarterly* 60 (1973): 185–293.

Schurz, Carl. *The Reminiscences of Carl Schurz*. 3 vols. New York: Doubleday, Page, 1916.

Reznikoff, Charles, ed. *Louis Marshall, Champion of Liberty: Selected Papers and Addresses*. 2 vols. Philadelphia: Jewish Publication Society, 1957.

Richards, B. G. *The American Jewish Congress: Jewish Communal Register*. New York: Kehillah, 1918.

Rudavsky, David. *Reform in America: Modern Jewish Religious Movements, a History of Emancipation and Adjustment*. Edited by Jacob B. Agus. New York: Behrman, 1967.

Sandburg, Carl. *Abraham Lincoln*. 6 vols. New York: Scribner's, 1945.

Schachner, Nathan. *What Price Liberty?* New York: American Jewish Committee, 1946.

Straus, Oscar S. *Under Four Administrations*. Boston: Houghton Mifflin, 1922.

Szakowski, Zosa. "The Alliance Israaelite Universelle and East-European Jewry in the 60s." *Jewish Social Studies* 4 (1942): 139–59.

———. "The Alliance Israelite Universelle in the United States, 1860–1949." *Publications of the American Jewish Historical Society* 39 (1950): 389–443.

———. "Emigration to America or Reconstruction in Europe." *Publications of the American Jewish Historical Society* 42 (1952): 157–88.

Tarshish, Allan. The Board of Delegates of American Israelites 1859–1878." Master's thesis, Hebrew Union College, 1934.

Tupper, Evelyn, and McReynolds, Geo. *Japan in American Public Opinion.* New York: Macmillan, 1937.

Urofsky, Melvin. *Zionism from Herzl to the Holocaust.* New York: Doubleday, Anchor Press, 1976.

Voss, Carl Hermann, ed. *Stephen S. Wise, Servant of the People: Selected Letters.* Philadelphia: Jewish Publication Society, 1969.

War and Peace: The Public Papers of Woodrow Wilson. 2 vols. Edited by Ray Stannard Baker and Wm. E. Dodd. New York: Harper, 1927.

Wiernik, Peter. *History of the Jews in America.* New York: Jewish History Publishing Co., 1931.

Williams, Wm. A. *Russo-American Relations, 1781–1917.* New York: Octagon Press, 1971.

Winter, Carl G. "The Influence of the Russo-American Commercial Treaty on the Rights of American Jewish Citizens." *Publications of the American Jewish Historical Society* 41 (1951): 163–94.

Wolf, Simon. *The American Jew as Patriot, Soldier and Citizen.* Philadelphia: Levytype, 1895.

———. *The Presidents I Have Known from 1860 to 1918.* Washington, D.C., 1918.

———. *Selected Addresses and Papers of Simon Wolf.* Cincinnati: Union of American Hebrew Congregations, 1926.

———. *Some of the Personal Reminiscences at Home and Abroad.* Washington, D.C., 1914.

Index

Abrahams, Lewis, 36, 83, 85–86; and Simon Wolf, letter to Secretary Charles Foster, 85

Abrogation of the Russo-American Commercial Treaty of 1832, 151–56, 158–59, 179

Adas Israel Congregation, 35

Adler, Cyrus, 13, 94–96, 103, 105, 127, 150, 166; *The Voice of America on Kishineff,* 150

Adler, Samuel, 63, 65

Alien contract labor, 106–7, 132

Alliance (Jewish Alliance of America), 85

Alliance Israelite Universelle, 37–40, 93

American attitudes to immigration, 38–39, 83–91, 100–104, 121–25, 133–39

American fears of increased Jewish immigration, 80–88, 90, 92–94, 100–101, 106–8, 121–24, 129–33, 135–43, 153–54, 158

American Hebrew, 122

American Israelite, 36

Americanizing the Jewish immigrant, 80, 85, 107, 136–39

American Jew as Patriot, Soldier, and Citizen, The: Wolf's essays on patriotism, 125, 178–79

American Jewish attitudes toward immigrants, 39–41, 48, 80–81, 83, 85–86, 88–90, 99–102, 106–8, 121–25, 127–29

American Jewish Committee, 13–14, 19–21, 94–97, 102–3, 105, 124, 127–28, 130, 145, 151–52, 154–57, 159, 162–64, 167, 180

American Jewish Community, 13–14, 19–21, 24–25, 27–29, 31–32, 36–38,

40–41, 48–49, 61–63, 79, 83–87, 95–96, 98, 102, 106–7, 123, 136–39, 147–50, 153–54, 163–67, 178–80

American Jewish Congress, 165–68; also referred to as Congress Movement 163–64, 166; Congress Organization Committee, 164–66, 168

American Jewish Historical Society, 166

American nativism, 84, 87–88, 133–39

American patriotism: as staple of Wolf's thought, 18–19, 96, 100, 147, 150, 156, 158, 165, 167, 178–79

American press: Wolf's reactions to, during the Civil War, 29–32

American Zionists, 149, 162–66, 174

Anglo-Jewish press: Wolf's uses of, 17, 33, 46, 65, 107

Anti-Semitism, 25, 27–29, 47, 79–84, 88–89, 94, 99–101, 133–35, 142, 145–48, 161, 163, 173–75, 179

Anti-Zionism, 98, 166–72, 174–75, 180

Anti-Zionist petition, 171

Arabi Bey: and Wolf's reactions to Egyptian rebels, 71–72

Arthur, Chester, 81

"Assassination of President Lincoln, The," 52

Assisted immigrant/public charge provisos, 84–85, 91, 100–108; Wolf as specialist in, 84–86, 91, 100–107, 128, 131

Atlanta Hebrew Orphan Asylum, 12

Attempts at Jewish congregational unity, 62–69, 81–83

Bacon, Robert, 146–47

Badeau, Adam, 31–32, 34
Baker, Lafayette C., 27
Balfour Declaration, 161, 169
Baron de Hirsch Fund, 85, 87
Barondess, Louis, 127
Basle Program, 162
Batcheller, George, 74
Bates, Edward, 26
Bath, Felix, 154–55
Behar, Nissim, 93
Belknap scandals, 54–56
Bendell, Hermann, 54
Benjamin, Judah P., 21
Bennett, William, 102–3
Berkowitz, Henry, 171–72
Bettman, Bernhard, 152
Bien, Julius, 89n.88
Bijur, Nathan, 127
Bingham, John A., 21–22
Blaine, James G., 73, 84, 142
Blair, Montgomery, 26
Blood libel accusations, 78, 148
Bloom case, 178
B'nai B'rith, 11–12, 24, 30, 36–41, 45, 47–48, 59, 88–94, 105, 127, 149, 159, 164–65, 178
Board of Charities of the District of Columbia, 12
Board of Delegates of American Israelites, 28–29, 37–41, 43, 48, 61–63, 65–66, 67–69, 80; its transformation by Wolf into new organization, 11, 61–69, 89
Board of Delegates on Civil and Religious Rights of the Union of American Hebrew Congregations, (Board of Delegates of the Union), 11, 68–69, 83, 89, 94–96, 101, 104–5, 121, 127, 129–30, 139, 141, 144, 150, 155, 161, 166, 178; and Wolf's *Reports*, 83, 104, 130, 143, 147, 161, 179
Boas, Franz, 123
Booth, John Wilkes, 20, 22, 52
Borne, Ludwig, 125
Boston sailor case, 95–96
Boston Transcript, 31–32
Brandeis, Louis D., 109, 162–65, 168–69; Wolf's opposition to, 164
Breckenridge, Clifton R., 143
Brentano, Henry, 20

British Foreign Office: reaction to Morgenthau Mission, 169
Brussels Conference: and Romania, 48–49
Bryant, William Cullen, 29
Buchanan, James, 21, 151
Buchner, Adolphe, 43–45
Burnett, John, 129–30
Burnett Immigration Bill, 132
Butler, Benjamin F., 29–31, 42

Cable, Benjamin W., 106–7
Call, Wilkinson, 143
Cannon, Joseph G., 102–4, 130, 132
Carr, Wilbur J., 136
Carroll Street prison, 27
Chandler, William, 86–87
Charles, Prince of Romania, 45
Chase, Salmon P., 26, 30
Chicago: Wolf's background in, 20–21, 35
Christian and Eleanor Ruppert Home for the Aged, 12
Civil War, 23, 26–29, 125, 140
Clark, Walter C., 178
Cleveland, Grover, 50
Cleveland, Ohio: Wolf's background in, 19, 20, 22, 25, 40, 44–45, 51
Clymer, Heister, 55–56
Cohen, Josiah, 68
Cohen, Meyer, 135, 151
Committee on Civil and Religious Rights of the Union of American Hebrew Congregations, 69, 80
Congressional Immigration Commission, 124
Conkling, Roscoe, 54
Conley, Jim, 134
Cortelyou, George B., 122–23, 156
Corwin, Thomas, 26, 176
Council of The Union of American Hebrew Congregations: Wolf's control of, 67–69, 81–83
Cowen, Philip, 122, 157n.59
Cox, Samuel, 77, 89, 142
Crémieux, Adolphe, 17, 37–40, 62
Curtin, Andrew, G., 36–38
Czarist alliances during W.W.I: American Jewish reaction to, 163
Czarist policy: toward American Jews,

93, 140–44; toward Jews, 141–43, 146–
48, 151, 156; toward Russian Jews, 36–
38, 79–84, 92–94, 122, 140–43, 146–
48, 151, 156, 158–59

Davis, James, 137–39
Day, William Rufus, 135
deGiers, Nicholas, 142
de Hirsch, Baron Maurice, 17; de Hirsch
Fund vital to Wolf's immigrant causes,
85, 87
de Manasce, Behar, 72
Democratic Party, 21–22, 45, 151; and
democrats, 150–51; and Wolf as alternate to Democratic National Convention, 21
Department of Commerce, 101, 105–7
Department of Labor, 122, 137–38, 158
Dickinson, J. M., 178
Dillingham, William P., 102, 124, 129–
30, 136–37; Dillingham-Burnett Bill,
130; and Dillingham Immigration Bill,
132
Disraeli, Benjamin, 124–25
Douglas, Stephen A., 44
Dual allegiance, 161, 163–64, 166, 179–
80

Earle, Charles: Wolf's resort to decision
by, 102–3, 106–7
East European Jewry, 36–44, 47, 80–86,
88–90, 93–94, 100–101, 126, 141, 152;
and central European Jewry, 162; and
north European Jewry, 125–27
Eckstein, David, 40, 53, 70
Egypt: Wolf's problems as consul in, 71–
74, 78; Wolf's social life in, 74–78
Einhorn, David, 63–64
Elkus, Abram, 90–91, 105–6, 127. See
also Kohler, Max: "Brief in the Matter
of Hersh Skuratowski"
Ellinger, Moritz, 39–40, 65–67
Ellis Island, 89–91; its Commission, 90–
91
Evaluations of Wolf's writings, 11–12,
125, 167, 178–79
Evans, Elwood, 39
Ezekiel, Moses, 59

Fahmy Pasha, 73–74
Farman, Elbert E., 73

Federation of American Zionists, 162
Felsenthal, Bernhard, 179
Fish, Hamilton, 37–38, 42–44, 46, 48
Foreman, Gerhard, 21
Foster, Charles, 84–85, 105–6
Foster, John, 141–45
Francis, David R., 160
Frank, Leo M., 134–35
Frankel, Lee K., 121–22
Frankfurter, Felix, 168
Freemasons, 12
Freiberg, J. Walter, 152, 171
Freylinghuysen, Frederick T., 81
Friedenwald, Herbert, 13, 155, 164;
controversy with Wolf, 155, 164
Friedman, Lee M., 76
Furth, Jacob, 152

Galveston Movement, 106–8
Gardner, Augustus P., 102, 130
German-American Alliance, 12, 109,
183n.6
German-Americans, 12, 34, 36, 52–54,
56–57, 62, 107, 177
German-American societies, 12, 34
German anti-Semitism: Wolf's criticism
of, 18, 56
German-Jewish newcomers: their search
for communal unity, 62–63
Goldfogle, Henry, 127, 150–51
Gotthold, Florence Wolf, 59
Gotthold, Frederick, 59
Gotthold, Newton, 26
Grant, Julia, 34
Grant, Madison, 136
Grant, Ulysses S., 24–25, 30–38, 44–46,
49, 52–53, 58, 66, 70; and office-
seekers, 35–36, 53–55; and Peixotto's
mission to Romania, 45–46; and rela-
tionship to Wolf, 34–36, 38
Greenebaum, Hannah, 20–21
Greenebaum, Henry, 20
Guild, Curtis, 153–56

Hackenburg, William B., 135
Hale, John, 25
Hall, Prescott, 99
Hamlin, Hannibal, 33, 42
Hammond, John Hayes, 157
Hance, Joseph C., 22
Harrison, Benjamin, 50, 83

Harrison, Burton, 151
Hart, Abraham, 20
Hay, John, 26, 88–89, 92, 145, 149–50, 176
Hayes, Rutherford B., 11, 35, 56–58, 70, 176; Wolf's political involvement with, 11, 49, 56–57, 176–77
Hearst, William Randolph, 150, 204n.32
Hebrew Emigrant Aid Society, 80
Hebrew Grant and Colfax Club, 32
Hebrew Immigrant Aid Society, 17, 105, 127, 136
Hebrew Union College, 65, 67
Heine, Heinrich, 124–25
Herzl, Theodor, 17
Hinzweiller, Bavaria, 18, 52–53, 71, 75
Hirsch, Samuel, 63
Hitchcock, Frank Harris, 156
Holmes, Oliver Wendell, 135
House, Edward M., 167
House Committee on Immigration and Naturalization, 127
Howard, Otis O., 54
Hughes, Charles Evans, 135
Hunt, William Henry, 81
Hurd, Frank, 22
Husband, Walter W., 123

Immigrant belief in democracy: Wolf's adherence to, 18, 52–53, 63, 136–37
Immigrant classification, 86–87, 90–91, 121–23, 133, 135–38
Immigrant deportation, 80–81, 101, 104–8, 132, 136–37, 193–94n.38
Immigrant distribution: Wolf's efforts toward, 85–87, 92, 106–7
Immigrants' Protective League, 87
Immigration: of East-European Jews (primarily from Russia), 28, 38–41, 80–86, 93, 99–102, 121, 125, 127–33, 136–37, 140–43, 147, 153, 158; and literacy provisos, 86, 102–3, 129, 133; racist nature of, 123–25, 130 33, 135–39; of Romanian Jews, 48–49, 88–89
Immigration Bill of 1891, 83
Immigration Bill of 1907, 102–4
Immigration Bill of 1924, 138
Immigration Bureau, 95, 100, 105, 121–22, 124, 128–29
Immigration Commissions (of 1904, 1907, 1910), 103–4, 123, 127, 129;

Wolf's reactions to, 91, 101–5, 125, 127–28, 133
Immigration Law of 1921, 137
Immigration Restriction League, 99
"Influence of the Jews on the Progress of the World, The," 35
International Order of B'nai B'rith. *See* B'nai B'rith
Isaacs, Abraham S., 82
Isaacs, Myer S., 28, 43–45, 66, 82
Ismailia, 76
Israeli, Pinhas, 96
Izvolsky, Alexander, 147

Jacobs, Joseph, 94
Jastrow, Marcus, 171
Jewish Alliance of America (Alliance), 85
Jewish contributions to civilization: Wolf's estimate of, 18, 29, 54, 125–26, 156, 162, 179
Jewish demands at Versailles, 170–71, 173–75
Jewish Immigrants' Information Bureau (Industrial Removal Bureau), 86, 106–7
Jewish masses: demands for equality of treatment, group rights, and Zionist recognition, 162–65, 173
Jewish Messenger, 40
Jewish Times, 33, 36, 38, 40, 63–67, 69
Johnson, Albert, 136–37
Johnson, Andrew, 29–31, 33
Judd, Norman, 42

Kahn, Julius, 171
Kaskel, Caesar, 28
Keene, Laura, 25
Kehillah, 164
Kempinski, Hermann, 144
Kerenski, Aleksandr, 167
Kesher Shel Barzel, 12
King-Crane Commission, 172–73, 175
Kishineff affair, 92, 94, 148
Kishineff Petition, 92, 148–50
Knox, Philander C., 153, 158
Koenigsberg Central Frontier Committee, 39
Kohler, Max, 13, 47, 86–87, 90, 104–8, 123–24, 137–39, 166, 173, 189; and Elkus, "Brief in the Matter of Hersh Skuratowski," 105–7, 123–24, 129;

Jewish Rights at The Congress of Vienna, 170; and Wolf," *Jewish Disabilities in the Balkan States*, 166–67, 170
Kraus, Adolph, 94, 152, 159, 164, 168
Kreisman, B., 48

Laffon, 73
Lamar, Joseph R., 134
Lamsdorf, V. N., 146
Landman, Isaac, 171, 175
Lansing, Robert, 160, 168–69
League of Nations, 173
Leeser, Isaac, 30, 63
L'Egypte, 73
Levi, Leo N.: his relations with Wolf, 88–92, 149, 204n.32
Levi, Sol, 68
Liberal Immigration League, 101
Lilienthal, Max, 62
Lincoln, Abraham, 11, 22–23, 25–28, 176; and Jews, 26, 28, 176; and meeting with Wolf, 26; and office-seekers, 23–24, 176
Littauer, Lucius N., 89
Lodge, Henry Cabot, 86, 99, 102–3, 122, 124–27, 135
Loeb, William, 103
London Standard, 148

McCook, George W., 23
McCormick, Richard C., 54, 146, 148, 150
Mack, Julian W., 124–25
McSweeny, Frank, 121
Magnes, Judah L., 127
Maimonides College, 65–67
Marshall, Louis, 13, 93–94, 97, 105, 127, 129, 133–35, 154, 163–66, 170, 173–75, 179–80
Menorah Monthly, 50
Metcalf, Victor H., 96
Minority Treaties, 98, 173–74
Montefiore, Claude G., 172
Montefiore, Moses, 17
Moore, William, 42
Morgenthau, Henry, 171, 175
Morgenthau Mission, 167–69
Moses, Adolph, 20, 24, 32; and Wolf's role in Order No. 11, 32
Multinational states: Wolf's views of, 125, 166, 173–74

Nagel, Charles: Wolf's friendship for, 107–9, 130–31, 158
Neely, Alexander L., 22
"Nestor of American Jewry," 181
New Philadelphia, 20
New York College Convention, 67–68
New York Evening Post, 29
New York Hebrew College, 68
New York Herald, 27, 37

Ochs, Adolph, 155
Olney, Richard, 143
Order No. 11, 24, 27–32, 62
Orth, Godlove S., 42
Osman (Moslem caliph), 73

Page, Walter H., 169
Pale of Settlement, 79, 141
Paris Peace Conference: and group rights for Jews, 170
Passport controversy, 143–47, 150, 154, 157–59, 179
Peixotto, Benjamin F., 20, 40, 44–51, 62, 166; and Wolf's attitude toward Romanian Mission, 45–49
Peixotto, Hannah S., 50–51
Phagan, Mary, 134–35
Phelps, William W., 77
Philipson, David, 171–72
Powderly, Terence V., 17, 121–22
Pseudonyms for Wolf: "Lupus," "Lupus Washingtoniensis," "Showmar," 13, 36, 180

Quota Laws of 1921 and 1924, 137–38
Quota system of immigrant admissions, 91, 129, 137–38; Wolf's reaction to, 137–38

Radical Republicans, 29–30
Rawlins, John A., 32, 34
Rayner, Isidore, 145
Readers' Digest, 169
Reconstruction era, 29–30; Wolf's benefits from, 31–33
Recorder of deeds post, 33–36, 44, 51, 52–53, 57–58, 60–61, 69–70, 177
Reform Judaism, 11–12, 18, 61–65, 80–81, 126, 160–62, 171; its anti-Zionist views, 161, 171; Reform Jewry, 163, 178

Report (of the Board of Delegates of the Union), 83
Report (Senate House Conference, 1891), 143
Report . . . to Investigate the Condition of the Immigration Station at Ellis Island, 90–91; and Wolf's testimony, 91
Republican party, 11, 21–22, 32–33, 45–46, 56, 58, 156, 163, 177
Restrictionist approaches to immigration, 39–41, 48, 83–91, 99–101, 104–7, 121, 124–25, 129, 133, 135–39, 153, 158
Rice, Henry T., 122
Riddle, Albert G., 32–33
Riddle, Nicholas, 147–49
Rockville, William W., 133
Romania, 42–45, 89, 146, 166, 174, 176; its anti-Semitism, 92, 100, 166–67, 189nn.71–74; equal rights for non-Christian populations in, 166; Wolf's views on, 42–49, 71–74, 88–89, 145, 189nn.71–74
Romania and Russia: Secretary Hay's and Wolf's hopes for a naturalization convention and/or non-discriminatory trade treaty with, 88, 92, 125, 146–47, 152
Romanian Jewish immigration, 81, 88–90, 92
Roosevelt, Theodore, 89–90, 145–46, 149, 156–57; his relations with Wolf, 11, 89, 101, 145–46, 149
Root, Elihu, 146–47, 151
Rosnosky, Isaac, 96
Ruppert, Jacob, 102–3
Russian doctrine of perpetual allegiance, 140–41, 143–45, 147, 151–52
Russian Revolution, 166–67
Russo-American Commercial Treaty of 1832, 140–42, 145, 147, 151

Sabath, Adolph, 127
Sabbath School Union, 65
Salomon, Edward S., 20–21, 30, 39, 53, 62, 70
Sami, Mahmoud, 71
Sandburg, Carl, 176
Sanders, Leon, 127
San Francisco, 40, 43–45, 103
Sargent, Frank P., 88, 90, 99, 102, 177; Wolf's friendship for, 177

Schiff, Jacob H., 13, 93, 106–7, 127, 152–53, 163, 165, 168
Schillerbund, 12, 34
Schuetzenverein, 34
Schulteis, H. V., 87
Schurz, Carl, 37, 42, 57–58, 71, 177
Schuyler, Eugene, 37
Seligmans (bankers: Jesse and Joseph), 44–45
Senior, Max, 171
Senner, Joseph H., 87
Separation of church and state: Wolf's adherence to theory of, 91, 126, 178
Seward, William H., 26
Shephard, Alexander R., 57
Sherman, John, 42, 144
Sherman, William T., 27, 44, 177
Sigel, Franz, 53, 62
Slaton, John, 134
Smith, Caleb B., 26
Smith, Charles E., 142
Sneersohn, Hayim Z., 44–45
Solomons, Adolphus, 12, 36–37, 83
Some of the Personal Reminiscences at Home and Abroad (essays devoted to Wolf's personal recollections), 77
Sprague, William, 42
Stafford, Wendell Philips, 11
Stanton, Edwin M., 23, 26–27, 30
State Department, 37–38, 45–49, 61, 88–89, 93, 123, 140–41, 143–48, 150, 152–60, 172, 179; Wolf's communications with, 46, 48, 72–75, 81, 89, 93, 123, 141–47, 149–50, 154–59, 178
Statue of Religious Liberty, 34–35
Stein, Philip, 152
Stewart, William, 45
Straus, Oscar, 13, 50, 94, 96–97, 149, 154, 156–57, 165
Sulzberger, Cyrus, 13, 166
Sulzberger, Mayer, 67–68, 95–97, 152–55, 166; his controversies with Wolf, 96–97, 155
Sulzer, William, 151
Sumner, Charles, 42

Taft, William H., 11, 109, 130, 133, 151–54, 156–58; his friendship for Wolf, 11, 109, 155–59, 172, 178, 196n.38
Talaat Pasha, 168
Temperance Movement: Wolf's reaction to, 56–57, 70

Tenure-of-Office Act, 30–31, 33
Tewfik Pasha, 72
Treaty of San Remo, 175
Tumulty, Joseph P., 168–69

Uhrichsville, Ohio: Wolf's background
  in, 19–20, 21
Union of American Hebrew Congregations, 35, 64–69, 82–83, 94–95,
  105, 139, 178
United Hebrew Charities, 80–82, 84–85,
  101
United States and Russia: Wolf's concerns about, 89, 146, 158
United States Census Bureau, 122
United States Industrial Commission,
  86–88
United States Supreme Court, 12, 30,
  134

Vance, Zebulon C., 171, 177
Voorsanger, Jacob, 164

Walker, Francis, 135
Walter, Father Jacob, 12
Washington, D.C., 23–24, 57, 130
Washington Chronicle, 27
Washington Hebrew Congregation, 12,
  24–25, 64–65, 67
Washington Jewish Community, 24–25
Washington Literary and Dramatic Asso-
  ciation, 25–26
Washington Territory, 39–41
Watchorn, Robert, 100–101
Watson, Tom, 133
Weber and Kempster: *Report,* 83–84
Weizmann, Chaim, 169
Welles, Gideon, 26
White, Andrew, 148
Wickersham, George W., 107
Wilenkin, Gregory, 157
Williams, E. R., 95
Williams, William, 89–91, 106, 109
Willman, Andreas, 53
Wilson, William B., 131–32
Wilson, Woodrow, 132–33, 159, 163,
  169, 171; his relations with Wolf, 148,
  165
Wise, Isaac M., 63–67
Wise, Stephen S., 168–69
Witte, Serge, 147–48

Wolf, Abram and Elias, 19
Wolf, Adolph Grant, 34
Wolf, Amy Lichtenstein, 189 n.88
Wolf, Benjamin and Rosa, 19
Wolf, Caroline Hahn, 22, 51, 59, 77
Wolf, Simon
—his achievements, 176–78
—his ambivalent attitudes toward abrogation of the Russo-American Commercial Treaty of 1832, 146–49, 152,
  154–55, 158–59, 179
—as anti-Zionist, 161–66, 170–72, 174–
  75, 180–81
—his approaches to interfaith relations,
  12, 19, 54, 78, 126, 179–80
—his attitudes toward the law, 12, 104–
  5, 108–9, 128
—as B'nai B'rith representative, 11, 24,
  27, 30, 36–41, 45, 47–48, 59, 62, 88–
  89, 90–95, 102, 105, 127, 149, 159,
  164–65, 178
—his contentions against anti-Semitism,
  12, 18, 25, 27–29, 31–33, 42–49, 56,
  66, 71–74, 79–81, 88–90, 125–26, 145,
  150–51, 178–80, 189 nn.71–74
—his delay of passage of literacy bill,
  101–4
—his efforts to help the Republican
  party, 45, 52, 56–57, 89, 150–51, 158
—his efforts to reverse immigrant deportation, 84–86, 99–101, 104–7, 128, 130–
  32, 136, 138–39, 178, 193–94 n.38
—his emphasis on equal rights for all,
  125, 138, 142, 144, 163, 166, 170,
  196 n.38
—failure of his 1869 immigration plan,
  39–41, 65, 151
—as founding member of American Jewish Historical Society, 170
—his frustrations with Czarist policy, 12,
  36–38, 79–81, 83–90, 92, 94, 99–101,
  104–5, 140–48, 150, 152, 156–59, 179
—and Max Kohler, heir apparent as
  chairman of the Board of Delegates,
  13, 104, 180
—his lobbying techniques, 13–14, 41,
  44–45, 66–68, 81–85, 97–98, 102–3,
  107–8, 128
—his methods of accommodating bu-
  reaucrats, 30–33, 98, 104–9, 130–31,
  136–37, 144, 147–48, 154–58, 164,
  173, 176–78

—his opposition to the American Jewish Congress, 164–66, 168

—his opposition to the classification of immigrants, 91, 122–27, 136, 138

—his opposition to the legal enforcement of Americanization and registration of aliens, 137–39

—and patronage, 35–36, 44, 52–54, 61

—his reaction to the Civil War, 23, 26–27

—his rebuttal of restrictionist views on immigration, 38–41, 48, 83–88, 92–93, 99–101, 104–8, 121–28, 132–33, 135–39

—his relations with the American Jewish Committee, 13–14, 94–98, 102–3, 105, 124, 127, 129–30, 151–53, 155–57, 167, 170, 179–80

—his relations with Adolph Kraus, 94, 152, 159, 164, 168

—his relations with Louis Marshall, 154–57, 166–68, 170, 179–80

—his request for postponement of the American Jewish Congress, 168

—his role in the "Brief in the Matter of Hersh Skuratowski," 105–6, 124

—his self-estimate, 77, 101

—as spokesman for the American Jewish community, 12, 19–22, 24–25, 27–33, 36–42, 51, 65–69, 83, 92, 95, 108–9, 125, 138–39, 143–47, 166, 168, 177–79

—his testimony before United States Industrial Commission, 87–88

—his whitewashing Grant's record in the matter of Order No. 11., 30–32, 35, 77, 104, 125, 178–79

—works: *The American Jew as Patriot, Soldier and Citizen*, 178–79; *Annual Reports of the Board of Delegates*, 83, 104, 130, 143, 147, 161, 179; *Jewish Disabilities in the Bulkan States* (with Kohler), 166, 170; *The Presidents I have Known from 1860 to 1918*, 30; *Selected Addresses and Papers of Simon Wolf*, 183 n.3; *Some of the Personal Reminiscences at Home and Abroad*, 77

Wolfenstein, Samuel, 68

Yale, William, 172

Zionism, 161–65, 168–72, 175